THE

NEXT

ENLIGHTENMENT

THE

NEXT

ENLIGHTENMENT

Integrating East and West in a New Vision of Human Evolution

WALTER TRUETT

ANDERSON

ST. MARTIN'S PRESS 〰 NEW YORK

THIS BOOK IS DEDICATED TO

STEVE BERKOV, LINDA BRANDON, ABE LEVITSKY,

and all the others.

THE NEXT ENLIGHTENMENT.
Copyright © 2003 by Walter Truett Anderson.
All rights reserved. Printed in the United States of America.
No part of this book may be used or reproduced in any manner whatsoever
without written permission except in the case of brief quotations
embodied in critical articles or reviews.
For information, address
St. Martin's Press,
175 Fifth Avenue,
New York, N.Y. 10010.

www.stmartins.com

Library of Congress Cataloging-in-Publication Data
Anderson, Walt.
    The next enlightenment : integrating East and West in a new vision of human
evolution / Walter Truett Anderson—1st ed.
        p. cm.
    ISBN 0-312-31769-7
    1. Religious awakening. 2. Spirituality—Psychology. 3. Human evolution—
Religious aspects. 4. East and West. I. Title.
BL476.A53   2003
291.4'2—dc21   2003041352

FIRST EDITION: AUGUST 2003

1   3   5   7   9   10   8   6   4   2

CONTENTS

ACKNOWLEDGMENTS

Thanks to my agent, Regula Noetzli, for much-appreciated hard work and good advice. Thanks also to the Foundation for the Future, for support of a research project that is reflected in several portions of this book.

Pulling Buddha's Tooth

I have read that the Indian prince Gautama Shakyamuni, who became known as the Buddha (literally the enlightened one), was cremated after his death in the year 480 B.C., and that his followers discovered among the ashes two teeth—apparently the only ones the Buddha had left in an age innocent of floss and fluoride—and preserved them as relics. One was taken south to Sri Lanka, where it is enshrined in the Temple of the Tooth at Kandi. The other went north to the ancient kingdom that is now Pakistan, was later brought to China, moved from place to place over the centuries, and now reposes in a sumptuous building—the Tooth Relic Pagoda—on the outskirts of Beijing.

This is, to say the least, a somewhat ironic development, because among the core ideas of the Buddha's message to the world—the matters about which he was enlightened—were the warnings that everything changes, human identity is illusory and transient, and attachment to anything (especially anything material) is the ultimate foolishness. The devout Buddhists, by preserving and enshrining the Buddha's teeth, demonstrated that they had rather missed the point of his teachings. Theirs is a far gentler example of point-missing than the variety demonstrated by the Christians who have oppressed, tortured, and slain countless human beings in heavy-handed service to the Prince of Peace, but it comes down to the same thing.

Growing Up in the Universe

Buddhism is but one of many schools of thought built around the proposition that ordinary maturity is not the ultimate stage of human development. In various accounts, most of them emanating from the East, we hear that it is possible—with serious application, some good guidance, and maybe a bit of luck—to go through a major psychological transition and become in a sense a different kind of person. Such transitions are said to be as complex and striking—and sometimes as difficult—as growth from childhood to adolescence, or from adolescence to adulthood. The big difference is that they don't happen to everybody; most people remain suspended all their lives in a state sometimes called a kind of waking slumber. The transition beyond that state is variously described as awakening, liberation, realization, or enlightenment. The literature of the Sufis sometimes describes it as "remembering yourself."

The basic proposition of these traditions is that everyday consciousness—the I-centered monologue we all run most of the time, the sense of looking out from inside our heads at an external and separate world—may be quite adequately adjusted to society, but it is somehow out of touch with the universe. And not only out of touch with the universe but, in a sense, out of touch with ourselves, the larger dimensions of our being, and the immediate, in-your-face data of our own experience.

The basic propositions of this book are that (a) the Buddhas, Sufis, and other Eastern mystics were on to something—something of enormous importance both to individuals and to the species as a whole, and (b) that something can be understood—perhaps better understood, in fact—without becoming a convert to any of those traditions. Today's world—this globalizing, postmodern, knowledge-based, multicultural, scientific, high-technology age—can be stressful and confusing in many ways, but it is still a remarkable time in which to be alive and human. It presents us with an opportunity to engage in a new way with new information the ancient challenge to understand what we are, and grow up.

What the knowledge of our own time now enables—and requires—us to discover is that there are indeed other ways of being in the world, and that the discovery of them is not merely a "religious experience" achievable by limited numbers of people within the boundaries of certain ancient disciplines, but it is rather a natural process of human growth, a psychological development undergone by many people outside of those contexts—one that does involve a radical shift of personal perspective but does not involve paranormal or supernatural experience (that's what's really radical about it), and is potentially within the reach of all human beings. It is more a maturation of vision, accompanied by a reorganization of conscious (and probably unconscious) thought, in which you see yourself and the world differently.

We usually are satisfied to think of maturity as growing up within a culture to fit a particular society's roles, rules, and expectations. The kind of maturity called enlightenment is more a matter of growing up beyond the culture. Enlightened, liberated people—people who have begun to realize, to remember themselves—may well live quietly and respectably within their society, but they know that its structures are the products of fallible beings, only one of many ways to manage human interaction, and that its canon of universal truths is only one of many ways to describe the world.

Such a shift may be described as spiritual growth—but it's not necessary to think of it that way and I don't think it's even particularly helpful.

Liberation Without Spirituality

A word about words: I notice that many people have grown wary of the word "religion" in connection with deeper feelings and grander thoughts about our place in the cosmos. And I can't say I blame them. The word carries so much baggage now—so much hierarchy, so much mythology left over from dead cultures, so many doubtful dogmas, so many cranky old men bearing armloads of Thou Shalt Nots. The word "spiritual" is taking its place and has rapidly become so popular that it now carries its own load of baggage. If you don't know what kind of baggage I mean, go stroll through the New Age section of your nearest bookstore. I don't plan to make much use of it here, because too many of the things that come under the heading of spirituality—astrology, faith healing, reincarnation, channeling, and so forth—really have nothing to do with what this book is about. Those things may or may not happen—it's a big universe, and I have not been granted the last word on what is possible in it—but I don't find them particularly interesting. Also, in popular usage "spiritual" is commonly taken to mean a way of thinking opposed to, or at least different from, science and rationality, whereas what I want to explore in these pages is a view of enlightenment that is illuminated by science and rooted in the rational traditions of Western thought.

So I have more or less dropped the word spiritual from my own vocabulary—stored it in the attic along with "paradigm" and a few others that have so outgrown their usefulness that they are best not used except in very limited and precise ways—and we should find it quite easy to explore the subject of higher levels of human growth without relying too heavily on them. I also want to make it clear that, although I will frequently cite concepts from Buddhism and other Eastern traditions, these traditions are not the central subject of this book. They are important chapters in the history of the larger human struggle toward freedom and sanity that *is* the subject of this book, and they deserve our respect, but I neither encourage nor discourage any extensive study of them. The advantage to exploring them is that they provide valuable and useful windows through which you can look at your life; the disadvantage is that in studying them it is easy to become so fascinated by the window that you lose sight of the view. What we need to do is develop a wider perspective, from which we can see both Eastern and Western developments beginning to converge on a new view of the human condition.

My purpose is to provide some pieces of that wider perspective: a new enlightenment project with enough breadth of vision to encompass both the core concepts of Asian enlightenment traditions and the rational/scientific heritage of the European Enlightenment. I hope that this book will help develop a clearer understanding of the kind of psychological growth that has been called enlightenment, and perhaps encourage some people and groups to think about how that might be brought more effectively into the mainstream of society. This will involve exploring ideas that have emerged in the Western world in the recent historical past and are now surfacing dramatically in such fields as physics, the brain sciences, and constructivist/developmental psychology. Many trends of modern Western science, psychology, and philosophy are much more compatible with ancient Eastern ideas about human consciousness than you might expect. Enlightenment, as described in the core teachings of disciplines such as Buddhism, is a clear perception and appreciation of what is right in front of us all the time. It is not other-worldly; it is this-worldly. I quote the ninth-century Tantric poet Saraha, whom I particularly enjoyed when I began years ago to explore Buddhism:

> Than knowledge of This there is nothing else.
> Other than This no one can know.
> It is This that's read and This that's meditated,
> It's This that's discussed in treatises and old legends.
> There is no school of thought that does not take This as
>   its aim.[1]

I will encourage you, reader, to look up occasionally from these pages; consider whatever is before you and around you, and remind yourself that This is the subject matter of this book. When I talk about the human condition—and I will—I am not talking about an abstract philosophical concept, but about the conditions of your life and mine, here and now. There is a lot to be learned about This—and how we look at it, and what we think about it—and that kind of learning is central to the process of growing up. I won't go all the way with the famous Socratic pronouncement that the unexamined life is not worth living—hell, any life is worth living—but would rather say that the unexamined life is not fully lived. If we don't use the marvelous gift of reflective cognition—our ability to think about thought itself, to look with fresh eyes at our own consciousness and our own thought processes—we remain unfinished business. I suspect that this proposition is going to become congenial to more people as human lifespans continue to lengthen, which they are highly likely to do, and more people begin to think seriously about personal development in adulthood—a lifetime of growing up in a way that involves questioning *what* we are and how we may develop beyond *where* we are.

The Larger Project

People usually talk about enlightenment as an event in the growth of individual people—which it most certainly is—and it would be impossible to discuss the subject fully without exploring it from that perspective; it is a deeply personal matter, and parts of this book will be addressed directly to individuals who are thinking seriously about their own growing up. But much more is involved here than just a self-help project; the challenge of the next enlightenment is not only the further development of individuals but also the further development of the human species. We are talking about something that is better described as an evolutionary project.

Evolution was not part of the worldview of the Asian civilizations, such as India in the time of the Buddha, within which the idea of enlightenment originated. The early mystics clearly had a social purpose, hopes of improving the human condition over time, but they had nothing really comparable to the evolutionary worldview that now informs our thinking. They were embarked upon an evolutionary process, but without a concept of evolution. There's nothing unusual about people setting out on important explorations without a very good map of the territory (see Columbus), but of course the enterprise changes when the map does—and the map has changed spectacularly; we now live in a different context of time and space.

Today we can best understand both the problem addressed by the Asian enlightenment traditions and the solution they proposed as stages along the road of human cultural evolution. The early mystics identified a place where the human species had gotten stuck in its development, and proposed a way out.

The problem is generally signaled by the word "ego," meaning not just vanity, greed, arrogance, and all the other moral shortcomings that we associate with that word, but rather the structure of cognition that creates a foundation for them. Ego is primarily created and maintained by symbolic systems such as language—our process of describing ourselves *to* ourselves. Unlike all other creatures, we live in a world of symbols, and we have a hard time with it. Our difficulties are compounded by our ability to see how inseparable language is from reality, how much of life is shaped by our descriptions.

The solution proposed by Buddhism and other disciplines is to investigate your own cognitive process so deeply, persistently, and acutely that you begin to see how it works and are thereby liberated from its snares. "Free from the domination of words you will be able to establish yourselves where there will be a 'turning about' in the deepest seat of consciousness by means of which you will attain self-realization of Noble Wisdom," says one of the Buddhist texts.[2] The person who succeeds in this effort has completed the evolutionary transition that commenced tens of thousands of years ago, when human beings first began to communicate information symbolically and store such information in their brains. We gained a great deal with the development of language—we became human—but language is a tool that uses us as much as we use it. We are all held captive by our invention, and we will never be free or even fully human until we have made ourselves its masters and not its subjects.

Enlightenment, then, is an evolutionary project, one that was begun long before evolution itself was understood. How successful has the project been so far? Well, not very. Study of the traditional enlightenment schools undoubtedly enabled many people to gain a deeper understanding of their own minds, and it has contributed greatly to the world's heritage of art and philosophy. But most people—even in civilizations dominated by the traditions of liberation—never quite managed to break free. Countless spiritual schools have degenerated into guru-worship cults and empty religious establishments perpetuating their rituals, prejudices, and rules of behavior. Despite the pious vow to liberate all beings that is regularly repeated by students of Buddhism, many teachers operate under the dismissive conviction that all beings are not capable of being liberated, and that the best thing to do is to speak only to those who show some ability to receive the message. Thus the author of *The Secret Oral Teachings in Tibetan Buddhist Sects* explains that the secrecy lies in the listener, not the teacher: "One may proclaim on the high road the Teachings considered secret, they will remain 'secret' for the individuals with dull minds who will hear what is said to them, and will grasp nothing of it but the sound."[3] No doubt this is a valid empirical observation, based on something every teacher of every subject has discovered: that—whatever the lesson to be learned, however skillfully it might be presented—some people just don't seem to *get* it. But it tacitly accepts that only a limited number of people will ever make it into the enlightenment boat. Its project is individual growth, not cultural evolution.

The West hasn't done a whole lot better. We have taken some giant steps along the evolutionary path (the biggest was the Darwinian step, the discovery of evolution itself), and the modern era has given rise to a surge of movements aimed at freeing the human mind from its own fetters—yet our job is far from done. We remain largely ego-ridden people in ego-ridden societies that school us in delusion from kindergarten onward; celebrate delusion in art and literature; and elevate the most consistently, heroically deluded to the highest levels of wealth and power.

Breaking through that ego-centered way of looking at the world is a difficult endeavor. It is one that many people willingly undertake because they sense that the breakthrough is close to the heart's most passionate desire. But it also invokes some of our deepest fears—that we may lose ourselves, rend apart the warm cocoon of certainty that our roles and beliefs weave around us, and cease to be what we thought we were. Most fearful of all, we might even cease to want the things we have always wanted.

My conviction, my purpose in writing this book and advocating future activities of research and education that will go far beyond it, is that there is nothing to lose—precisely nothing—and, as the old revolutionaries used to say, a world to win.

Richard Bucke, the Canadian psychiatrist who wrote the somewhat dated but still useful book *Cosmic Consciousness,* was as far as I know the first person to view enlightenment as an evolutionary phenomenon. Writing only a few decades after the publication of *The Origin of Species*—and inspired by a powerful enlightenment experience of his own—he proposed that evolution on Earth could be understood in three stages: the evolution of consciousness (in animals), the evolution of self-consciousness (in humanity), and the emergence of cosmic consciousness. He also predicted that cosmic consciousness would appear more and more frequently, until the whole human race had reached that stage. And, like a true New Ager, he expected it to happen soon: "This new race is in act of being born from us, and in the near future it will occupy and possess the earth."[4]

I have never much liked the term "cosmic consciousness" for some reason (it strikes me as being a bit trippy) but I have to grant that it is a precise description of the phenomenon: people *do* in fact become conscious of the cosmos in a new way, and of the fact that they are it. Also, although Dr. Bucke wisely avoided saying exactly what he meant by "the near future," he obviously overestimated the speed of the transformation he was trying to describe. Such an evolutionary transition has never happened before, and we really have no idea of how long it might take. That is one of the many questions that a twenty-first-century examination of the evolution-enlightenment thesis must explore.

I have spoken of a new project, the next Enlightenment, in which the insights of both Eastern mysticism and Western rational empiricism serve as the foundation for a new understanding of the universe and our place in it, or, to put the matter a bit differently (in a way that I hope will become clear as we proceed), of human consciousness and the universe's place in it. This project is already under way; I am not its proposer or inventor. The task I set out for myself in this book is part description, part prescription; part journalism and part exhortation. I will try to identify some of the lines of activity that are already involved in the project, note some of the ways they fit together, and point out areas where important work remains yet to be done. The main themes of this exploration are what I call the Big Three: cosmology, identity, and epistemology; how you think about the universe, who you think you are, and what you believe about belief.

Where I'm Coming From

Enlightenment is an inherently slippery subject—elusive, full of paradoxes, never quite capable of being contained within boxes of words. Yet, with all due respect for its indescribability, I feel obligated to be clear—as clear as words permit—about my concept of it and personal experience with it.

I stumbled into my first experience of this sort at the age of thirty, one night while quietly reading a book of essays about psychology. I felt something open up within me, clearing the way for a powerful and long-lasting surge of feelings; these feelings were all one thing, but I can't describe that thing with any single word in my vocabulary of mental events. It was simultaneously a feeling of intellectual discovery; of enormous joy and peace; of love (just love, not for anything or anybody in particular); of sharpened sensory perceptions (I have described this as rather like having your windshield washed, or the wax removed from your ears); and of relief. The last was perhaps the most mysterious part of the experience, because I had not been particularly aware of anything that I needed to be relieved *from.*

I hadn't been involved in any serious exploration of Eastern mystical traditions up to that point, nor did I know much of anything about Abraham Maslow's studies of peak experience, or Fritz Perls' ideas about psychological health as a matter of getting into closer touch with the senses. All that came afterward. My process in the years that followed was a good example of what some psychologists call "reflective learning." Instrumental learning is the kind in which you pursue a course of study and then change as a result of it; in reflective learning the study comes after the change, when you try to figure out what you have figured out.

I certainly would not describe as an enlightened being the young man who then began to explore meditation disciplines, group therapies, and various schools of psychology, nor am I interested in applying that designation to myself now, except in the sense that I am about to define. It is a definition that has to do with the speed of the process, and also with the idea that enlightenment and non-enlightenment are not mutually exclusive.

There's some difference of opinion in the Eastern traditions about how long it takes for enlightenment to happen. Some see it as a gradual growth process that takes place over the course of a person's life. Others favor the sudden and complete transformation, *satori,* the thunderbolt of insight: You open your eyes, kick the ego's ass out the door, and never look back. I choose to stand courageously on both sides of this dispute. Those "aha" experiences do happen: I have had them and know others who have had more dramatic ones than my own. But the process never ends. There is always room for more reflective learning, always the opportunity to expand understanding of the larger context—the universe, no less—within which the individual restructuring of consciousness takes place. I am unimpressed by gurus who don't acknowledge that they have anything to learn; that signifies to me a pernicious sort of ignorance. It then follows that there is no absolute line to be drawn between enlightened and unenlightened people, or, for that matter, between gurus and seekers: Everybody has something to teach and something to learn.

I see enlightenment as a growth process in which a restructuring of cognition takes place, a shift—sudden or gradual, quite possibly a bit of both—that involves a changed understanding of the universe, of self, and of truth. A completely unenlightened person (who I don't believe exists) would be completely devoid of any sense of, or experience beyond, everyday, I-centered consciousness. The completely enlightened person (who I don't believe exists either) would have completely taken leave of the world of egos and social beliefs and customs. I think that Western discussions of enlightenment tend to rely too heavily on the idea that enlightenment and ego-centered consciousness are two entirely different things, mutually exclusive. We might do better, and come much closer to what people actually experience, to think of them as complementary. For many people—as we'll see in later chapters in which we look at specific cases—the enlightenment experience opens the door to a more supple consciousness that has room for ego-centered cognition as well as a much wider sense of self that can as accurately be called no-self. Think of it as being able to use both arms, whereas in the past you had two of them but only knew how to use one—or, to stretch the metaphor a bit—didn't know the other one was there.

In this book I will deal with enlightenment as a process that may unfold slowly, or in sudden leaps, or in some combination of the two—and the enlightened person as one who has some understanding of that process and is actively engaged in living and deepening it. There are many degrees of enlightenment, of course, as many as there are people. The human mind is endlessly intricate and varied, and yet far from being fully understood by any school of thought, East or West. That being the case, we really aren't justified in making too many pronouncements about who is or who isn't enlightened, or who is more or less enlightened than somebody else. I especially want to avoid the kind of spiritual hero-worship that is all too common among explorers and seekers. Enlightened people do not know all things, and they do not glow in the dark. Enlightenment happens to real, flawed human beings; they remain real, and remain flawed—at least insofar as the concept of flaws is of interest to them. Yet there is a basic common characteristic among those who have entered that terrain—a recognition that everyday, I-centered consciousness is only one way of organizing cognition (far from the best one), and that other ways are available to us at all times. This doesn't mean that I-centered cognition disappears entirely from the individual's thought processes—that ego is vanquished, as some of the spiritual literature has it. Ego is not a thing but rather a general and not entirely precise term for certain cognitive operations. And, as we'll see when we get into what's happening in the worlds of psychology and brain research, cognition is capable of doing a number of different things at the same time.

The View from the West

Although this is a work of synthesis, bringing together themes from East and West, it definitely and deliberately approaches the intersection from the Western side, and within the framework of an evolutionary story.

The plot of my story is essentially this: Life evolves on the planet and, eventually, develops consciousness—many kinds of conscious life forms. In one species the evolutionary process jumps to a new level with the development of a new kind of consciousness, marked by a capacity for self-reflection and symbolic communication—language—that becomes vastly more complex and sophisticated than the communications strategies known to other species. Language is so powerful a tool, with such a great capacity to aid survival and further development, that it begins to shape the biological evolution of the species: Homo sapiens develops a larger brain because individuals with better symbol-processing abilities have much better chances of surviving and reproducing. Language becomes central to cognition, internal as well as communicative. People frame their personal fantasies and plans in words, and they employ words to fashion all the things that make a society—laws, rituals, literature, history.

This is a wonderful development, and with it people essentially create a new world, and new concepts of themselves. The individual has a life story, a name, names of ancestors, a story about the society of which he or she is a part. In some places personal identity extends beyond life with myths of immortality and belief in the soul.

Much is gained, but there is a price to be paid: People become so involved in their identity-narratives that they become lost in them like some brilliant builder who constructs a wonderful maze of gardens and buildings and then cannot find his way out of them into the world beyond—who indeed forgets that there is a world beyond.

In this world of words individuals become identified with the narrative of self—the internal parade of needs, greeds, agendas, vanities, and resentments called the ego. They also accept the structures of their particular society—with its categories of class, tribe, religion, nationality, and gender; its values and beliefs; its stories about the world—as if they represented some transcendent cosmic order rather than the all-too-human creations of a particular time and place. And they learn to reify—to make things out of processes.

But there are always people who see through this maze to a greater or lesser extent, experience their insight as liberation, and seek to liberate others. These efforts are sometimes institutionalized into religions, and at other times they are carried out by individual teachers or ephemeral groups, leaving little or no record behind them. In the West the efforts have been associated with the work of philosophers and, more recently, psychologists, humanists, and scientists.

Some of these visionaries are beginning to talk about an evolutionary project—perhaps at times a touch too loosely, as if it were a task we fully understood or could bring off in a year or two. It is a project that involves constructing a more spacious worldview, one that includes among its many elements a growing understanding of human cognition itself, and of the role of language (and other symbolic systems such as visual images) in structuring our reality. It involves an ability to stand apart from the concept of self, and to see beyond the structures of society. Searching for appropriate metaphors—an important part of the project, because straightforward descriptions don't always work—some seize upon examples from the realm of nonhuman nature, such as the biological model of the chambered nautilus.

The nautilus is a marine mollusk, in structure somewhat resembling a snail. But snails don't get around much, whereas the nautilus travels enormous distances underwater. As the nautilus grows, from time to time it constructs a new and larger chamber in its shell, moves into it, and seals off the smaller chamber it had previously called home. In the nineteenth century this caught the fancy of Oliver Wendell Holmes, who wrote a poem about it that was much quoted at the time:

> Still, as the spiral grew,
> He left the past year's dwelling for the new,
> Stole with soft step its shining archway through,
> Built up its idle door,
> Stretched in his last-found home, and knew the old no more.

Holmes took the nautilus' example to be a "heavenly message" with excellent advice on how human beings should proceed through life:

> Build thee more stately mansions, O my soul,
> As the swift seasons roll!
> Leave thy low-vaulted past!
> Let each new temple, nobler than the last,
> Shut thee from heaven with a dome more vast, . . . 5

The words sound old-fashioned—I can't imagine Holmes at one of those slam gatherings where people shout poetry at one another—but the metaphor is a good one. People and societies progress by building more spacious cognitive worlds, expanding their boundaries—"pushing the envelope," in today's organizational jargon—and moving beyond the limited perspectives of the past. And this work is done not only by the traditional Eastern disciplines that we generally associate with enlightenment but also by Western scientists, philosophers, artists, psychotherapists. It is everybody's business.

I have nothing whatever against the Eastern enlightenment traditions, but we need to remember that they, too, are structures of words and images, products of specific cultures. Unlike most religious doctrines they present themselves—at least the best of them do—not so much as bodies of eternal truth but rather as sets of tools and guidelines for developing a more spacious view of reality. The guidelines can easily become dogmas, however, and the person who is trying to grow needs to be aware of that tendency—and to remember that the subject is This, and that nobody owns it.

PART ONE

FIVE MODERN LIBERATION

MOVEMENTS

In the latter centuries of the modern age, in a Western world shaking itself free of political and religious absolutism, and stirring with discoveries and inventions, there began to emerge the outlines of an evolutionary project, a new trajectory for the human species.

In the following pages we will look at five different movements—one in the eighteenth century, one in the nineteenth, and three in the twentieth—each of which took steps in that direction:

- The Enlightenment, in which the notion of progress became a predominant theme and people were encouraged to think for themselves and to question all dogmas—most definitely including those of established religions.

- The Darwinian movement, which offered powerful evidence in support of two disturbing ideas: that we live in an ever-changing universe—not merely created in the remote past, but continually in process of creation—and that we are integrally and inseparably a part of all life on Earth.

- Psychoanalysis, a sequel to Darwinism, in which a further connection was made between the human mind and its biological origins. The conscious mind—the evolutionary process—became conscious of the unconscious and saw the ego as a fragment of the self rather than its entirety.

- Existentialism, haunted by Neitzsche's powerful yet puzzling command to "become what you are," which challenged all received truths and wrestled with the nature of Being—the supreme mystery, the ultimately unanswerable question. The existentialist movement also led to new psychological theories and therapies based on the proposition that we repress not only thoughts of sex and violence but also our very sense of being.

- The human potential movement of the 1960s and 1970s, in which Eastern mysticism and Western psychology flowed together and the vision of a grand and immediate transformation of the human species became—for better and for worse—something akin to a political ideology.

Each of these was a liberation movement in its own way, an attempt to stretch the boundaries of human consciousness and move beyond narrow visions of the person. Each brought messages that were welcomed as such by some, rejected and ignored by others. And all, in their various ways, are still with us. They are essential building blocks of the next Enlightenment, as the human evolutionary project enters a new stage.

CHAPTER I

Enlightenment, European Style

The identity, which we ascribe to the mind of man, is only a fictitious one.
— DAVID HUME[1]

What objects may be by themselves, and apart from the receptivity of our senses, remains completely unknown to us. We know nothing but our manner of perceiving them.
— IMMANUEL KANT[2]

Our personal lives and the lives of societies are a continual process of change; this is one of many things that we all know, sort of, but don't know deeply enough. And to make matters even more interesting, there are also second-order changes: accelerations, leaps to another level, and occasionally the appearance of radically new ideas about change itself. Second-order changes are emergents, not merely continuations of what has been going on so far. They're surprises that can't be predicted from the state the system was in prior to the change.

The cultures of both East and West are rich with accounts of second-order changes in the lives of individual people: the Bible tells of revelations, the Greeks spoke of *metanoia,* the Zen masters teach the doctrine of *satori.* Some of these changes are described as instantaneous, others as deep and gradual unfoldings, but they are always seen as profound transitions in which a person becomes fundamentally different in some major way from what he or she had been before. Today such change is studied by developmental psychologists, who know that personal growth isn't simply a matter of accumulating information according to what you might call the architectural model, adding pieces according to a predetermined plan. It's also a series of restructurings in which you form new and different concepts about yourself and the world—including new concepts about personal growth.

The second kind of progress, social, historical growth, is described by such terms as Michel Foucault's "episteme" and Thomas Kuhn's ever-popular "paradigm shift." An episteme, for Foucault, was the underlying set of rules that framed the thinking of a specific society at a certain stage of its history—and was occasionally replaced by a new episteme. A paradigm shift for Kuhn was one of those revolutionary upheavals when the members of a scientific community, forced by new evidence to change their minds about some essential feature of the natural world, began to see things differently, form different theories, and find things in their research that an older paradigm had not been able to explain. After such a paradigm shift, according to Kuhn, comes a period of first-order change in which researchers accumulate new information consistent with the new paradigm. These terms (particularly "paradigm shift") have been so promiscuously overused that they no longer have much value—and yet societies do change their prevailing worldviews, sometimes on a large and heroic scale. Such changes are a common and natural part of the history of civilizations as much as they are the growth of individuals. They are also wonderful generators of political and intellectual conflict as they set liberals and conservatives, radicals and reactionaries, hucksters and heroes to arguing about how much change is desirable, how soon, and in what direction.

The past few centuries have been a time of remarkable first-order changes in the everyday realities of human life and even more remarkable second-order changes in how people think about change itself. Some of these changes really define the beginning of the modern era. In the Western world, the Middle Ages was a long period in which life seemed to grind on through endless cycles, little was known of the past, and the future promised to stretch on with more of the same until the angelic horns would finally blow at Judgment Day. Toward the end of that era, people began to revise their ideas about how they were located in space and time. If there was ever a new episteme, that was it.

The new orientation in space is the easier part of this epistemic change to understand, more clearly readable in the pages of history. Human beings were becoming increasingly footloose; developments in shipbuilding and navigation were making it possible for explorers to travel far beyond land on the high seas and soon literally around the world, bringing back news of distant civilizations, vast oceans, and heretofore unknown territories. The early modern era was a time not only of exploration but also of mapmaking and printing. Even the stay-at-homes could study Mercator's map of the world—as awesome an intellectual achievement in its time as the sequencing of the human genome in ours, and a whole lot easier to figure out—and browse through Ortelius's first atlas, or read that smashing sixteenth-century bestseller, *Mundus Novus,* the story of Amerigo Vespucci's adventures along the coastlines of South America. In the process of study their mental maps took on a new clarity and scope, and their minds ventured out into the vastly larger world that the navigators had found for them.

As that new sense of geographic space spread throughout the world, so did a new perception of time and history. The ancient view of time as cyclical was overtaken by what sociologist Goran Therborn calls "the discovery of the future," a recognition that the basic conditions of life *changed,* that there was not only a New World out there across the ocean but also new worlds continually appearing everywhere as the future revealed itself—"an open, unbuilt site never visited before, but a place reachable and constructible."[3]

Those unfolding landscapes of space and time were the spacious environment within which the Renaissance and the Enlightenment flourished. The former brought exuberant visions of life's possibilities; the latter an outburst of scientific discovery, social dissent, and philosophical exploration that at some points produced concepts of *personal* enlightenment much closer to what we find in Eastern traditions than today's spiritual seekers may suspect. It isn't entirely coincidental that we use the same word in English—enlightenment—for the Eastern concept of liberation from illusion and the Western concept of liberation from ignorance.

The March of the Philosophes

The European Enlightenment wasn't only a concept, of course; it was also a *Zeitgeist,* a period of time with a distinct personality, and it was first and foremost a movement. As it gained momentum its leaders, particularly the boundlessly energetic *philosophes* of France, formed a loose community, something like what today we would call a network. It had its cliques and loners; it had some deep philosophical differences, especially the schism between empiricists and idealists; and it had no lack of strife and rivalry. But the various writers, academicians, scientists, aristocrats, politicians, and renegade clergymen who formed the movement shared a sense of common purpose—they saw themselves as united in a noble cause. This understanding stretched across national boundaries: it was the Age of Enlightenment in Great Britain and the United States, the *illuminismo* in Italy; the *siècle des lumières* in France, and the *Aufklärung* in Germany. The *philosophes* and their allies believed that the time had come to bring the final end to the Dark Ages, debunk superstition and dogma, and create a new and more hopeful sense of human nature and the possibilities of civilization. In the words of the encyclopedist Denis Diderot, the movement's objective was nothing less than to "change the general way of thinking."[4] They wanted a new episteme, built on the discovery of the future but going well beyond it, in which human beings would for the first time deliberately transform themselves and create the conditions of life in the decades ahead.

Their project took them inevitably into an extensive running battle with established religions. Although the Reformation and Counter-Reformation had been shaking up the power structures of the Christian world for some two centuries before the *philosophes* and their allies emerged as a major force, the kind of religious freedom most of us in the West take for granted today was nowhere to be found in Europe. Official state religions—whether Catholic or Protestant—were the norm, and religious authorities had real power, which they exercised with great enthusiasm. The persecution of dissent was vigorous in most of the great monarchies: On the Continent people were still being put to death for sacrilege and sorcery, and even in relatively open-minded England life could be difficult for anyone whose faith was not that of the established church.

However, despite its strong reformist bent and general skepticism, the Enlightenment was not simply an antireligious movement. Even Sir Isaac Newton—the scientific ikon of the age, whom some of the *philosophes* considered to be the greatest man who ever lived—was a devout believer who saw his work as advancing the cause of Christianity. Most of the intellectuals of the Enlightenment considered themselves to be religious in some sense of that word, and they had all been reared and educated within a civilization saturated with Christian belief. But they were dedicated to the free exercise of the mind and favored a more relaxed, tolerant, and nondogmatic form of religion. They tended to regard many of the official teachings as little more than primitive superstitions—in some cases rather silly and in others downright dangerous.

The doctrine of original sin was especially uncongenial. Both Catholic and Protestant churches taught that humanity had been naturally corrupt since Adam and Eve got into trouble with God for disobeying his orders. This was a proposition that the authorities no doubt sincerely believed, but it just happened to serve nicely in support of both religious and secular power structures: It was—said the church—necessary for people to follow the teachings of religious leaders in order to save their souls and escape eternal damnation. It was equally necessary—said the state—for people to submit to the power of monarchs (endowed with divine right) who would benevolently but forcefully hold down their animal natures and guide them along the paths of righteousness.

The concept of original sin worked wonderfully well for defenders of the status quo, but not so well for reformers; it just wasn't hospitable to ideas about improving the conditions of human life for the living, and religious authorities were likely to regard any exercise of reason as evidence that the wily Devil was playing games with the human mind again. If people were inherently, naturally corrupt, it followed that there were definite limits to their ability to better themselves. In fact, too much concern for improving their conditions was missing the true point of mortal life, which was to seek salvation in the hereafter.

The prevailing view of the Enlightenment was that human beings were essentially good—or at the very least were capable of self-improvement—and that the means to improvement was the free exercise of reason. The Baron d'Holbach, for example, insisted that religious teachings had it all wrong in holding original sin to be the cause of evil and misery in human affairs: "Men," he wrote, "are unhappy only because they are ignorant; they are ignorant only because every thing conspires to prevent their being enlightened; they are so wicked only because their reason is not yet sufficiently unfolded."[5]

Although d'Holbach stood at the most radically anticlerical wing of the Enlightenment, that particular statement pretty well expresses the mainstream view of the movement: Humanity would improve—perhaps even achieve utopian perfection, a sort of Salvation on Earth—through the disciplined and unfettered application of its capacity for rational thought.

The kind of science that had led Newton and Copernicus and Galileo to new comprehension of the natural world was now to be applied in the realm of human affairs. Toward the end of the eighteenth century the term "social science" appeared in the vocabulary of Enlightenment thinkers. It was the ancestor of the social sciences that are now part of the curriculum of modern universities everywhere, but with a much more proactive thrust. The object was not merely to understand social conditions but to apply that understanding in practical ways to change those conditions for the better. Knowledge—won and tested with scientific rigor—would be the shining key to social progress.

The Apostles of Progress

It's hard for us now to realize that there was a time when the idea that the world changes, and might even change for the better, was a stunning, shining-new concept. Scholars argue about whether people in classical Greece and Rome or in the Middle Ages had any idea of progress at all: Some claim that expressions of such a concept can be found in the works of various philosophers. Others find the evidence that it was a driving force in social life very scanty, and doubt that any such concept had much of an effect on the lives of the majority of people. Sociologist Robert Nisbet believes that the idea of progress was never entirely absent from Western thought, but concedes that it underwent a remarkable surge of vitality at a fairly recent stage of history. "During the period 1750–1900 the idea of progress reached its zenith in the Western mind in popular as well as scholarly circles. From being one of the important ideas in the West it became the dominant idea, even when one takes into account the rising importance of other ideas such as equality, social justice, and popular sovereignty— each of which was without question a beacon light in this period."[6]

The tangible signs of progress—the explorations, discoveries, and inventions; the spread of knowledge and prosperity—were so much in evidence that it is hardly surprisingly that people began to think there was an underlying natural law at work, something comparable to those Newton had discovered. The inevitability of progress was an idea whose time had come, and it made a dramatic entrance in December of 1750, when a twenty-three-year-old student named Anne-Robert Turgot delivered a public lecture at the Sorbonne entitled "A Philosophical Review of the Successive Advances of the Human Mind." There may have been other ideas of human advancement in the past, but this was a *modern* idea, based on Turgot's survey of what was known of human history and his scientific search for a unifying pattern: "The natural philosopher forms hypotheses, observes their consequences. . . . Time, research, chance, amass observations, and unveil the hidden connections which unite phenomena."

And what such investigations revealed was an onward-and-upward march of human betterment in which "manners are softened, the human mind enlightened, isolated nations brought together; commercial and political ties finally unite all parts of the globe; and the total mass of humankind, through alternations of calm and upheaval, good fortune and bad, advances ever, though slowly, toward greater perfection."[7]

Some aspects of Turgot's thesis sound terribly naive today. He was unselfconsciously ethnocentric, never really questioning whether what looked like improvement to one group of people might not look so bright to another. But his lecture wasn't just giddy boosterism. It took into account the ignorance and folly of human life, the backward steps and the distance yet to be traveled. That was what gave such conviction to its enormously optimistic conclusions about the general direction of change.

The young student's lecture was one of those remarkable statements—like Martin Luther's two centuries before—that somehow catch the spirit of the time and open the floodgates for an outpouring of new thought. After Turgot came a long parade of thinkers with ideas about how humanity progressed: Adam Smith with ideas of progress through economic freedom, Thomas Jefferson and the other American founders with ideas of progress through political change, Immanuel Kant with ideas of progress through advanced understanding of the nature of truth. One of the most dedicated apostles of progress was the Marquis de Condorcet, who wrote an adulatory biography of Turgot and proclaimed him the discoverer of the "law of progress." For Condorcet, progress *had* to happen and keep happening and was firmly built into the order of the universe: "Nature," he wrote, "has set no term to the perfection of our human faculties, that the perfectibility of man is truly indefinite; and that the progress of this perfectibility, from now onwards independent of any power that might wish to halt it, has no other limit than the duration of the globe upon which nature has cast us." Condorcet became a dedicated supporter of the French Revolution, so passionately committed to its democratic promise that he wrote the lines above while he was in hiding from Jacobin police. He finally died in prison, probably a suicide, and would have been dragged to the guillotine by his fellow revolutionaries if he had not taken his own life. But his faith in progress never wavered.

The Enlightenment's faith in the law of progress was so powerful that some people even began to believe there was progress in the biological realm. This was in some ways the most revolutionary idea of all, since it challenged the centuries-old prevailing view that all species of life had been given their forms and places in the Great Chain of Being by God at the time of the original creation of the world, that God's work in that department was done, and they would continue to exist forever in exactly the same forms and places without alteration. This view was summed up nicely by the Abbé Pluché, who wrote shortly before the Enlightenment began: "Nothing more, therefore, will be produced in all the ages to follow. All the philosophers have deliberated and come to agreement upon this point. Consult the evidence of experience; elements always the same, species that never vary, seeds and germs prepared in advance for the perpetuation of everything . . . so that one can say, Nothing new under the sun, no new production, no species which has not been since the beginning."[9] According to this view, there was neither appearance of new life forms nor extinction of those that existed.

A different view emerged in the eighteenth century. In Germany, the philosopher Gottfried von Leibnitz put forth the idea of the "progress of the whole universe," and in France the naturalist Georges Louis LeClerc, Comte de Buffon, estimated that the earth had existed for about thirty-five thousand years before humankind appeared and that nature was in a continual state of development.

One of the most enthusiastic promoters of the idea of biological progress was the English physician Erasmus Darwin, who was also a tireless student of nature and the author of gigantic scientific studies such as the two-volume, 1400-page work entitled *Zoonomia, or, the Laws of Organic Life*. Dr. Darwin also wrote works that might best be described as scientific poetry, some of which, like the long poem titled *The Temple of Nature*, contain surprisingly modern accounts of evolutionary change:

> Organic Life beneath the shoreless waves
> Was born, and nurs'd in Ocean's pearly caves;
> First forms minute, unseen by spheric glass
> Move on the mud, or pierce the watery mass;
> These, as successive generations bloom,
> New powers acquire, and larger limbs assume;
> Whence countless groups of vegetation spring;
> And breathing realms of fin, and feet, and wing.[10]

The eighteenth-century vanguard of evolutionary thinking—Buffon, Erasmus Darwin, and others—could speculate about progressive change in the realm of nature. They could even describe it—but they couldn't prove it. It would remain for Erasmus Darwin's grandson Charles to bring about a major shift in the way people thought about evolution, by offering a persuasive and well-researched explanation of how it worked.

Selfless in Scotland, Prescient in Prussia

Another kind of progress was being made in the eighteenth century, a philosophical voyage into uncharted seas of uncertainty about the nature of thought, our ability to gain absolute truth, the continued existence of the objects we see around us, and even the reality of the self as a continuing entity. This line of thought—which we associate mainly with two philosophers, David Hume and Immanuel Kant—expressed in some ways the eighteenth-century critical spirit, but took it further than most of the *philosophes* dared or wanted to go. Voltaire and d'Holbach mainly wanted to debunk religious dogma and elevate science; Hume and Kant raised questions about the claims of science as well. In their explorations they took Enlightenment thought far beyond simple scientistic rationalism. ("Scientism," by the way, is a fussy but useful word used to describe the religion of science, the belief that it is the one true path to reality.) Kant and Hume brought into the Western world a few ideas that sound today very much like Asian mysticism, others like postmodern constructivism, and still others like the strange speculations of contemporary scientists about the relation between, or perhaps the inseparability of, cosmos and consciousness.

There were two distinct and somewhat contentious streams of thought in eighteenth-century philosophy, empiricist and idealist: the empiricist view of sensory experience as the ultimate key to reality versus the idealist veneration for abstract reasoning supported by the Platonic view of ideas as the ultimate reality. Hume's accomplishment was to take empiricism to its outer limits; Kant's was to create an ambitious conceptual edifice that claimed to reconcile empiricism and idealism, philosophy and science.

David Hume, born in Edinburg in 1711 to a family of the minor landed gentry, was a man of many parts. He was not only a philosopher but also an economist (a good friend of Adam Smith), an historian, a librarian, an essayist, and a diplomat. His best-known and most influential work is *A Treatise of Human Nature,* in which he attempted to apply the scientific methods of Isaac Newton to human thought and in the process advanced some ideas that scientists, then and now, find quite disturbing. Contemporary scholars argue about whether the *Treatise* is a work of psychology or a work of epistemology, but Hume was operating in those blessed times before the invention of academic disciplines and did not need to worry about that argument; he was simply trying to understand how we form our concepts about the world. Hume became one of the leaders in the Enlightenment's most ambitious project: the rational mind's investigation of the rational mind.

Immanuel Kant was born in Königsberg, East Prussia, in 1724, son of a humble saddle-maker. He became a student at the local university and, after many years of ill-paid work as a private tutor, a professor. He was also a man of wide-ranging interests who studied, taught, and wrote about physics, astronomy, geography, anthropology, and numerous other subjects. Kant is generally regarded as a greater philosopher than Hume, as he made the more lasting impact on the world, but his major works would never have taken the form they did without the influence of Hume, whose writings, Kant said, roused him from a "dogmatic slumber."

The two great thinkers of the Enlightenment never met. If they had, they would undoubtedly have found much to talk about, but they would have made an odd couple. Hume was a plump and amiable man, who enjoyed good food and good company and adapted comfortably to life in Paris during his years there as secretary to the embassy. Kant was slender and short, scarcely five feet tall, a man of eccentrically regular habits, of whom it is said that his neighbors could set their clocks by the moment he emerged for his daily afternoon walk. He spent his whole life in Königsberg, except for a short stint as a teacher in a town some thirty miles away, and declined a prestigious professorship in Berlin because it seemed too far from home.

Hume worked in the tradition of British empiricism, elaborating on the ideas of John Locke and Bishop George Berkeley, and frequently tipping his hat to Isaac Newton. He took the empiricist insistence on deriving knowledge from sensory experience further than his predecessors, and the *Treatise,* published when he was only twenty-six, was regarded by many as heretical and shocking. It challenged such commonly accepted notions as cause and effect. How do we know that one thing causes another? Hume asked. Surely there are things that happen in the present that probably proceed from other things that happened in the past and lead to things happening in the future. But we have no direct sensory evidence leading to a clear idea of the cause and effect *connection,* he said, and must "beat about all the neighboring fields" in the hope of stumbling across it. What we are left with is an inference, not a certainty. Hume also made short order of the soul and the very idea of any immaterial entity. He even challenged the idea of the mind, since we don't see that, either. What we see are things taking place within it; the mind is a "kind of theatre, where several perceptions successively make their appearance. . . ."

Had Hume ever been exposed to Zen Buddhism, he might have appreciated the famous parable in which the student comes to the master saying that his mind is troubled and asking that it be pacified.

"Show me your mind," says the Zen master.

"Sir, I cannot."

"There. I have pacified your mind."

Hume's most Zenlike idea, the challenge to the continuing identity of the self, is based on his view of consciousness as a series of experiences that we connect inferentially. Hume pointed out that the continuing self—like the cause-and-effect relationship between different events—is something we assume but do not experience directly. "What then," he asked, "gives us so great a propension to suppose ourselves possest of an invariable and uninterrupted existence thro' the whole course of our lives?" He concluded that "the identity, which we ascribe to the mind of man, is only a fictitious one." Our experiences may be real when they happen, but the idea of a continuing, coherent, experiencing *self* is definitely a construction. Ego is illusion, in other words—and this from a Scottish skeptic. Hume thus managed to penetrate singlehandedly one of the most persistent illusions of human thought, an achievement that seems remarkable in some ways and yet more or less predictable from a strict empiricist approach. The observation that the only empirically verifiable self is that which exists at the moment was really a rather simple one, and not even entirely original. It was more or less the same as what you find in the fragments of Heraclitus, who wrote about the ephemeral nature of our existence before the time of Socrates. Nevertheless, the observation was revolutionary—so much so that Hume himself did not seem to have fully grasped the importance of it. His statements about the self take up only a small portion of the *Treatise*.

Kant agreed with some of Hume's ideas, disagreed with others, and went well beyond some of them. He agreed with the empiricists on the importance of sensory experience as a necessary condition of knowledge, but he insisted that the human mind comes equipped with a priori forms of sensibility that are hardwired—as we might say today. Among them are concepts of space and time, and of causality. His elegant bridge between radical empiricism and scientific realism was the distinction between things in themselves—the world we sometimes describe as "out there," existing in its own pristine condition, apart from human cognition—and the events of human consciousness. He called the former noumena, the latter phenomena. He insisted that noumena are real—without them there would be no phenomena—but nevertheless they are not what we experience, and they are not the raw data out of which scientific discoveries (such as Newton's) are made. He applied this distinction to all science, and also to Hume's doubts about the self. There is, Kant supposed, a real noumenal self—but we never experience it; we experience only the phenomenal self, the events of daily consciousness.

Although both men tore away a lot of comforting certainties, neither seems to have been plunged into existential despair about it. Hume remained cheerful and good-humored even after he learned that he had a fatal stomach cancer, and perhaps his resilience was consistent with his ideas: If you don't have a soul you can't be too worried about its career in the hereafter, and if you don't have a continuing self you can't be too worried about losing it. Kant was also a sociable man in his somewhat monastic way, and he wrote about experiences of the sublime, the infinite and boundless beauty of the world, as though he knew the territory.

It isn't my intention here to turn the amiable Scottish scholar and the clock-watching little Prussian professor into Asian gurus. They deserve to be understood as products of their own time and place. But there was more going on in that time and place—eighteenth-century Europe—than we give credit. Hume's radical empiricism (in practice very much like meditation) remains a priceless tool for examining and questioning assumptions, such as a continuing self that does the experiencing while somehow remaining separate from the experience. Kant gave us a way of regarding the discoveries of science as valid, yet at the same time putting human consciousness in the center of the universe we study. As a contemporary scholar puts it: "Kant changed the very meaning of 'metaphysics' or 'first philosophy' from the first-order study of the supernatural or incorporeal realm of being to the second-order study of the way human inquiry itself makes possible its access to whatever subject matter it studies."[11]

Looking Forward, Looking Back

The general verdict of contemporary historians is that the Enlightenment has long since run its course, the *philosophes* have done their work—with some success, some failure—and the torch has passed to other generations of intellectual vanguard. In fact, when the term "postmodern" came into general use as a descriptive term for the new state of cultural affairs that was emerging in the later years of the twentieth century, some writers explicitly defined postmodernity as what came after the final end—even collapse—of the Enlightenment project. It was not the impishly antiestablishment skepticism of the *philosophes* that seemed to be out of date but rather their conviction that intellectual accomplishments would reveal the right way to find the truth, and thus get all right-thinking people on the same page. Central to their idea of progress was that it would be achieved as more people became free of ignorance and joined in the project of finding the universally agreed-upon truths about how to live and run sensible societies. David Harvey, in an influential account of postmodernity, writes:

> The Enlightenment project . . . took it as axiomatic that there was only one possible answer to any question. From this it followed that the world could be controlled and rationally ordered if we could only picture and represent it rightly. But this presumed that there existed a single correct mode of representation which, if we could uncover it (and this was what scientific and mathematical endeavors were all about), would provide the means to Enlightenment ends. This was a way of thinking that writers as diverse as Voltaire, d'Alembert,

Diderot, Condorcet, Hume, Adam Smith, Saint-Simon, August Comte, Matthew Arnold, Jeremy Bentham and John Stuart Mill all had in common.[12]

That observation could be extended to Kant as well, even though his epistemology was extremely sophisticated, because it still aimed toward a universal truth—universal at least for the entire human species. In his earlier work Kant had written about other planets and their possible populations; apparently he believed that a priori ideas might not be the same for other intelligent life forms, and that the best we could hope for would be specieswide, scientific certainty. In the passage quoted at the beginning of this chapter, he noted that we do not perceive things in themselves: "We know nothing but our mode of perceiving them—a mode which is peculiar to us, and not necessarily shared in by every being, though, certainly, by every human being. With this alone have we any concern."

Toward the end of the nineteenth century, the idea that there was only one possible mode of representation began to break down. The categorical fixity of Enlightenment thought was increasingly challenged in the twentieth century and ultimately replaced by an emphasis upon divergent systems of representation—things perceived and known differently by different human beings. Harvey identifies some of the factors in this shift: the impact of modern art, the turn in linguistics to new ways of thinking about the connection between words and their objects, Einstein's theories with the increasing influence of non-Euclidean geometry, and the Marxist challenge that consciousness was shaped by the conditions of production. I would add the rise of anthropology with its view of cultural relativism, the emergence of intellectual movements such as the sociology of knowledge, research in the brain sciences that view truth as partially created by human cognition rather than simply discovered by it, and the ongoing process of globalization and changes in information and communications technologies that bring us all into daily confrontation with realities different from our own.

The Enlightenment's exuberant agenda of getting everybody to think rationally, and its assumption that rational thinking would lead straight ahead to a well-ordered society, now seem naive and simplistic. But it was a productive and courageous liberation movement that boldly took on the twin tyrannies of religious dogma and political power. Although some of its lessons have had to be unlearned in succeeding centuries, we are all—for better or worse—its children. Without the freedom from religious dogma that the eighteenth-century Enlightenment helped to win, we would not be at liberty to explore the kind of twenty-first-century Enlightenment that I propose to describe in these pages.

In an essay titled "What Is Enlightenment?" Kant called on all people to break free from slavish dependence on the thinking of others and have the courage to use their own minds. He offered *Sapere Aude* ("dare to know") as the motto of enlightenment.[13] A stirring battle cry. Although the Age of Enlightenment gave way to other liberation movements, it serves well for them all.

CHAPTER 2

Meeting Cousin Mushroom

In the light of the science of evolutionary biology which Darwin
founded, man is seen not just as a part of nature, but as a very
peculiar and indeed unique part. In his person the evolutionary
process has become conscious of itself.

— J U L I A N   H U X L E Y [1]

If Mr. Darwin can demonstrate to us our fungular descent, we
shall dismiss our pride, and avow . . . our unsuspected cousinship
with the mushrooms.

— B I S H O P   S A M U E L   W I L B E R F O R C E [2]

From the time of the great global explorations onward, the modern era has been marked by a series of epistemic upheavals—
times when people were challenged to revise their bedrock beliefs
about how the world worked, how things had been in the past, and
might become in the future. Of these upheavals, none was more contentious than the events following the publication in 1859 of Charles
Darwin's book *The Origin of Species by Means of Natural Selection, or,
The Preservation of Favoured Races in the Struggle for Life*. It had
what a contemporary observer called a "convulsive effect" in England, and, over a century and a half later, some groups are still fighting a rearguard action against what it brought into being—a
worldview of connection and change in which the human species is
seen as integrally related to all biological life and all biological life as
continually in transition. The concept of evolution took humanity a
long and frightening step away from the certainties of the medieval
world, and toward the still-forming consciousness of the twenty-first
century.

The Great Chain of Being

In order to appreciate the nature of this revolution, it's necessary to have an idea of the worldview that Darwin challenged, and how deeply it was rooted in the consciousness of Western civilization.

For over two thousand years, scientists and philosophers had been building a concept of the order of life on Earth, the concept known as the Great Chain of Being. The American philosopher Thomas Lovejoy, who wrote a history of the concept, finds it was foreshadowed in the thought of Socrates and Plato and expressed in rudimentary form by Aristotle's descriptions of a hierarchy of organisms—each level of life having all the powers of those below it on the scale, as well as some additional power of its own that differentiated it.[3] The biblical account of how God created all the kinds of birds, beasts, and finally humans in six days, was also foundational to what developed over the centuries into a huge edifice of thought, uniting theology, philosophy, and an ever growing body of scientific research. It envisioned all the forms of earthly life ascending through levels of complexity to humankind, and then upward from humanity to the angels and to God. There were, of course, many disputes about the details of this arrangement, but on the whole it was a powerful, elegantly organized, and widely held view of the living world that made it entirely possible for a student of nature to be both a scientist and a good Christian.

In the eighteenth century the Great Chain worldview was at its zenith, as were two basic concepts that had come to be associated with it. One was the principle of plenitude—that God had created everything it was possible to create. The other was the belief that this plenitude was an unchanging state of affairs. The two were really one as Lovejoy explains. The principle of plenitude was "inconsistent with any belief in progress, or, indeed, in any sort of significant change in the universe as a whole. The Chain of Being, in so far as its continuity and completeness were affirmed on the customary grounds, was a perfect example of an absolutely rigid and static scheme of things."[4] A writer early in the eighteenth century pointed out that if the arrangement had been satisfactory to God when he created it, it should remain so: "God *cannot hereafter* create any new Species of Beings; because, whatever it is good for him to create in time, it was equally good from all Eternity."[5]

Yet, even in this proud moment when the Great Chain worldview was at its most powerful, some thinkers were beginning to revise it. Lovejoy describes this as a *temporalizing* of the Great Chain—moving it out of the status of the unchanging and eternal into the world of change. Influenced by the *zeitgeist,* a growing attractiveness of the idea of progress, a small but growing number of people began to wonder if all of creation were not somehow in motion: "The *plenum formarum* came to be conceived by some, not as the inventory but as the program of nature, which is being carried out gradually and exceedingly slowly in the cosmic history."[6]

Darwinian Foreplay

So *The Origin of Species* was not simply a bomb dropped on an unsuspecting public. The idea of evolution was already blowing in the wind, and had been expressed—at least in a very rudimentary form—by others. Writing over a century before *The Origin* appeared, Leibnitz had stated his belief that "we must recognize a certain perpetual and very free progress of the whole universe, such that it is always going forward to greater improvement."[7] Other philosophers had expressed similar ideas, and so had scientists such as the Comte de Buffon and the French biologist Jean-Baptiste Lamarck. Lamarck—whose major book was published in 1809, the year of Charles Darwin's birth—argued that the organs of animals changed according to how they were used (or not used) and that these "acquired characteristics" were passed on to subsequent generations. Several decades before Charles Darwin published his groundbreaking book, there was already a lively and sometimes contentious debate in the world of biology between "evolutionists" and "immutabilists." The evolutionists were definitely in the minority, but they were an influential minority, confident that they were on the cutting edge of understanding.

Geological research was doing its part to prepare the way for the intellectual revolution that *The Origin* was to bring about. Charles Lyell's *Principles of Geology,* published in the 1830s, offered strong evidence that the earth was much older than it would be had it been created on the date (October 23, 4004 B.C.) that British theologians had come to accept as the day when God went to work. Lyell's discoveries and those of others who built on them would be essential to forming an idea of a much, much older world—old enough for evolution to have taken place in it according to the Darwinian account.

Yet another sort of evidence to shake the immutabilist worldview was provided by the occasional discovery of species of animal life that no longer existed. Fossils of extinct prehistoric species such as dinosaurs and mastodons were being unearthed, studied, and biologically classified. This evidence would seem to controvert the theological doctrine of the Great Chain of Being, which held that all life forms existed exactly as they had at the time of creation, with no emergence of new species nor the disappearance of old. For many people in the early nineteenth century, such discoveries prepared the way for accepting an evolutionary worldview; others, however, avoided any such discomfort by explaining that these were simply animals that had been created by God at the same time as all the others, but then had failed to get into Noah's Ark during the great flood.[8] (I sometimes muse on this as a wonderful way of explaining away a difficulty, and also find it enjoyable to contemplate what a great seagoing Jurassic Park that Noah would have had if he succeeded in getting a few dinosaurs and mastodons onto the boat.)

Erasmus Darwin believed in evolution as strongly as some people believed in Genesis, and his writings about the origins and transitions of life on earth, although poetic and speculative—and regarded by some critics as little more than fantasy—were read by many people. They helped to get the idea of evolution into general circulation well before the doctor's grandson presented it in the form of a careful and amply documented scientific study.

And then there was Alfred Wallace, the naturalist who was working toward the same general evolutionary ideas that Darwin made famous, and whose journal article entitled "On the Law Which Has Regulated the Introduction of New Species," published in 1855, stimulated Darwin to get busy and prepare his own work for publication, after a delay of fourteen years following his famous voyage aboard the *HMS Beagle*. He then completed his book in a little over one year, and *The Origin of Species* was published in 1859.

The most disturbing idea associated with *The Origin*—that the human species was a part of the evolutionary process and probably descended from nonhuman life forms—wasn't really in the book. Darwin only suggested that "much light will be thrown on the origin of man and his history" as a result of future research, and wrote about the subject at great length in a later work, *The Descent of Man*.[9] The subject of human origins jumped so quickly out of the pages of *The Origin of Species* into the heat of a huge public controversy because many people already had a pretty good idea of the concept of evolution and its human implications. What they experienced upon encountering *The Origin of Species* was, as one historian observes, "not the shock of discovery but rather the shock of recognition."[10] And the shock, even though it had been sneaking up on Western society for a century or more, was profoundly disturbing when it finally hit.

Convulsion

It was shocking in at least four different ways: politically, scientifically, theologically, and psychologically.

The political implications of *The Origin* were subtle, but not so subtle that people failed entirely to notice them. There was a fairly obvious parallel between the biological order described by the Great Chain of Being—all species of life, from the most humble to the most exalted, going about their business in their God-given econiches—and the British class system in which "knowing one's place" and faithfully "keeping one's station in life" were praised as the greatest of civic virtues, even as obedience to divine will. "'Tis impossible that all should be rulers and none subjects," reflected one prominent English theologian.[11] Another, Soame Jenyns, could write:

The universe resembles a large and well-regulated family, in which all the officers and servants, and even the domestic animals, are subservient to each other in a proper subordination; each enjoys the privileges and perquisites peculiar to his place, and at the same time contributes, by that just subordination, to the magnificence and happiness of the whole.[12]

It's hardly surprising that Karl Marx, who was living in London at the time of Darwin, wrote to a friend saying: "Darwin's book is very important and serves me as a basis in natural selection for the class struggle in history. . . ."[13]

In the world of science, Darwin's ideas were met with a variety of responses, ranging from enthusiastic acceptance to mild skepticism and quibbling to outright hostility. The leading enthusiasts were Joseph Dayton Hooker and Thomas Henry Huxley, the latter known as "Darwin's bulldog" because of his enthusiasm for attacking critics of evolution. The quibbles included worries about whether Darwin's theorizing met the standards of inductive science as well as more technical questions that could not really be resolved until the twentieth century with the emergence of genetics and the "evolutionary synthesis" of Darwin and Mendel. The outright hostility is nicely exemplified by John Obadiah Westwood, professor of zoology at Oxford, who proposed that the university establish a permanent lectureship for the exposure of the fallacies in Darwin's work. It was a difficult moment for Western science, which was strongly rooted in the Cartesian-Newtonian view of the scientist as observer—standing apart from natural phenomena and objectively studying them. The more explicit became the question of where Homo sapiens belonged in the evolutionary story, the less tenable this stance became.

The theological shock is, of course, the best-known aspect of the reaction to Darwin's ideas, and, although the controversy about evolution is sometimes represented as little more than a conflict between scientific fact and religious doctrine, it was never really that simple. There were clergymen who accepted Darwin's ideas and scientists who rejected them, and there were people such as Adam Sedgwick, a clergyman and geologist, who criticized Darwin on both scientific and religious grounds. In a review of *The Origin,* Sedgwick charged that Darwin had completely abandoned solid science: "Each series of facts is laced together by a series of assumptions, and repetitions of the one false principle. You cannot make a good rope out of a string of air bubbles." And in a letter to a friend he revealed religious concerns that were inseparable from the methodological critique. Darwin's book, he wrote, was "a system embracing all living nature, vegetable and animal; yet contradicting—point blank—the vast treasury of facts that the Author of Nature has, during the past two or three thousand years, revealed to our senses. And why is this done? For no other solid reason, I am sure, except to make us independent of a Creator."[14]

The most determined and dedicated of the evolution-bashers was Samuel Wilberforce, bishop of Oxford, and it was the famous clash between Wilberforce and T. H. Huxley that presented to the world a dramatic if somewhat overstated image of the Darwinian conflict as a *mano a mano* between religion and science.

This took place in the summer of 1860 at the annual meeting in Oxford of the British Association for the Advancement of Science, where the proceedings included the reading of a paper on the impacts of Darwinian ideas. The paper, thunderously dull by most accounts, was followed by a lively discussion between Wilberforce and Huxley that led to a much-quoted—and probably misquoted—exchange of barbs. Accounts vary, but apparently Wilberforce said something to the effect of asking Huxley whether it was through his grandfather or his grandmother that he claimed his descent from an ape. Huxley's response was that he would rather be descended from an ape than from Bishop Wilberforce—or perhaps the somewhat milder rejoinder: "I would rather be the offspring of two apes than be a man and afraid to face the truth." Quotes of such events are never precisely accurate, but as a recent Darwin biographer notes: "Whatever the exact words, Huxley struck back as forcefully as he knew how. Insulting a bishop was, a century and more ago, a very rare practice; insulting him in public, in his own diocese, was even more so. Lady Brewster fainted at the shock. Most of the audience applauded."[15]

Bishop Wilberforce may have been bested on that occasion, but he was as tenacious a battler as was Huxley, and he kept up the campaign against Darwinian heresy for the remainder of his life. It ended in 1873 when he was thrown from his horse and died as his head hit a stone, prompting Huxley to remark that it was the first time reality and the Bishop's brains had ever come into close contact.

The Deeper Disturbance

It's interesting that so much of the outrage expressed against Darwin by Wilberforce and other critics had to do with the issue of whether the human species were also a product of evolution and therefore connected, as though by family ties, to all other forms of life. This was the core of his insulting remark to Huxley. It was also a major theme in a review of *The Origin* that Wilberforce wrote for the influential *Quarterly Review,* in which he referred archly to "our unsuspected cousinship with the mushrooms," and wondered whether it was credible "that all favorable varieties of turnips are tending to become men."[16]

Although Darwin had only hinted at the matter of humanity's place in the evolutionary scheme of things in *The Origin,* Huxley, ever ready to advance the argument, gave two lectures on the subject in Edinburgh and published them in 1863 under the title *Evidence as to Man's Place in Nature*.[17] Arguing from a detailed study of the anatomical similarities between humans and the higher apes, Huxley asserted unequivocally that Homo sapiens was a product of evolution. Later in the same year the geologist Charles Lyell offered further support for the human-animal connection in *The Geological Evidences of the Antiquity of Man*[18], and in 1864 Alfred Wallace, the less famous co-discoverer of evolution, published an article entitled "The Origin of Human Races and the Antiquity of Man Deduced from the Theory of 'Natural Selection'."[19] Other works along the same lines followed, and as they did it was no longer possible for anyone to avoid grappling with the proposition that human life had evolved out of earlier forms of life.

Ego and Evolution: Something Lost, Something Gained

The concept of evolution forced into human consciousness two dis-turbing—and enlightening—ideas: One was the idea that we live in an ever-changing universe, not merely created in the remote past but continually in process of creation. The other was the idea that we are integrally and inseparably a part of all life on earth, and indeed related to the monkeys and the mushrooms. To assimilate these two ideas fully—which is part of the work of the twenty-first century—is to restructure fundamentally our vision of what we are.

The effort to accept and appreciate the Darwinian message is remarkably similar to the struggle that accompanies individual growth and change. Personal growth always involves letting go of something; every letting-go feels like a loss and is the precondition to a greater gain. What humanity loses is the rather simple biblical image of its starring role in the creation. What it gains is a far more signifi-cant place in the universe because we can see that we are not only a part of nature but also a conscious part of it. Human thought is obvi-ously the product of evolution; in the discoveries of Darwin, as Julian Huxley put it, evolution became conscious of itself. That a descendant of the apes, a distant cousin of the mushrooms, should begin to figure out how life itself evolved is a story no less wondrous than Genesis, humbling in some ways and exalting in others, and made even more awesome as we come to understand that it is a story not yet fully told.

Darwin was not only a discoverer but a liberator, enabling those who were willing to break free of a specieswide egoism that had set humanity apart from the rest of life, and to take a place in the complex and ever-changing biological processes of an evolving planet.

Although the Darwinian worldview is often dismissed as coldly scientific, replacing the reverence of the religious account of creation with a bleak story of mechanistic development amid endless struggle, the tone of Darwin's own work, full of poetry and wonder, belies this. In *The Origin* he wrote of the great Tree of Life, "which fills with its dead and broken branches the crust of the earth, and covers the surface with its ever-branching and beautiful ramifications." In one description of the beauties of life's varieties he asked:

> How have all these exquisite adaptations of one part of the organization to another part, and to the conditions of life, and of one organic being to another being, been perfected? We see these beautiful co-adaptations most plainly in the woodpecker and the mistletoe; and only a little less plainly in the humblest parasite which clings to the hairs of a quadruped or feathers of a bird; in the structure of the beetle which dives through the water; in the plumed seed which is wafted by the gentlest breeze; in short we see beautiful adaptations everywhere and in every part of the organic world.

The late cultural critic O. B. Hardison was a great admirer of Darwin's prose, and commented on the above: "*Exquisite, perfected, beautiful, humblest, plumed, gentlest.* The world described by these adjectives is not cold, alien, or indifferent. It is a work of art."[20]

CHAPTER 3

The Dark Matter of the Mind

I can assure you that the hypothesis of there being unconscious mental processes paves the way to a decisive new orientation in the world and in science. —SIGMUND FREUD[1]

We do not know how far the process of coming to consciousness can extend, or where it will lead. —CARL JUNG[2]

The exploration of the unconscious by Sigmund Freud and his followers in the twentieth century was a great step forward in the evolution of human consciousness, although it isn't customarily thought of that way. A conscious mind that thinks it is the whole mind is as maimed and incomplete as an ego identity that thinks it is the whole person.

So Freud, like Darwin, was a liberator. His contribution, like Darwin's, can be regarded from different viewpoints—either as a debasement of humanity or as an advancement. Freud himself, the original headshrinker, preferred to view it as a demotion. In a famous comment on his own work, he claimed that Copernicus and Darwin had each blown a great hole in human vanity: Copernicus by showing that the earth was not the center of the universe, Darwin by destroying our supposedly privileged place in creation. And psychoanalysis, he said, was a comparable shot at our collective self-esteem, in seeking "to prove to the ego that it is not even master in its own house, but must content itself with scanty information of what is going on unconsciously in the mind."[3]

Freud did discover (and thought he had mapped, although that part of his contribution remains controversial) a vast new domain of human cognition that lurks heavily, like the dark matter of the universe, in and around our consciousness. In so doing he revealed that even though the ego may not be as big a deal as it thinks it is, the mind is far more spacious and mysterious than we had ever imagined.

As a path of liberation, psychoanalysis is in some ways comparable to Buddhism and in other ways strikingly different from it. It does appear that the ego that Freud describes is roughly similar to what the texts of Buddhism and other enlightenment traditions mean by the same term. But the Eastern and Western prescriptions for what to do about it differ strikingly. John Engler, a psychologist and teacher of Buddhism, gives an excellent summary of both the similarity and the difference:

> Both Buddhist psychology and psychoanalytic object relations theory define the essence of the ego in a similar way: as a process of synthesis and adaption between the inner life and outer reality, which produces a sense of personal continuity and sameness in the felt experience of being a "self." In both psychologies, then, the sense of "I"—of personal unity and continuity, of being the same "self" in time, in place, and across states of consciousness—is conceived as something that is not innate in personality, not inherent in our psychological or spiritual makeup, but that evolves developmentally out of our experience of objects. The "self" is literally constructed out of our object experience. What we take to be our "self" and feel to be so present and real is actually an internalized image, a composite representation, constructed by a selective and imaginative "remembering" of past encounters with the object world. In fact, the self is viewed as being constructed anew from moment to moment. But both systems further agree that the self is not ordinarily experienced this way. The sense of self is characterized rather by a feeling of temporal continuity and sameness over time.
>
> The fate of this self is *the* central clinical issue in both psychologies. But the fate of this self is also an issue on which the two psychologies under consideration seem diametrically

opposed. From the perspective of psychoanalytic object relations theory, the deepest psychopathological problem is the *lack* of a sense of self. The most severe clinical syndromes—infantile autism, the symbiotic and functional psychoses, the borderline conditions—represent failures, arrests, or regressions in establishing a cohesive, integrated self.

In contrast, from the Buddhist perspective the psychopathological problem is the *presence* of a self and the feeling of selfhood. According to Buddhist diagnosis, the deepest source of suffering is the attempt to preserve a self, an attempt that is viewed as both futile and self-defeating. The severest form of psychopathology is precisely *attavadupadana,* the clinging to personal existence.

The therapeutic issue in psychotherapy and psychoanalysis is how to "regrow" a basic sense of self or how to differentiate and integrate a stable, consistent, and enduring self-representation. The therapeutic issue in Buddhism is how to "see through" the illusion or construct of the self.[4]

Engler believes the two schools of psychology reveal themselves to be essentially compatible despite this difference—compatible if you look at both Freudian-style psychological health and Buddhist-style enlightenment as stages in the growth of the individual. As Engler sees it, you have to be somebody before you can be nobody, and the development of a healthy ego at one stage of personal development can be regarded as preparation for letting go of it—actually, learning to see it and in some ways see through it—at another stage.

Buddhism is very much concerned with boundaries—between self and other, organism and environment, person and cosmos. Its objective is not exactly to break down or destroy your personal boundaries; it's more a matter of enabling you to discover for yourself that they are largely illusory. Underlying is a somewhat subtler and more difficult learning task, which is discovering the boundaries are also to some degree invisible—that our sense of separateness is so taken for granted, so deeply woven into the fabric of reality, that we are scarcely aware of its presence. Therefore, we are hardly likely to be aware that there is anything about the way we construct reality that might be questioned, investigated, or changed.

Freud was also concerned with boundaries and his theories on that subject can only be understood in an evolutionary context, as an effort to comprehend not only the development of the individual but also the progress of the human species.

Evolutionary Continuities and Discontinuities

It is hard to imagine that there could ever have been a Freud without a Darwin. Freud began his work only a few decades after the publication of *The Origin of Species,* and the whole edifice of psychoanalysis is essentially a story about the problems encountered by an intelligent animal—still with powerful links to its primal past—trying to become a civilized human being.

The three main characters in this evolutionary saga were described by Freud as id, ego, and superego. The interactions and, of course, the conflicts among the three formed the dynamics of the human psyche. Understanding this conflict revealed the causes of neurosis and the path to a cure. Although he did not particularly call attention to it, two of the three players came from beyond the boundaries of the self as it had normally been understood: one from prehuman nature and the other from civilized society. So the Freudian story is not just about the person living within nature and society. It is also about primal nature and modern society coexisting within the person—not entirely harmoniously, either—yet largely beyond the ken of the conscious, rational mind that thinks it *is* the person.

The id—and the Darwinian influence is most visible here—was described by Freud as the inner animal: "everything that is inherited, that is present at birth, that is fixed in the constitution—above all, therefore, the instincts, which originate in the somatic organization."[5] The id is needy and uncivilized, "a cauldron full of seething excitations," totally ignorant of any sense of good and evil, or of morality.[6]

The ego—in German the *Ich,* or "I"—arises at a later stage in the development of the human individual. It represents the organism's need to deal with external reality. Its purpose is essentially to serve the needs of the id, but whereas the id is pure primal need, the ego has an increasing ability to learn from experience and consider the possible outcomes of different lines of action.

The superego grows out of this process, and in some ways overdoes it. It is the individual's personal police force, censor, and sometime Grand Inquisitor. And Freud was quite explicit about what the super-ego was and where it came from; it was the agent of social repression, the internalized authority of civilization. In *Civilization and Its Discontents,* Freud offered a powerful metaphorical account of how the superego takes on the task of controlling the rowdy, aggressive, and deeply antisocial impulses of the id:

> What means does civilization employ, in order to inhibit the aggressiveness which opposes it, to make it harmless, to get rid of it, perhaps? . . . This we can see in the history of the development of the individual. . . . His aggressiveness is introjected, internalized; it is, in point of fact, sent back to where it came from—that is, it is directed towards his own ego. There it is taken over by a portion of the ego as super-ego, and which now, in the form of "conscience," is ready to put into action against the ego the same harsh aggressiveness that the ego would have liked to satisfy upon other, extraneous individuals. The tension between the harsh super-ego and the ego that is subjected to it, is called by us the sense of guilt; it expresses itself as a need for punishment. Civilization, therefore, obtains mastery over the individual's dangerous desire for aggression by weakening and disarming it and by setting up an agency within him to watch over it, like a garrison in a conquered city.[7]

No wonder Freud saw his theories as a reduction in the stature of the ego's place in the world. The poor thing was trapped, sandwiched between the wild, libidinous id and the harsh, repressive superego. Obviously there is some truth in his account of our psychological inner conflicts. Who hasn't felt the crunch between inner impulses of sexual desire, anger, or aggressiveness bumping up against the opposing desire to be a responsible and respectable person? Still, Freud's powerful view of inner psychological turmoil is not the last word on the boundary issues—the all-important question of how we differentiate between what is me and what is not.

Freud saw the therapeutic process as a struggle toward greater differentiation, a stronger sense of the boundary between self and environment, self and other. The rational ego would reclaim some of the fierce energy from the id ("where id was, there shall ego be" was one of his classic pronouncements on this subject) and would also free itself from some of the oppressive power of the superego. In so doing it would become more autonomous and effective, yet always somewhat at odds with nature and society.

The American psychologist Jerome Bruner thought there might be a quite different way of looking at it, however—that Freud had in a sense misinterpreted his own theory. In a seminal journal article Bruner argued that Freud's discovery of the unconscious could be regarded not as a diminution of Homo sapiens and a break with the past but rather as the establishment of a new continuity, part of a long effort by leading thinkers in the West to integrate humanity into the world and the cosmos.

Bruner described the "first continuity" as established not by Copernicus but by Greek philosophers in the sixth century B.C. One of these, Anaximander, saw humanity as part of a physical world that was "continuous and monistic," governed by the common laws of matter. Darwin, he said, established the second continuity, one between humans and the animal kingdom, a necessary precondition for Freud's work. According to Bruner, Freud then established several more continuities: the continuity of organic lawfulness, so that "accident in human affairs was no more to be brooked as 'explanation' than accident in nature"; the continuity of the primitive, infantile, and archaic as coexisting with the civilized and evolved; and the continuity between mental illness and mental health.[8]

So we can look at psychoanalysis as integrative rather than disintegrative, and at Freud's theories as links rather than as prescription for a battle against nature and society. As psychohistorian Bruce Mazlish summarizes:

> In this version of the three historic smashings of the ego, humans are placed on a continuous spectrum in relation to the universe, to the rest of the animal kingdom, and to themselves. They are no longer discontinuous with the world around them. In an important sense, once humans are able to accept this situation, they are in harmony with the rest of existence. Indeed, the longings for a sense of "connection" seen in early nineteenth-century romantics and all "alienated" beings are, unexpectedly, partially fulfilled.[9]

In the book quoted above, Mazlish goes on to discuss yet another discontinuity that we have yet to recognize as illusory, the boundary between humans and machines. That's a fascinating and important line of thought, suggesting a reorientation of the human self-image far beyond any contemplated by enlightenment traditions of the past. We'll look again at that continuity in a later chapter; at this point I'll stay with the specific contribution of psychoanalysis.

Freud's Primal Horde: Disciples, Dissenters, and Defectors

Freud was a brilliant man and a powerful personality. He built, more or less single-handedly, an impressive body of theory that still stands as the main intellectual resource of the international psychoanalytic establishment. He effectively presented his ideas to the world, debated with his critics, and trained a body of devoted followers. He also begot a number of rebellious offspring who departed from his circle to launch their own schools of psychotherapy. Some historians have drawn a parallel between his own life as founder of the psychoanalytic movement and his speculation about a defining incident in the distant primitive past when a group of men rebel against a powerful patriarchal chieftain, kill him, and eat him.

Freud's legacy, more than that of any major thinker of the modern era, is understandable only with reference to the rich contributions from people who began as his students and ended as his adversaries. Among the most powerful of these were Alfred Alder and Carl Jung, both trusted lieutenants who came to differ from Freud in major and irreconcilable ways. Alder denied the very existence of the unconscious. Jung defied Freud's staunch atheism and went on to build a huge body of psychological theory and practice based on the view of psychotherapy as a search for unity with God. And there was a host of lesser dissenters and school-builders as well, among them Wilhelm Reich. He sought to synthesize psychoanalysis with Marxism, managed in the process to get himself expelled from both the International Psychoanalytic Association and the Communist Party, built a body of work based on treating the body as well as the mind, and ended his days as a madman in an American prison. Later came the neo-Freudians such as Erich Fromm and Karen Horney, the existentialists, and many others who were in some measure influenced by psychoanalysis. They would no more have built their theories without Freud than Freud would have built his without Darwin, but their ideas and practices were too far from the Freudian canon even to be described as neo-Freudian.

The most famous and influential of the problem children, Carl Jung, had much to say about the self and boundary issues. Jung was the most devoutly religious of all the renegades—yet it was a curious and idiosyncratic kind of religion he offered. He once said of himself that if he had put forth his ideas in the Middle Ages he would have been burned at the stake. His works certainly reflect his Protestant faith and heritage, but they are also full of references to demons and pagan deities.

In Jung's systems the self is the totality of one's being, encompassing both ego and the unconscious, and the goal of therapy—indeed the goal of human life—is the union of the self with the totality of *all* being, with the collective unconscious, and with God. The development of the sense of self as a separate individual is the task of the first half of a person's life, and the integration with the infinite is the task of the mature individual.

As anybody who has encountered Jungian thought will immediately recognize, I am considerably simplifying the main thrust of an enormously complex body of theory—densely populated with archetypes, gods and demons, mythic beings, concepts drawn from mythology, Eastern religions, and ancient doctrines such as gnosticism, alchemy, and astrology. Whether Jung's work is an improvement on Freud's or merely an elaboration is a question I will leave to the psychological partisans. He certainly went well beyond Freud in viewing the boundary between self and other as vague, porous, and in some sense illusory. The self includes the unconscious, and the unconscious is boundless. Jung wrote often of the collective unconscious that links all minds at their deeper levels; it is, he said, "the foundation of what the ancients called the 'sympathy of all things.'"[10] Later in the same work he identified God and the unconscious as synonymous terms for the same thing.[11]

What Does Psychotherapy Do?

Although Freud, Jung, and most other major thinkers in the field described their efforts as scientific and insisted on presenting their theories and techniques as rigorously tested and objectively correct, there are really very few scientifically indisputable facts about the workings of the human mind. The various Freudian and post-Freudian theories do not easily lend themselves to the methods of hard science, and attempts to measure the effects of approaches to therapy have never been conclusive. Some psychologists of a more hard-nosed persuasion regard all the theories and therapies of psychoanalysis—Freudian, Jungian, and other variations—as totally meaningless and ineffective.

I think there is a great deal of useful wisdom in the best work of Freud, his followers, and his wayward offspring, and that psychotherapy is often of great benefit. But I don't see much neatness of fit between the mechanisms described in the theories and what actually takes place in the mind of a person undergoing psychotherapy.

One perspective on this is offered in an interesting and suggestive study on the effects of psychoanalysis that I came across some decades ago—the work of Herbert Fingarette of the University of California at Santa Barbara. Fingarette was by no means one of the debunkers of psychoanalysis; yet, in his research with people who had undergone analysis he found outcomes that, while quite positive, didn't sound like anything described in the Freudian literature. In fact, he noted that the theoretical works and scholarly journals had very little in the way of nontechnical accounts of the *feeling* of the subjective experience of former patients after successful analysis. When Fingarette asked his research subjects about such feelings, many reported various experiences, particularly attitudes toward the problems they encountered in everyday life, that were quite different from the way they had been before therapy—and in some ways these experiences were remarkably similar to those reported in the literature of mysticism.

In a paper entitled "The Ego and Mystic Selflessness," one research subject, a woman identified as Katherine, described changes in her emotional responses to Alice, a woman with whom she had once had some stormy personal conflicts. Asked by Fingarette about her present desires in connection with Alice, she replies: "Well, I don't have any desires now. I used to want Alice to be shown up in her true colors, to have people see how wrong she was. Now I just don't think about it. I just act. I get along." She also discussed her lack of hunger for praise from others, which had formerly been of great importance to her, and said: "All the competition's sort of left, too. I'm calmer; I don't try so hard."[12]

A psychoanalyst or a representative of many other schools of Western psychotherapy might respond: "Aha! Katherine's ego has been strengthened. She now has more self-esteem, a more solid sense of her own value that makes her less threatened by the acts of other people, less needful of praise."

A follower of Zen or other schools of Eastern thought might respond with equal conviction: "Aha! Katherine's ego is being extinguished. She is no longer attached to its little dramas, snared into conflict with other people, or concerned about her self-importance."

Who would be right? Is it one or the other—or both?

Fingarette explored another area of confusion and apparent contradiction: Katherine's responses could easily be interpreted as the expressions of a sort of wimpy, unemotional person—but she wasn't that way at all. She still had feelings and opinions that she expressed freely, and she was deeply engaged in the business of life. But somehow everything was different—and it was extremely difficult if not impossible to describe in any clear and final way just what the difference *was*. Katherine "finds herself forced to use locutions which she realizes are unusual, contradictory, inadequate, and in constant need of corrections which are in turn bound to be inadequate. It is clear that she is trying to put something into language which the language is not equipped to communicate in any routine, news-reporting fashion." He pointed out that the writings of Eastern mystics are often equally inscrutable, insisting that the state of enlightenment is not merely the withdrawal from consciousness and/or from the world of ordinary human experience that is so often described.

The problem, Fingarette concluded, lay in language, what he called the "language of self," which is not up to the task of communicating enlightened states of consciousness in a way that can be unambiguously understood by a person who has not experienced similar states. And the main thrust of his argument is that successful psychoanalysis often guides people into perceptions and feelings of nonattachment that are quite similar to those of Eastern mysticism, even though that's not the stated goal of psychoanalysis.

All of this suggests four things to me: One, that in any psychotherapeutic process there is much more going on than what is prescribed in the formal theoretical literature of whoever is doing the therapy.

Two, that the client or patient is an active participant in the process, and perhaps more in charge of what happens than the therapist is. Three, that even the client is not fully aware of what is happening because much of the process is unconscious and/or not capable of being unambiguously described in words. Four, that the drive toward enlightenment—let's describe it here as the drive to house the ego in a wider framework of understanding—is at work in everybody, and likely to be nourished by any therapeutic process that is not itself (as I'm afraid some are) toxic and destructive.

The Freudian Gift

Julian Huxley observed that in the light cast by evolutionary biology, the science Darwin founded, humankind is seen as not just a part of nature, but a very peculiar and indeed unique part. In humankind the evolutionary process became conscious of itself. If that's a useful way of looking at Darwin's contribution—and I believe it is—then we can think of Freud's contribution as showing our connection to nature in yet another dimension. The conscious mind—the evolutionary process—becomes conscious of the unconscious, and becomes aware of the ego, which it had formerly taken to be the totality of the self, as a rather fragile fragment bobbing about on a vast sea of primal energies.

Freud didn't make much of the idea that the ego is socially constructed (a part of his discovery more implicit than explicit), and it remained for later thinkers, such as Engler, Bruner, and Mazlish to draw it out and explore its implications. I think the constructivist aspect needs to be drawn out and explored still further because it shows us a path beyond conventional psychoanalysis and suggests work that is yet to be done.

Another piece of work for future psychologists will be to gain a wider understanding of the several mental forces generally grouped under the heading of "the unconscious," and especially to understand more about the role played by the unconscious in the progress of individuals toward higher levels of cognitive development. The Freudian

view of the unconscious as primarily irrational is already being challenged on several fronts (as we'll note in later chapters) and perhaps
in the twenty-first century we will have a more comprehensive
understanding of human growth, one that recognizes developmental
processes—enlightenments—that are at work in us all the time,
whether we are consciously aware of them or not.

CHAPTER 4

Existence Lost and Found

Two ways, in general, are open for an existing individual: *Either* he can do his utmost to forget that he is an existing individual, by which he becomes a comic figure, since existence has the remarkable trait of compelling an existing individual to exist whether he wills it or not. . . . *Or* he can concentrate his entire energy upon the fact that he is an existing individual.

— SØREN KIERKEGAARD[1]

Become what you are!   — FRIEDRICH NIETZSCHE[2]

The existentialists of the early twentieth century were in a sense the heirs of the Enlightenment, but their own legacy has a darker tone and a harder edge. Whereas some of the *philosophes* had looked forward with high hopes to a revolution in France, the existentialists looked back on it and contemplated the horrors it had unleashed: the tumbrels, the Terror, and Napoleon's mad binge of conquest. Some of the major works of existentialism were written in the 1930s, when Europe was in the midst of an economic depression and moving toward a second world war; others were written in the aftermath of that war—the war that had brought the Holocaust and ended with atomic bombs exploding in the skies over Hiroshima and Nagasaki, and much of Europe in ruins. The existentialists had all the skepticism of the Enlightenment—they took it well beyond Hume and Kant, in fact—but none of the optimism, and no confidence whatever in the inevitability of progress. Yet they delivered a powerful and essentially positive message: that we are free—more free than we suspect, more free than we may wish to be—and that it is possible to awaken to this state of freedom and to act on it through an unflinching confrontation with human life in all its enormous mystery and even its apparent meaninglessness.

Like the *philosophes,* the existentialists wanted to cut through myth and dogma and get at the raw bone of things; their subject matter was *being* itself. Existentialism points straight to the ultimate and awesome fact that that there is something instead of nothing. We exist, and our existence precedes anything we may think or say about what we are; we are not, as Jean-Paul Sartre declared in his challenge to religious belief, creatures who come accompanied by instruction books on how to live, with our essence already defined in the mind of God:

> Atheistic existentialism, of which I am a representative, declares . . . that if God does not exist there is at least one being whose existence comes before its essence, a being which exists before it can be defined by any conception of it. That being is man or, as Heidegger has it, the human reality. What do we mean by saying that existence precedes essence? We mean that man first of all exists, encounters himself, surges up in the world—and defines himself afterwards. If man as the existentialist sees him is not definable, it is because to begin with he is nothing. He will not be anything until later, and then he will be what he makes himself. Thus, there is no human nature, because there is no God to have a conception of it. Man simply is. Not that he is simply what he conceives himself to be, but he is what he wills, and as he conceives himself after already existing—as he wills to be after that leap toward existence. Man is nothing else but that which he makes of himself. That is the first principle of existentialism.[3]

Sartre was the best-known of the existentialists, a world-famous figure in the early post–World War II years when he and Simone de Beauvoir presided over the intellectual life of Paris. Yet he did not really speak for the movement as a whole, and neither did anybody else. In fact, there is no strong consensus among historians of existential thought that there ever *was* a coherent existentialist movement—

or, if there was, who was a member and who wasn't, when it began, and when it came to an end.

Most accounts of this nonmovement identify as its forebears Søren Kierkegaard and Friedrich Nietzsche—both of whom wrote in the nineteenth century and sounded themes that would haunt the thinkers of the twentieth. What these two men created in their work—according to Karl Jaspers, himself a leading philosopher of the existentialist period—was not a movement or a system but rather a new atmosphere:

> They passed beyond all of the limits then regarded as obvious. It is as if they no longer shrank back from anything in thought. Everything permanent was as if consumed in a dizzying suction: with Kierkegaard by an otherworldly Christianity which is like Nothingness and shows itself only in negation . . . and in negative resolution; with Nietzsche, a vacuum out of which, with despairing violence, a new reality was to be born. . . .
>
> In a magnificent way, penetrating a whole life with the earnestness of philosophizing, they brought forth not some doctrines, not any basic position, not some picture of the world, but rather a new total intellectual attitude. . . . This attitude was in the medium of infinite reflection, a reflection which is conscious of being unable to attain any real ground by itself. No single thing characterizes their nature; no fixed doctrine or requirement is to be drawn out of them as something independent and permanent.[4]

Existential Attitudes

Existentialism was more an attitude than a movement, and the attitude expressed itself in diverse ways: There were atheistic existentialists like Sartre and there were Christian existentialists like Gabriel Marcel. There were left-wing existentialists (Sartre was an avowed Marxist for many years, although he could never bring himself to join the French Communist Party) and right-wing existentialists, most notably Martin Heidegger, who saw the rise of Adolf Hitler as the dawn of a new era. "The refusal to belong to any school of thought, the repudiation of the adequacy of any body of beliefs whatever, and especially of systems, and a marked dissatisfaction with traditional philosophy as superficial, academic, and remote from life—that is the heart of existentialism," wrote Walter Kaufmann, a leading historian and interpreter of existentialist works.[5]

Yet, even though the people we call existentialists were anything but a matched set, they shared a common preoccupation that justifies the use of the label: their profound concern with existence itself. They wanted to draw our attention to the presence and the grandeur of being, to awaken us from the slumber of taking it for granted. This preoccupation is evident in the titles of some of their works—Sartre's *Being and Nothingness,* Jaspers' *Reason and Existence,* Gabriel Marcel's *The Mystery of Being,* Heidegger's *Being and Time*. In their various ways they reminded us that we do not really know what we are or where we came from, that being itself is the supreme mystery, an ultimately unanswerable question, and, as Marcel put it, that a mystery is not at all the same thing as a mere problem:

> A problem is something which I can meet, which I find complete before me, but which I can therefore lay siege to and reduce. But a mystery is something in which I am myself involved. . . . A genuine problem is subject to an appropriate technique by the exercise of which it is defined: whereas a mystery, by definition, transcends every conceivable technique. It is, no doubt, always possible (logically and psychologically) to degrade a mystery so as to turn it into a problem. But this is a fundamentally vicious proceeding, whose springs might perhaps be discovered in a kind of corruption of the intelligence.[6]

Heidegger did talk about the "problem of being" and even seemed to believe that it could in a sense be resolved. Yet he didn't mean that we would find a satisfactory answer to what he called the basic question of metaphysics—"Why there is any being at all and not rather nothing?"—but rather that people could somehow be brought into deeper contact with "the truth of Being," which he believed had been lost in the modern world. Heidegger is the most difficult, impenetrable, and mystical of the existentialist thinkers, he wrote in a dense and convoluted style, yet clearly had a passionate desire to reach his readers deeply and directly to bring about a transformative experience. Perhaps he could have communicated his vision more effectively if he had spoken from his own personal experience as did Kierkegaard and Nietzsche—and occasionally he did lapse into poetry—but his prose remained pure *Herr Professor*. Reading it was more likely to put people to sleep than to awaken them.

I suspect that Heidegger had flashes of deep personal insight into the truth of being—and for him it was Being, capitalized, more or less the equivalent of God—but they were not something he knew how to impart to others. Walter Kaufmann calls Heidegger "for all his faults, one of the most interesting philosophers of our time," and goes on to say that his greatest fault—even greater than the opaqueness of his style or his infatuation with Nazism—was a certain lack of vision: "After everything has been said, he really does not have very much to say."[7] I am more inclined to believe that Heidegger did have something to say but didn't know how to say it, and that his work—like much of existentialism as well as many of the works of Eastern mystics—is best taken as a finger pointing the way toward something that readers must discover for themselves.

Heidegger was interested in phenomenology, an intellectual movement launched by his colleague Edmund Husserl, which aspired to devise methods to study the structures of consciousness, the reality of the "life-world." The movement was in a sense a response to Kant's idea that we only experience phenomena, not things apart from human consciousness. All right, said Husserl, we will simply "bracket" the question of whether or not something in consciousness is real and study human "being" itself. Phenomenology would be a science of experience. This movement was a powerful recognition of the need to investigate human experience in order to investigate the world, and it still survives in various journals and societies. But in some ways as the natural sciences took over the experimental study of the objectified world and psychology took over the study of consciousness, it led to the marginalization of academic philosophy.

Existential Theologies

The question of God was never far from existentialist thought. How could it be otherwise for people who wrestled with the mystery of being, who lived in a society that for centuries had called itself Christian and believed that the Bible contained the definitive answers to how and why we came to be? God had been a central issue for both of existentialism's contentious ancestors—for Kierkegaard, who insisted on the need to submit to the authority of Christ, and for Nietzsche, who called Christianity the "immortal blemish of mankind" and wrote in *Ecce Homo* that after contact with a religious man he always felt the need to wash his hands.

Marcel was one of the religious existentialists but—like Kierkegaard before him—his faith was not of the comforting, Jesus-loves-me variety. Marcel wrote more of hope than faith, and that hope was not based on any certainty to be found in religious dogma but rather was a way of being, a choice that could be made amid the vast and even terrifying uncertainty of existence.

The religious existentialists were passionately concerned with the morality of relationships. However, the morality they offered was not based on any code of ethics or tablet of do's and don'ts. Rather, it came out of the conviction that a confrontation with the truth of our mysterious being—the plunge into the depths of experience that is advocated, in different ways, by all writers of existentialism—leads not only to a deeper sense of self but also to a different way of being with others. This idea comes across most clearly in the work of Martin Buber, particularly his classic *I and Thou*.

Buber was an Austrian philosopher with an extensive education in the heritage of Western philosophy—all the classic philosophers from the Greeks onward—but he was also steeped in the lore of a mystical movement called Hasidism that had been influential among Eastern

European Jews in the eighteenth and nineteenth centuries. His accomplishment was to draw out of that ancient tradition a set of themes and concepts that became a powerful influence in twentieth-century theology, especially among liberal Protestants, as well as in psychotherapy and organizational development. There are people today in marriage-counseling programs and corporate personal-development groups who are influenced by his ideas, although they may never have heard of Martin Buber, much less of Hasidism.

Like Heidegger, Buber longed for a rediscovery of the truth of Being. Unlike Heidegger, he was quite clear about where and how to seek it: in the here and now, and in the authentic encounter with God, other human beings, and nature. The basic aim of Hasidism was the resacralization of everyday existence, so that religion becomes not merely a matter for the Sabbath and holy days but also a constant search for the deeper dimensions of life. That same aim in Buber's writing proved to be remarkably compatible with existentialism's emphasis on the immediate present. God is not to be talked about or understood through theoretical discourse—even through scripture—but is to be found in the present time and place. God is "the mystery of the obvious that is closer to me than my own I."[8] And inseparable from that sense of the power of the present is the insistence upon the power of recognizing the divine mystery of other people. Walter Kaufmann says of Buber that he finds in the other "what Blake finds in a grain of sand and in a wild flower: infinity and eternity—here and now." He succeeds in "endowing the social sphere with a religious dimension."[9]

Buber's distinction between the I-Thou and the I-It relationship is his most famous concept, and although it is highly idealized, it has had a remarkable impact in the world, well beyond the limited number of people who have actually read Buber's work.

The I-Thou relationship is seen as the true meeting of human beings in which both parties are fully present and open to one another, free of expectations, judgments, strategies, and selfish agendas: "Nothing conceptual intervenes . . . no prior knowledge and no imagination; and memory itself is changed as it plunges from particularity into wholeness. No purpose intervenes . . . no greed and no anticipation; and longing itself is changed as it plunges from the dream into appearance. Every means is an obstacle. Only where all means have disintegrated encounters occur."[10]

Despite the lofty tone of such pronouncements, Buber had his practical side. He realistically recognized the need for the more instrumental I-It relationships, in which people interact on the basis of prescribed social roles, concepts, purposes, or goals. He granted that we all must enter into such relationships, and can live productively and comfortably in them, but at the same time he insisted that we should never accept them as all of life: "Without It a human being cannot live. But whoever lives only with that is not human."[11]

Buber had studied Hindu, Buddhist, and Taoist thought and, more than any of the other existentialist writers, he comes extremely close at some points to the Eastern mystics. His descriptions of moments of deep insight—suggestive, although a bit elusive and inscrutable— sound at times very much like the equally suggestive and elusive descriptions of Satori experiences in Zen Buddhism. In both cases, the descriptions take those experiences to be of supreme importance. For example:

> There are moments of the secret ground in which world order is beheld as present. Then the tone is heard all of a sudden whose uninterpretable score the ordered world is. These moments are immortal; none are more evanescent. They leave no content that could be preserved, but their force enters into the creation and into man's knowledge, and the radiation of its force penetrates the ordered world and thaws it again and again. Thus the history of the individual, thus the history of the race.[12]

There are other similarities: One is Buber's insistence that the only God worth worshipping is a God that cannot be described, which is close to the Taoist doctrine that the Tao that can be described is not the true Tao. Another is his injunction to let go of all ideas and preconceptions in order to enter into the I-Thou relationship, whether with God or another human being. This is strongly reminiscent of the Zen "Drop it" koan, and it makes the same point: In order to come into a fuller and wider experience of life it may be necessary to let go of conceptual baggage that, however useful up to a certain point, cannot be carried into the new terrain.

But there was an important difference between Buber's thought and the main themes of Far Eastern mysticism. Buber had read extensively in those sources, and he was strongly convinced that they spoke for a path he did not want to take—into the "thou art that" of Hinduism, the no-self of Buddhism. He wanted separateness, not mystical union—not with God, not with nature, not with another human being. Separateness was necessary in order for encounter to matter. "We . . . are resolved to tend with holy care the holy treasure of our actuality that has been given us for this life and perhaps for no other life that might be closer to the truth. In lived actuality there is no unity of being."[13]

This separateness was important to Buber and deserves to be respectfully noted. But I am not sure whether it means as much in practice as he believed. I'm more inclined to think that, if it turns into the kind of issue people argue about in philosophy seminars, it is better allowed to let fall to the floor.

Existential Therapies

Few of the writers we think of as existentialists were particularly happy with the job description of philosopher. They did not aspire to create huge systems of thought to be pored over and dissected in the universities. They wanted to touch people, shake them out of their lethargy, change their ways of feeling and seeing the world. Existentialism is basically about consciousness and its transformation, and the history of existentialism is the history of a search for methods—ways of waking people up, guiding them toward the confrontation with the reality of their own lives.

Naturally, many people associated with existential thought turned to the arts, Europe's approved pathway to those deeper levels. Some wrote poems; Marcel wrote plays; Sartre wrote plays and novels and won a Nobel Prize for literature, which he refused to accept. Many existentialists were also interested in psychology, particularly the psychoanalytic movement that was such a powerful force in the thinking of the times. Psychoanalysis was a theory, but it was also a method—a structured encounter between two people, patient and analyst, that had as its aim to change the patient's understanding of himself, her way of being in the world.

Existential psychology emerged at about the same time as psychoanalysis, the two moving along roughly parallel tracks—separate, not quite equal, contentiously different in some ways, and quite similar in others. Certainly, both owed a philosophical debt to Neitzsche, whose work was widely read and discussed in Vienna in his time, and whom Freud once described as a man who "had a more penetrating knowledge of himself than any other man who lived or was ever likely to live."

In *Being and Nothingness,* Sartre talked extensively about a new approach to therapy called existential analysis. Although the ideas were interesting, they were also highly abstract and not particularly clear; Sartre presented a theoretical framework, not a method for putting it into practice. He undoubtedly had an influence on the various practitioners who called themselves existential therapists, but the existential movement that did emerge and become a force in the world of psychology owes more to Buber than to Sartre.

The most influential innovator of really new ways of doing psychotherapy was Jacob Levy Moreno, a Romanian-born psychiatrist who in Vienna in the mid-1920s began creating a variety of new social forms, rituals, and practices that were aimed at realizing Buber's goal of bringing about more authentic interactions among human beings.[14] Moreno edited a literary magazine, to which Buber was a contributor, founded an avant-garde theater group called the Spontaneity Theater (a forerunner of later forms of improvisational drama), and began experimenting with psychotherapy done in groups rather than in the one-to-one form that had been standardized by Freud. Eventually he developed what was to become his lifelong mode of therapy and the ancestor of the many group and action therapies, such as encounter groups, sensitivity training, and gestalt, that came along later. Moreno called it psychodrama, a group process in which the therapist, acting as a director, guided the creation of small plays, enactments of real or sometimes imagined scenes from the life of the patient. The patient was the protagonist and co-creator of the scenes. The other participants were sometimes the audience, sometimes supporting players in the dramas that were enacted, other times a kind of chorus commenting on the play. While the rules of Freudian analysis discouraged the "acting out" of neurotic symptoms, it was precisely what Moreno encouraged. He sometimes called his therapy "spontaneity training." His prescription was not so much to be cured or better adjusted but to become more fully alive, and in his major work *Who Shall Survive?* he described himself as a good example of a person who followed his own advice:

> I wanted to show that here is a man who has all the signs of paranoia and megalomania, exhibitionism and social maladjustment, and who can still be fairly well controlled and healthy, and indeed, of apparently greater productivity by acting them out than if he would have tried to constrain and resolve his symptoms—the living antithesis of psychoanalysis.[15]

Moreno's therapeutic system, his attitude toward his own life, and his somewhat peculiar personality (and it was that; I knew him fairly well in his later years) were a living expression of Neitzsche's exhortation to become what you are.

Other schools of existential psychotherapy were less exuberant than Moreno's but no less grounded in the basic view that psychotherapy had to grapple in some way with such basic issues of being. Many pioneers in the field recognized that the existential philosophers were talking, however abstractly, about something relevant to the painfully real experiences of ordinary people trying to make sense of their lives in an increasingly uncertain world. They borrowed ideas from existentialism to develop a new approach to psychotherapy, much different from psychoanalysis.

Existential psychologists such as Rollo May thought Freud had kind of missed the point of repression—which is that we don't just repress thoughts of sex and violence but our very sense of being. May placed great importance on a certain kind of psychological break-through he called the "I am" experience. This was not so much an insight, the goal in most therapies, or even the catharsis sought by Moreno and other action therapists. He described how this actually took place in the lives of patients, such as a young woman who was illegitimate. Her mother had told her, in moments of anger, that she had tried unsuccessfully to abort her, and other relatives had told her she should never have been born. Obviously she had a heavy load to bear, and a major turning-point in her therapy was described in the memory of a specific experience:

> I remember walking that day under the elevated tracks in a slum area, feeling the thought, "I am an illegitimate child." I recall the sweat pouring forth in my anguish in trying to accept that fact. Then I understood what it must feel like to accept, "I am a Negro in the midst of privileged whites," or "I am blind in the midst of people who see." Later on that night I woke up and it came to me this way, "I accept the fact that I am an illegiti-mate child." *But* "I am not a child anymore." So it is, "I am ille-gitimate." That is not so either: "I was born illegitimate." Then what is left? What is left is this, *"I am."* This act of contact and acceptance with "I am," once gotten hold of, gave me (what I think was for me the first time) the experience "Since I Am, I have the right to be."[16]

Such experiences, May believed, were not the end of all the patient's problems but rather a necessary precondition to growth. In his book *The Discovery of Being* he wrote: "In the broadest sense, the achieving of the sense of being is a goal of all therapy, but in the more precise sense it is a relation to oneself and one's world, an experience of one's own existence (including one's own identity), which is a prerequisite for the working through of specific problems. It is, as the patient wrote, the 'primary fact'."[17]

This idea—that emotional illness involves not only the inner conflicts famously described by Freud but also, at a deeper level, a loss of contact with one's own sense of being alive—runs through all of existential psychology. Different people stated it in variations: Abraham Maslow became a student and chronicler of "peak experiences." Frederick Perls placed more emphasis on getting in touch with emotions and the senses. And both believed that a successful outcome of therapy could be not merely the dour adjustment to society's constraints offered by the followers of Freud but a powerful and vivid rediscovery of life, a reawakening. Such experiences, when people discovered the immediate reality of their own existence, were extensively described in the case histories of existential therapy.

Although most of the existential psychologists were inclined to honor Freud and grant the importance of his discoveries (May himself was trained as an analyst, as was Perls) they were also skeptical about many aspects of Freudian theory, particularly in relation to the unconscious. They didn't doubt that it existed; they just doubted that it was as thoroughly mapped out and explained as Freud and others of his school believed. "The unconscious ideas of the patient," said Erwin Straus, "are more often than not the conscious theories of the therapist."

May was highly critical of what he called the "cellar" view of the unconscious while at the same time he disagreed with the briskly scientific rationalists of American psychology who wanted to throw out the concept altogether: "I would propose, rather, that being is indivisible, that unconsciousness is part of any given being, that the cellar theory of the unconscious is logically wrong and practically unconstructive, but that the meaning of the discovery—namely, the radical enlargement of being—is one of the great contributions of our day and must be retained."[18]

And May was one of many therapists who, in building the philosophical foundations of their practice, noticed striking similarities between existentialism and Asian enlightenment traditions. "The likenesses between these Eastern philosophies and existentialism," he wrote, "go much deeper than the chance similarity of words. Both are concerned with ontology, the study of being. Both seek a relation to reality that cuts below the cleavage between subject and object."

After the Revolution

Existentialism was in part a cultural fad, and as such its day has passed. The cafe-lounging existentialists of the early post–World War II years were displaced in the public consciousness by the beatniks of the 1950s, then by the hippies of the 1960s, and subsequently by a long parade of other sensibilities and other antiestablishment lifestyles. But no other movement of its kind has tried so persistently to push us into confrontation with our own experience, with what we find when we look deep within ourselves, and also with what we do not find.

CHAPTER 5

East Meets West in the Hot Tubs

The previously robotized corpses begin to return to life, gaining substance and beginning the dance of abandonment and self-fulfillment; the paper people are turning into real people.

— FRITZ PERLS[1]

We do not need a new religion or a new bible. We need a new experience—a new feeling of what it is to be "I".... The most strongly enforced of all known taboos is the taboo against knowing who or what you really are behind the mask of your apparently separate, independent, and isolated ego.

— ALAN WATTS[2]

After the 1950s, existentialism lost some of its vanguard cachet—but none of its vitality. The same ideas and passions emerged again in the United States, often under new names. In fact, a good case could be made that existentialism was the unofficial philosophy of the 1960s.

The extended happening we call the 1960s does not quite coincide with the decade. It was about 1964, as I recall, that the happening began. There was a palpable sense of liftoff, as though we were setting forth on a space flight from the rather inhibited world we had known in the 1950s. That feeling, and the various styles and enthusiasms that went with it, continued well into the 1970s.

It's hard to say, now, exactly what were the events that made us feel that way, the components of that change of *zeitgeist*. Certainly one part of it was the quickening of political activity—the civil rights movement in the South, the Free Speech Movement at Berkeley, the movement to end the Vietnam War, and the causes that followed. We also saw the sudden blossoming of a new and rebellious youth subculture; I lived in Los Angeles then, frequently visited San Francisco, and discovered that the staid old Haight-Ashbury district was turning into a hangout of young people who called themselves hippies. Then there was the experimentation with drugs, the growing interest in Eastern religions, and, of course, rock and folk music. And then there were group therapies, all kinds of them, with much buzz about t-groups and sensitivity and encounter. Finally—coming as a thrilling surprise to those of us who lived on the West Coast—there was the heady conviction that we were not on the edge of things but in the midst of them. California was, as people began to say about that time, where it was at.

And what was it all about? Well, it was about political change, and it was about equality and civil rights. But it was most of all about freedom. Liberation. The words were everywhere: free speech, sexual freedom, women's liberation, men's liberation. Civil libertarians on the right, the Peace and Freedom party on the left. Turn on your radio and you were likely to hear singers proclaim the dawning of the age of Aquarius, the age of Aquarius where harmony and understanding, sympathy and joy abound, mystic crystal revelation and the mind's true liberation.

I was involved in these happenings in many ways, and one was journalism. I dug into what was going on, I researched and interviewed, I wrote articles and books. And as I explored the various movements—particularly the psychological/mystical one that was particularly evident in California—I found that the sixties were not the sharp break with the past that many people took them to be; they were more a resumption of something that had begun earlier and been interrupted.

There is a lineage of liberation movements, with particularly strong links between early-twentieth-century Europe and 1960s America. So many ideas that had excited Europeans in the years just before and after World War II, such as existentialism and Asian mysticism, now excited Americans who discovered them in the years of rock, revolution, and psychedelia—often with no sense of their histories. Theodore Roszak in *The Making of a Counterculture* identified among the leading mentors of the times the Zen popularizer Alan Watts and Paul Goodman, co-inventor with Frederick Perls of gestalt therapy. Watts had first been introduced to Buddhism in England in the 1930s, where he attended meetings at the Buddhist Lodge of London and socialized with the network of Europeans who were interested in Oriental philosophies and religions. Perls had studied psychoanalysis in Berlin and had been much influenced by European existentialism—in fact, he and Goodman had had some serious arguments about whether to call his new approach existential therapy.

Both Watts and Perls had emigrated to the United States and eventually to the West Coast, where they became star players in one of the most intriguing parts of the 1960s, the human potential movement. It's interesting to note that the term "human potentialities" originated with another transplanted European intellectual—Aldous Huxley, grandson of Darwin's bulldog and younger brother of the man who had described humanity as evolution becoming conscious of itself.

The New Dream of Transformation

Huxley, who was famous as an author of novels satirizing the British upper classes, settled in Southern California and took an interest in a number of things—including psychedelic drugs, novel psychotherapies, and Asian mysticism. In the process he formed and propagated the idea, which became a central theme in the age of Aquarius, that the human species was on the verge of a majestic leap forward, a self-propelled acceleration of its own evolution. In a way, his idea of an evolutionary project of psychological enlightenment was a revival of the dream of transformation that had so energized the apostles of progress two centuries earlier, but it was informed by Darwinian theory and contemporary ideas about applications of science and psychology. Around 1960 Huxley began a lecture tour, visiting college campuses and giving a lecture titled "Human potentialities." In it he said:

> The biologists have shown us that, physiologically and anatomically, we are pretty much the same as we were twenty thousand

years ago and that we are using fundamentally the same equipment as the Aurignacian man to produce incredibly different results. We have in the course of these twenty thousand years actualized an immense number of things which at that time and for many, many centuries thereafter were wholly potential and latent in man.

This, I think, gives us reason for tempered optimism that there are still a great many potentialities—for rationality, for affection and kindliness, for creativity—still lying latent in man; and, since everything has speeded up so enormously in recent years, that we shall find methods for going almost as far beyond the point we have reached now within a few hundred years as we have succeeded in going beyond our Aurignacean ancestors in twenty thousand years. I think this is not an entirely fantastic belief. The neurologists have shown us that no human being has ever made use of as much as ten percent of all the neurons in his brain. And perhaps, if we set about it in the right way, we might be able to produce extraordinary things out of this strange piece of work that a man is.[3]

Huxley had a lot of ideas about how this might be accomplished. He thought that psychoactive drugs could be used to increase human capacity for cognition, creativity, and feeling. He had heard about gestalt therapy, which was more about the development of awareness than the cure of neurosis and aimed to increase the patient's ability to be present in the here and now. He was interested in the work of the Freudian renegade Wilhelm Reich, and of neo-Reichians who used massage and exercises to release the energies that were trapped in the body by repressed emotion. Huxley's proposal, which he rather diffidently put forth in his lectures and writings, was that some institution might organize a project to evaluate all the known methods for actualizing human potentialities, and design a program of lifelong education based on them—something like the space program that had so captivated the public imagination—but this time seeking to explore the far reaches of the human mind and body. He had in mind a major university or foundation, but it didn't work out that way; instead, his ideas got caught up in the sweep of the sixties and became much more a part of the counterculture than the establishment.

Huxley's friend Gerald Heard had already tried to a launch a program for developing human potentialities, an experimental educational center in Southern California called Trabuco College. That enterprise had failed, but Huxley and Heard both gave their advice and encouragement to a couple of young Californians, Michael Murphy and Richard Price, who had similar ideas. Murphy and Price were taking over the management of a small hot-springs resort on the California coast and hoped to offer lectures and courses on some of the subjects that were beginning to percolate through the times. Huxley's synthesis was obviously influential: the first program of lectures at Big Sur Hot Springs—which they later named the Esalen Institute, taking the name from a local Indian tribe—was headed HUMAN POTENTIALITIES.[4]

It was clear from the very beginning of the Esalen Institute that its subject matter was going to be a blend of East and West: Asian religions, European-American philosophy and psychology. Among the first lecturers were historian Arnold Toynbee, who had predicted that the coming together of East and West would be a major event in human history; and existential philosopher Paul Tillich, who elaborated on that same theme to his audience in the little lodge on the Big Sur coast. Esalen was a crucible in which new ideas were shaped and tested and Asian practices such as meditation and *tai chi* were blended with lectures by existential-humanistic psychologists such as Rollo May and Abraham Maslow.

Esalen flourished, its public visibility aided by media coverage such as the special *Look* magazine issue on California that described the state as developing a new kind of society and perhaps "a new kind of person," and the ideas and practices developed there spread rapidly. Esalen-style "growth centers" sprang up everywhere and soon the major luminaries of the movement were traveling around the world, giving lectures,.conducting public demonstrations of their therapeutic methods, and leading encounter groups and sensory-awakening programs.

Psychology's Third Force

Running roughly parallel to the human potential movement—and at times virtually indistinguishable from it—was the humanistic psychology movement, a gathering of ideas and practices that ran counter to the prevailing schools of the time and brought a charge of distinctly 1960s sensibility into psychology departments and psychiatric hospitals. Abraham Maslow called this the "third force" to distinguish it from the Freudian and behaviorist schools that were then the most influential—the Freudian dominant in psychotherapy and the arts, the behaviorist dominant in the laboratories where psychologists busily ran rats through mazes in search of insight into what makes us do what we do.

Maslow, who taught psychology at Brandeis University, was a tireless researcher who wrote numerous papers and books, some of which became central to third-force thinking. But his greater contribution was in the role of what later became known as a networker: He collected ideas and maintained a large mailing list of friends and colleagues to whom he circulated articles and papers. He got people in touch with one another. He organized a conference at Old Saybrook, Connecticut, bringing together some of the leading thinkers in humanistic psychology. He helped to launch the *Journal of Humanistic Psychology* in 1961 and the Association for Humanistic Psychology in 1963.

In his writings, Maslow accused psychoanalysis and behaviorism of being handicapped by seriously stunted views of humanity: He thought the psychoanalysts unfairly represented us as neurotics driven by unconscious, irrational impulses, while the behaviorists reduced us to stimulus-and-response machines with no sense of personal will or volition; worse yet, they believed that the behavior of human beings could be understood by studying rats, worms, and pigeons. The social sciences and social progress in general, he believed, were hampered by such blinkered psychology, and they were seriously in need of a new vision. His response to the problem was to throw himself into research on the lives and behavior of healthy, fully functioning people—what he called "self-actualizing" individuals.

Self-actualization wasn't an easy syndrome to describe, as Maslow recognized; in general terms it meant "the full use and exploitation of talents, capacities, potentialities, etc." Such people, he said, "seem to be fulfilling themselves and to be doing the best that they are capable of doing," reminding us of Neitzsche's exhortation to "become what you are."[5] Some of the specific characteristics included:

Efficient perception of reality
Acceptance of self, of others, and of nature
Spontaneity
Problem-centering (rather than ego-centering)
Detachment and the desire for privacy
Autonomy and resistance to enculturation
Continued freshness of appreciation, and richness of emotional
    reactions
Frequency of peak or mystical experiences
Identification with the human species *(Gemeinschaftsgefühl)*
Deep interpersonal relations
Democratic character structure
Greatly increased creativeness
Certain changes in the value system[6]

Maslow had large hopes about the long-range impact that his studies might have on our ideas about human nature—and human possibilities. He wrote:

The study of such healthy people can teach us much about our own mistakes, our shortcomings, the proper directions in which to grow. Every age but ours has had its model, its ideal. All these have been given up by our culture; the saint, the hero, the gentleman, the knight, the mystic. About all we have left is the well-adjusted man without problems, a very pale and doubtful substitute. Perhaps we shall soon be able to use as our guide and model the fully growing and self-fulfilling human being, the one in whom all his potentialities are coming to full development, the one whose inner nature expresses itself freely, rather than being warped, suppressed, or denied.[7]

What Maslow had in mind—and what came into being in the 1960s—was more than a new school of psychology. He wanted a profound social change, a new episteme, and believed that a new kind of psychology could nourish a new kind of culture. And he believed that such a psychology was emerging—embodied not only in his own ideas but in those of numerous other dissenters. He numbered among the charter members of the third force a long list of post-Freudians, general semanticists, existentialists, phenomenologists, social critics, and philosophers. His goal, which he pursued doggedly and with considerable success until his death in 1970, was to link these various stirrings together and shape out of them a new force—not only in the world of psychology, but in all the world—a movement that would be dedicated to a new stage in human evolution.

Among the concepts that Maslow popularized were self-actualization; the hierarchy of needs, a proposition that as basic needs are satisfied we naturally progress to the satisfaction of higher ones, going eventually beyond material gratification to the search for self-actualization; and—closest to Eastern enlightenment traditions—the concept of "peak experiences." These moments of blissful discovery and elevated perception were, he said, a common part of the lives of self-actualizing people, and they were likely to happen in just about anybody at one time or another. They represented another vast dimension of human experience to which the prevailing psychologies of the time were paying little or no attention. As Maslow collected research on accounts of such experiences, he felt that he was entering a new terrain, undiscovered country within the bounds of his discipline but apparently well known beyond them: "I have found a particular kind of cognition for which my knowledge of psychology had not prepared me but which I have since seen well described by certain writers on esthetics, religion, and philosophy."[8]

Most accounts of the origins of the humanistic psychology movement name three major figures—Maslow, Rollo May, and Carl Rogers—as its intellectual leaders. But as the events of the 1960s unfolded and the movement grew in size and influence, a fourth major figure joined the pantheon: Frederick Perls. A man who had been named among the bit players in Maslow's list of currents in the third force became one of its best-known and certainly most interesting stars.

The Galloping Gestalt

Gestalt therapy, virtually unknown in 1960, was listed at the end of the decade as the sixth most common affiliation among American psychotherapists, having quickly passed such older and more published schools as the Jungian and the rational-emotive.[9] Part of its success undoubtedly had to do with its congeniality to the radical, revolutionary spirit of the times. Theodore Roszak wrote approvingly of gestalt as "one of the few schools of psychiatry that has been prepared to set society at large into the therapeutic scales and to find the way of the world wanting, a mad attack on human potentialities. Gestalt holds out for the inherent sociability of the whole human being, including his sexual and even his aggressive needs."[10]

Success came late in life to Perls. He was seventy when he arrived at the Esalen Institute and began the period of residency there that launched him and his mode of therapy into the limelight. He had been around: Trained as a psychoanalyst in Germany (where his training analyst at the time he left in 1933 was Wilhelm Reich), he lived and worked in South Africa for many years. He then came to the United States in 1946, where he developed his own form of therapy in the decades that followed. He participated in Moreno's psychodrama sessions in New York, practiced Zen meditation in Kyoto, and dabbled heavily in LSD when it became an available—and, for a time, legal— mode of psychological exploration.

And he always considered himself an existentialist. For Perls the goal of therapy was not adjustment but something much closer to Nietzsche's "become what you are," and the mode of therapy he developed hewed close to Buber's belief that life is to be lived in the here and now. When I interviewed Perls once in the mid-1960s he told me with his usual modesty that gestalt was the purest form of existentialism, much closer to the truth of our organic life than other varieties such as Sartre's.

Perls had had his own peak experience—probably many of them, but only one that he recorded in the autobiographical memoir entitled *In and Out the Garbage Pail.* In it he described something that had happened to him some twelve years before in Miami Beach:

> I was walking down Alton Road, when I felt a transformation coming over me. At that time I did not know anything about, nor had I ever taken, a psychedelic drug. I felt my right side getting cramped and nearly paralyzed. I started limping, my face got slack, I felt like a village idiot, my intellect went numb and stopped functioning altogether. Like a thunderbolt the world jumped into existence, three-dimensional, full of color and life—definitely not with a depersonalization, like life-"less" clarity—but with a full feeling of "This is it, this is real." This was a complete awakening, coming to my senses, or my senses coming to me, or my senses making sense.[11]

Those moments of the world jumping into sensory existence were what Perls sought to bring about in his therapy. He presented a dynamic personality and a powerful mode of therapy aimed at making the "discovery of being" happen—immediately and in public. It was derived from Moreno's psychodrama, but whereas Moreno staged scenes in which the patient (or protagonist in his terminology) confronted people playing the roles of significant others in his life, Perls had his patients play all the parts themselves. Typically he worked in a group, with the patient sitting in a chair that came inevitably to be known as the "hot seat," and one empty chair. The patient might choose to act out a dream, deal with a relationship, or state a problem. As he did, he would move back and forth between the hot seat and the empty chair, playing out the parts of whatever was being dealt with— a figure from a dream, another person, a part of his own body, a fragment of his own personality. As the little drama played itself out, Perls would function as a combination stage manager, observer, therapist and—often—acerbic critic. Most of all, he would direct the patient's attention to things that were taking place in the situation: the tone of voice, the use of a particular phrase or mannerism, the movement of a hand. He would encourage awareness and discourage analysis. He had no time to spare for dissection of the Oedipus complex, and I never heard any reference to early toilet training other than Perls' comment that the goal of therapy was to teach people how to wipe their own asses. The idea was that whatever was happening to the patient, whatever the "problem" was, was happening *here and now,* and all a part of the self.

Many of Perls' students and admirers saw gestalt therapy as a new form of meditation, active rather than passive. Claudio Naranjo, a Chilean-born psychiatrist who became a gestalt therapist and was also a student of Eastern religions, described gestalt work as having the three basic dimensions of meditation: "concentration on the actual, suppression of conceptual activity, and noninterference in the flow of experience."[12] What took place in gestalt therapy, he believed, was a shift of identity, an integrative leap beyond the ego:

Most central to it is the notion that we "disown" aspects of our personality by narrowing the boundaries of the ego. By drawing a boundary between what we call I and not-I in our processes, we give up responsibility, but we also become impoverished. The assumption in Gestalt therapy is that all that "happens" in us *is our doing,* yet is not the doing of the ego that may be talking at the moment—the particular personality fragment saying "I" in the name of the whole. It is instead the doing of our organism—the independent totality of our processes—and to the degree that we take responsibility for it, becoming aware of how *we do* it, we become our organism, our totality. . . . *we become what we already are,* unknowingly.[13]

Perls himself had experimented with Buddhist meditation. He spent two months at a Zen monastery in Kyoto and found it a positive experience, but he was doubtful about its effectiveness. Just as psychoanalysis tended to breed psychoanalysts, Zen, he said, tended to breed monks. Sitting meditation, he used to tell his students, was neither shit nor get off the pot. So although he claimed to have no Eastern ancestors for gestalt, it was clearly an approach that was—as no mode of therapy had been before—about This.

Freestyle Buddhism

Alan Watts was also a regular at Esalen, and he probably did more than any other person to introduce Buddhism to the United States— not only its basic ideas but also the congenial message that you did not have to follow any particular rules or swallow any dogmatic doctrines in order to make it a part of your life. You did not have to become a Buddhist. In his lectures and books he described Buddhism as the diagnosis of a universal ailment—an ego that narrows our range of consciousness and separates us from the world.

Watts had become powerfully attracted to Buddhism when he was a precocious teenage schoolboy in England. First he read about it, then he made contact with a circle of devotees of Eastern mysticism. He has written in his autobiography that the authorities of the school he was attending in Canterbury were so delighted to see one of their students taking an interest in anything resembling religion that they not only permitted but encouraged his studies.[14] He made regular trips to London to attend sessions of the Buddhist Lodge, became acquainted with the colorful and mysterious Madame Helena Blavatsky and other members of the Theosophical Society and, by the time he was twenty, had published his first book, *The Spirit of Zen*. In his London years, he also became acquainted with the work of the English psychoanalyst Trigant Burrow, who held to the strikingly Zenlike conviction that the ego was a socially implanted fiction rather than a valid psychophysical entity in its own right.

Later Watts emigrated to the United States where, somewhat to his own surprise and to those of people who knew him, he decided to enroll in a theological seminary and become an Episcopalian priest. He had chosen that denomination on the assumption that it would be as liberal as the Church of England had been—an assumption that he tested severely during his years in the priesthood and found to be incorrect. The church authorities might have tolerated his interest in Eastern religions, and perhaps even his rather active sex life if he had kept it hidden, but they could not tolerate his public advocacy of free love in his sermons at the chapel in Northwestern University where he officiated as chaplain. He left the priesthood and moved to San Francisco, where he taught Buddhism at an academy of Asian studies and became a sort of Zen guru to the writers of the Beat movement that was just getting under way.

By the time he began to give talks at Esalen and socialize with therapists such as Fritz Perls, he had already formed his own synthesis of Eastern mysticism with Western psychology and combined it with a freethinking Bohemian lifestyle—all of which made him particularly suitable for the role he carved out for himself in the 1960s.

Watts talked about any number of things; here I am going to touch on two of his ideas that are particularly relevant to the themes of this book: his characterization of Buddhism as psychotherapy, and his idea about a social taboo against enlightenment.

Many psychologists and psychotherapists were discovering Zen and drawing parallels between it and their own work—noting, for example, the striking parallels between Zen accounts of satori enlightenment experiences and the "Aha!" experiences that were frequently felt by patients in therapy when it all came together.

In *Psychotherapy East and West*, first published in 1961, Watts audaciously declared that Buddhism was a mode of psychotherapy, or at least it could be much better understood and approached along that path than by thinking of it as a religion in the Western sense.

A few years later he published another book, with the curious title of *The Book*. Its subtitle was: *On the Taboo Against Knowing Who You Are*. It was based loosely on the teachings of the Vedanta philosophy of Hinduism, but he insisted that he did not mean it to be taken as in any sense a textbook or on introduction to Vedanta; he described it instead as "a cross-fertilization of Western science with an Eastern intuition."[15]

Its central idea was, in a way, a revision of Freud's map of the psyche. Freud, remember, had described the superego as an introject, a social construct, society's rules and repressions come to live within us, like a garrison in a conquered city. Watts went a step further and described the ego—our very own sense of who we are—as equally foreign: "a hoax, or, at best, a temporary role that we are playing, or have been conned into playing, just as every hypnotized person is basically willing to be hypnotized."[16] This was close to the concept he had learned from Trigant Burrow decades before, but he put a Hindu spin on it by describing the whole play as a cosmic drama, with God disguising himself as separate beings. In this game some of the separate beings discover that they are not separate after all but rather God in hiding—and discover at the same time that everybody and everything else is God as well.

Watts may have overstated his case a bit with the use of the word "taboo," but I think he was quite correct in identifying the self as a social construct, not only the product of our early socialization but also continually and actively reinforced by society. And he was also correct in observing that, although enlightenment is considered in some circles to be a nifty idea and/or an enviable achievement, it is neither encouraged nor recognized by most of our social institutions, which tend to be rather more interested in the care and feeding of egos.

Watts was important in the counterculture not only as a popularizer of Zen and a synthesizer of Buddhism and therapy but also as a booster of psychedelics. He wrote eloquently in *The Joyous Cosmology* of his drug adventures and called them yet another synthesis—of science and religion. Psychedelics, he believed, might make possible the systematic exploration of modes of consciousness heretofore only hinted at in the difficult symbolism of esoteric art and literature. "If the pharmacologist can be of help in exploring this unknown world," he wrote, "he may be doing us the extraordinary service of rescuing religious experience from the obscurantists." For many, this sounded like a simple invitation to instant enlightenment through chemicals—an idea that has led to many discoveries and disasters. I don't know what was the discovery-to-disaster ratio, and I don't believe anybody else does, but I am certain that drugs must be accepted as part of our evolutionary enterprise. Learning how to live with the world's cornucopia of psychoactive chemicals remains a major piece of unfinished business in humanity's struggle to grow up.

The Paradigm (Sort of) Shifts

Euphoria was in the air in the 1960s. It was easy for people who attended workshops at Esalen, participated in encounter groups, or read any of the torrent of books that were pouring forth from its leaders to become convinced that a large-scale transformation of human consciousness was not just an agenda for work and exploration but a forecast of something that had to happen, was perhaps happening already, and would soon change the world.

So ideas such as the ones Aldous Huxley had so cautiously offered in his lectures began to form into a kind of ideology. It was all the more powerful because none of its advocates recognized it as such, and allowed their well-intentioned inspirational statements to turn into promises without quite recognizing what was happening, or what the dangers might be.

And whenever there were words to be chosen, they were words of uplift, hope, and golden promise. The 1965 Esalen brochure contained lines of the playwright Christopher Fry:

> Dark and cold we may be, but this
> is no winter now. The frozen misery
> of centuries breaks, cracks, and begins to move,
> the thunder is thunder of the floes,
> the thaw, the flood, the upstart spring.

It also contained an introduction by George Leonard, the magazine editor who had supervised *Look*'s special issue on California. He become a close friend of Esalen co-founder Michael Murphy and a devoted booster of the human potential movement. It began:

> Within a single lifetime, our physical environment has been changed almost beyond recognition. But there has been little corresponding change in how we, as individuals, relate to the world and experience reality. Such a change is inevitable, however—indeed, it is imminent.

Inevitable and imminent: those are strong words, the words of manifestos. Leonard went on to write a book entitled *The Transformation* that described the current period as unique in history, representing "the beginning of the most thoroughgoing change in the quality of human existence" since the beginning of civilization.[17] There appeared to be no doubt in Leonard's mind that this change could accurately be described as a societywide paradigm shift, and that the human potential movement was one of its leaders and shapers. A similar message with an even stronger emphasis on the paradigm shift theme was *The Aquarian Conspiracy,* published in 1980.[18]

Obviously, things haven't worked out at anything like the scale and speed that was suggested in the visionary literature of paradigm shift and transformation. The road looks longer now and the climb steeper, but the ideas and experiences opened up in the wild green years of the human potential movement were important and valuable parts of our progress along the evolutionary path. *Guru* and *satori* are in our vocabularies now, and many of the ideas and practices of existential and humanistic psychology have found their way into widely used and decidedly un-Bohemian counseling practices. Yet, however common-place such ideas may have become, many people still regard them as suspiciously subversive. We don't yet have a culture that fully inte-grates the wisdom of East and West in a way meaningful to the non-hip; it appears now that, if such a culture is to come into being, science—not just pharmacology, but the sciences of cosmology and cognition—will have much to contribute to it.

PART TWO

THE NEW MIRROR

OF SCIENCE

Images of science in the popular mind have long tended to conjure up visions of somebody studying an external object through an optical instrument: the lab-coated biologist peering downward through his microscope at a small specimen of life, the astronomer peering upward through his telescope at the stars and planets. Before that, and in a sense the granddaddy of all such visions, was René Descartes' picture of the human mind peering out from the pineal gland at the inert objects that surround it.

But some scientists have always known that they were inseparable from the objects they studied, and now more and more are moving toward the understanding that what we always study, in a sense, is ourselves. Consciousness is nature looking at nature. This is a major transition—Stephen Toulmin calls it "the death of the spectator"— in the evolution of human consciousness.[1]

One of the reasons I make minimal use of words such as "spiritual" and "mystical" in connection with the discussion of enlightenment is that those words tend to reinforce the assumption, held by many people in the West, that the subject is naturally akin to matters theological and supernatural and is therefore unapproachable through scientific investigation and rational cognition. Nothing could be further from the truth.

In the next few chapters we'll explore some areas of science—physics, cosmology, brain research—and some well-researched fields of psychology such as cognition, constructivism, and adult development. My aim will be to show how findings in these various fields are converging to produce a new worldview, a larger space of understanding—a more stately mansion, if you will—in which the concept of enlightenment becomes, although still mysterious, at least scientifically respectable.

Along the way I want to draw attention to the slipperiness of the traditional boundary line between physics and psychology. These two disciplines might seem entirely irrelevant to one another—and are still protected from illicit intercourse in academia—but they have much to say about how we experience the world, and perhaps more, if we allow both voices to be heard in the same room.

CHAPTER 6

Meeting Cousin Sirius

And then one day there came to be a creature whose genetic material was in no major way different from the self-replicating molecular collectives of any of the other organisms on his planet, which he called Earth. But he was able to ponder the mystery of his origins, the strange and tortuous path by which he had emerged from star-stuff. He was the matter of the cosmos, contemplating itself.   — CARL SAGAN[1]

The classical ideal of an objective description of nature is no longer valid. The Cartesian partition between the I and the world, between the observer and the observed, cannot be made when dealing with atomic matter. In atomic physics, we can never speak about nature without, at the same time, speaking about ourselves   — FRITJOF CAPRA[2]

A human being is a part of the whole, called by us the "Universe," a part limited in time and space. He experiences himself, his thoughts and feelings as something separate from the rest—a kind of optical illusion of his consciousness. This delusion is a kind of prison for us . . . Our task must be to free ourselves from the prison.   — ALBERT EINSTEIN[3]

Sigmund Freud's description of the Copernican revolution as a blow to human vanity is a memorable example of an idea that was gaining currency among leading thinkers of the twentieth century: the close connection between cosmology and identity, between the ideas we hold about the nature of the universe and our concepts of who and what we are. And what makes this insight particularly important to us in the twenty-first century is the obvious fact that cosmologies change profoundly over time, requiring human beings to make adjustments in their personal and collective self-images. The house of consciousness is continually being rebuilt, and at the present time—with science in the midst of an intense surge of cosmological discovery and theory-building—our concept of self is an open question in a way it has never been before.

Some of the findings of contemporary science are so strange, so different from our everyday understanding of reality, that the mind can scarcely grasp them. But at the center of what is now being discovered and discussed are a couple of major themes—connection and change—that are not so hard to accept in general terms, even though they take us far from where the mainstream of Western thought used to be, and where many people think it still is.

Evolution Big Time

The most important theme in the way scientists now think about the universe is the idea that it develops and changes over time. The universe evolves. The same general way of looking at biological life that caused such an upheaval when it was advanced by Darwin and his colleagues in the nineteenth century has now—rather quietly, with considerably less social upheaval—become the general way of looking at the entire cosmos. This is another kind of continuity, a view of everything that exists—us and the galaxies—as involved in some sort of *process*.

For most premodern peoples the universe—however it was conceived or believed to have been created—was regarded as a more or less unchanging entity. Timothy Ferris nicely sums up these ancient worldviews:

> If we were to express in a single word the principal liability of the prescientific philosophies of nature—if, to put it another way, we were to name the one among their shortcomings that science has done the most to repair—I think it would be that they presumed that the universe was *static*. Many thinkers dismissed change as an illusion. In this view, the manifestations of

time—"the moving image of eternity," as Plato called it—are noise, while what matters, the signal, is the invariant hum of eternal stasis. Others admitted that change occurs, but regarded it as trivial. They held that time moves in cycles, so that events, though they may seem unique and important from our limited point of view, are in the long run destined to repeat themselves, tracing out endless orbits of fatalistic destiny. The grinding of these eternal wheels, music to the ears of many a sophisticate, sounds through the works of Hesiod, Pythagoras, Plato, Aristotle, his student Eudemus, and many who followed them. Even the vast timescapes of Hindu belief, often invoked by science writers as foreshadowing today's astronomical figures—and the numbers *are* big; a thousand *mahayugas,* each lasting four billion years, make up but a single Brahma day—amount to little more than fitting larger cogs to the same old mechanism of eternal return. One reads in the ancient books of *rev*olution, but almost never of *ev*olution. Change occurs *in* the universe, but in the end amounts to nothing important, and the overall picture remains the same.[4]

And we have noted that even in the early part of the modern age and in the scientific West—in the years before Darwin and Wallace disturbed the peace—the hierarchy of organic life was regarded as a fixed entity. All creatures great and small had their places in the Great Chain of Being, while the larger arrangement of phyla and species remained static and stable, just the way God had made it at the beginning of time. That static vision of biological life is dead now, a victim of the Darwinian revolution, and now another revolution is under way—a cosmological revolution in which scientists piece together a story of a universe that was somehow born, and that somehow grows and changes.

Such a cosmology, however strongly supported by contemporary science, is pretty weird when you think about it. For that matter, I have yet to see an explanation for the existence of the universe—or existence at all—that *isn't* weird. Theological creation stories a la Genesis are weird; primitive mythological stories are weird; and scientific stories are *really* weird.

Around the middle of the twentieth century, there were two competing weird stories of how it all began. There was the weird "big bang" theory, according to which everything sort of popped into existence all at once, and the weird "steady state" theory, according to which the universe had no beginning and just expanded endlessly, with new matter continuing to drift into existence out of nowhere to make up for the density sacrificed by the process of expansion. The big bang theory seemed at first to be full of holes—not black holes, which hadn't yet been named or accurately described, but logical holes; there was, for example, the perplexing fact that some of the early astronomical evidence on which the theory was based seemed to indicate that Earth was older than the universe.[5]

Gradually better evidence accumulated, the big bang theory won converts, and the scientists began not only to talk more confidently about it but to venture descriptions of various events that must have taken place in the first few minutes. These, too, met with much skepticism, however; one theoretical physicist writes of attending a lecture at University College London in the late 1960s, where a professor was explaining that the discovery of cosmic microwave background radiation indicated that the universe had to have been composed of about 25 percent helium and 75 percent hydrogen in the first few minutes: "Everyone in the lecture hall fell about laughing, because they thought it was so absurd and audacious to talk about the first three minutes after the big bang, just on the basis of the discovery of this radiation."

He adds: "Now, of course, it is absolutely standard cosmological theory. We feel we understand the first few minutes of the universe very well."[6]

The whole story, which now spans some 14 billion years, tells of how the first-few-minutes mix of hydrogen and helium gases formed into spinning patterns of movement that became the galaxies, within which atoms collided and generated huge amounts of energy. The first stars were born and evolved through generation after generation, forging in their intensely hot interiors new elements, the whole periodic table, everything from oxygen to uranium. Some of these stars were surrounded by gas and dustlike particles of the heavier elements that they or other stars had created, which gradually formed into orbiting clumps of matter, absorbing energy radiated from the star. One of the clumps, settling into a semblance of its present shape after the cosmos had been going about its expansive business for some 10 billion years, was Earth: a storming, volcanic mass of cosmic debris, much of which had been forged in distant now-dead stars and sent spinning across the galaxy until it was swallowed into the solar system. Gases swirling about this clump of matter formed the primordial atmosphere, a noxious mix of compounds such as methane and hydrogen sulfide, and other gases condensed to form the first oceans. Amid the storms and volcanic activity, new and more complex molecules were formed, some settling into the oceans.

According to this cosmological story, some of these molecules began to copy themselves. The molecules that could self-replicate grew more numerous, of course, and their replication processes grew more complex and consistent. Copying systems became more sophisticated—kind of like new editions of your software—as molecules interacted and combined with other molecules, and in time the waters teemed with communities of them.

And at some point these communities of molecules began to exhibit the characteristics of what we would now call life. This was an astonishing development, one that science can describe in increasingly precise detail but cannot begin to explain. Some refer back to the French philosopher Henry Bergson's early book *Creative Evolution* and to the more recent and more scientifically respectable *Cosmogenesis* by astrophysicist David Layer.[7] In both books the central argument is that evolution innovates, bringing forth things that could not have been predicted before they appeared. Who would have thought that a bunch of mindless molecules stewing in the primeval oceans could have invented sex and death, and then could have managed to climb onto the land, fly in the air, survive huge global disasters such as volcanic eruptions, meteorites, and ice ages, and develop eventually into you, me, and all the other living things that inhabit the planet—that *are* the planet—as it goes its creative way?

This story of the growth of the universe, and of the life within it, is, of course, anathema to those who cling to the classic religious stories of creation. But as Eric Chaisson, one of the more eloquent exponents of the new super-science of cosmic evolution, points out, it's a story that is still being written and does not necessarily involve either dogmatism or atheism. However, it definitely does involve change and connection:

Evolution is hardly more than a fancy word for change—especially developmental change. Indeed, it seems that change is the hallmark for the origin, development, and maintenance of all things in the Universe, animate or inanimate. Change has, over the course of all time and throughout all space, brought forth, successfully and successively, galaxies, stars, planets, and life. Thus, we give this process of universal change a more elegant name—cosmic evolution, which for me includes all aspects of evolution: particulate, galactic, stellar, elemental, planetary, chemical, biological, and cultural. As such, the familiar subject of biological evolution becomes just one segment of a much broader evolutionary scheme stretching well beyond mere life on Earth. In short, what Darwin once did for plants and animals, cosmic evolution does for all things. And if Darwinism created a veritable revolution in understanding by helping to free us from the anthropocentric belief that humans basically differ from other life forms on our planet, then cosmic evolution is destined to extend that intellectual revolution by in turn releasing us from regarding matter on Earth and in our bodies any differently from that in the stars and galaxies beyond.[8]

And now the evolutionary story, which was mysterious enough even in the conventional summary I have given above, is becoming even more mysterious. Some of the theoreticians are talking seriously about multiple universes, and speculating about a kind of cosmic Darwinian natural-selection process by which new universes are continually being born and developing, with varying degrees of success, along divergent evolutionary pathways.

The view of the universe as conscious of itself—at least through the medium of human consciousness—has also gained a general currency, although there is a fair amount of quarreling about what this means or how it should be stated. The "anthropic principle," as it is generally described, comes in several packages with varying degrees of weirdness.

In its most innocuous and most widely accepted version, the anthropic principle merely notes that certain conditions need to have emerged in the course of cosmic evolution in order to make intelligent life possible—and suggests that it might be a fruitful course for future scientific study to explore and identify exactly what those conditions might be. This is sometimes called the weak anthropic principle, or WAP for short.

The strong anthropic principle (SAP) takes this view a giant step further by proposing that the laws of physics and the conditions of cosmic evolution were somehow designed to bring forth life. This is a view that many theoretical physicists, even those receptive to ideas about multiple universes, regard as scientifically unsound. Thus, Lee Smolin of Pennsylvania State University calls it "more religion than science," and adds: "I'm not surprised to find that several advocates of the strong form of the anthropic principle are writing books and papers connecting their belief in the anthropic principle with Christian theology."[9]

Then there is another version, sometimes called the final anthropic principle (FAP) and popular among science-fiction writers, which holds that once intelligent life appears in the universe it will continue to evolve and grow, shaping the universe to its own purposes. I don't personally find this at all outrageous—certainly not as much as the idea of multiple universes and in some ways less far-out than the SAP—but it has been heavily stomped upon by skeptics such as writer Martin Gardner, who some years ago dismissed it as the "completely ridiculous anthropic principle," or CRAP.[10]

How Anthropic Can You Get?

Anthropic principles abound, and their very multiplicity is an indicator of our awkward entry into a new way of seeing the world and being in it—the latter by far the more important part of the transition.

Classical physics, which molded my own construction of the world as I grew up, gave me to understand clearly that consciousness and the subject matter of physics were two different things. This was so built into the fabric of my reality that I didn't even know it was what I thought, or that there was any other conceivable way that anybody *could* think about it. I was a child of the modern era, my worldview formed by Newton's concept of atoms as hard, indivisible entities moving through a fixed background of time and space, and by Descartes' division of mind from matter.

Then, when I was a high school kid aspiring to become a nuclear physicist, I got hold of some of Einstein's work and absorbed (to the best of my intellectual ability) a revised universe in which time and space were relative and matter and energy were essentially the same. I found this heady stuff but in no sense disturbing—realities are pretty easily revised when you're fourteen or fifteen years old—and I can remember standing by the side of a road waiting for a school bus and contemplating the space-time continuum with what I can only describe as a kind of deep satisfaction, the way you feel when you are digesting a really good meal. I can't claim that I understood the concept all that well, but somehow it felt good to think about it.

However, that Einsteinian message didn't really shake up the Cartesian part of my classical worldview. I still understood that I was a mind in here looking at a universe out there on the other side of the road, and that consciousness was still one thing and physics—even a revolutionary physics—was something else.

Now even conventional cosmologists (even those who consider themselves to be hard-nosed, although cosmology is a tough field in which to remain an old-school, commonsense realist) are willing to take note of the indisputable fact that the evolutionary process of the universe did indeed lead to the appearance on Earth of conscious creatures—even creatures capable of studying the evolutionary process of the universe itself. The universe evolves, and we are it.

I mentioned above that there is a certain difference between seeing the universe this way and of *being* in it this way, the latter being the more difficult transition because it carries you into a *felt sense* of participation and connection that is also the path of enlightenment. The anthropic principle, even in its mildest form, makes common cause in our consciousness with the "Thou art that" of enlightenment traditions and the "become what you are" of the existentialists.

This is one of the ways that an emerging "big picture" of the whole cosmos runs parallel to the one that was expressed in ancient Asian philosophy, especially when we take it into our daily lives and allow it to become more than theory. And it was over twenty years ago that Fritjof Capra pointed out other parallels between East and West—this time involving new ideas that were emerging from the study of the smallest imaginable units of the universe.

East Meets West in the Cyclotron

Capra's book, *The Tao of Physics,* first published in the mid-1970s, was for many people the first stunning introduction to the idea that the science of physics wasn't just about rock-solid stuff "out there" in the landscape, and was in some ways remarkably similar to ideas about the universe found in Eastern disciplines such as Buddhism. But, as Capra pointed out, other scientists, including leading nuclear physicists such as J. Robert Oppenheimer and Neils Bohr, had been thinking in that direction since the 1950s. Both those pioneers had written about the impacts of their discoveries on human understanding of the universe.

Oppenheimer, director of the Manhattan Project, had said that the general notions about human understanding then being revealed by discoveries in atomic physics "have a history, and in Buddhist and Hindu thought a more considerable and central place. What we shall find is an exemplification, an encouragement, and a refinement of old wisdom."[11] Bohr also believed that parallels to atomic theory would be found in "those kinds of epistemological problems with which already thinkers like the Buddha and Lao Tzu have been confronted, when trying to harmonize our position as spectators and actors in the great drama of existence."[12]

Capra summarized his own view as follows:

In modern physics, the universe is experienced as a dynamic, inseparable whole which always includes the observer in an essential way. In this experience, the traditional concepts of space and time, of isolated objects, and of cause and effect, lose their meaning. Such an experience, however, is very similar to that of the Eastern mystics. The similarity becomes apparent in quantum and relativity theory, and becomes even stronger in the "quantum-relativistic" models of subatomic physics, where both these theories combine to produce the most striking parallels to Eastern mysticism.[13]

Since Capra wrote those words decades ago, the sciences of physics and cosmology have continued to evolve away from the Newtonian model: The big bang theory and the vision of an ever-expanding universe have moved steadily closer toward the mainstream, various experiments in quantum mechanics have revealed uncanny behaviors among subatomic particles, and perfectly respectable physicists now come to conferences and chat happily about other universes with different sets of dimensions.

Perhaps the reason we haven't *all* gotten off the Newtonian bus is that the other vehicle is moving too rapidly for us to get aboard. What we are dealing with here is not simply a so-called paradigm shift in which science moves from one settled description of how things are to a new, settled description of how things are—from Newton to Einstein. The new cosmology is a bit dicier than that, and far more mysterious, yet you don't need a Ph.D. in physics to join the post-Newtonian universe. You need only to grasp certain key images, such as the continually evolving universe and the quirkiness of subatomic particles, and to know that there are many unanswered questions. You need to understand that good old, everyday physics, although still handy when you want to hit a golf ball or get out of the way of a truck, is only one way of looking at things. And you need to notice that what scientists seem to want to communicate to us, when they turn to writing about their work, is a sense of wonder. In this vein Richard Dawkins, in a book entitled *Unweaving the Rainbow: Science, Delusion and the Appetite for Wonder,* writes:

> After sleeping through a hundred million centuries we have finally opened our eyes on a sumptuous planet, sparkling with color, bountiful with life. Within decades we must close our eyes again. Isn't it a noble, an enlightened way of spending our brief time in the sun, to work at understanding the universe and how we have come to wake up in it? This is how I answer when I am asked—as I am surprisingly often—why I bother to get up in the mornings.[14]

The modern age has often been described as a time of disenchantment, the wonder of primitive belief cruelly dispelled by the dull realities of science. Well, that's one opinion. I say you can be either enchanted or disenchanted, and your degree of enchantment will depend on how you decide to be in the universe. If you are merely in it as a detached observer, you may or may not summon up a breath of wonder when you contemplate, say, a photograph of a galaxy being born. If you are more fully in it, and have allowed yourself to consider deeply the amazing fact of being instead of not-being, you may also allow yourself to recognize that whatever force exploded into the big bang is at the moment thinking your thoughts and flowing through your veins. Unless you came from one of the other universes, you are what is happening in this one; and I find that an enchanting reality indeed.

In the days of Ptolomey or even Copernicus, cosmology was not an evolutionary science; today it is. The whole amazing Darwinian saga has been folded within an infinitely larger story, which is, among other things, a story about you and me and about change. Darwinian evolution connected us to all biological life; cosmology connects us to the universe. The late Carl Sagan never tired of saying that we are "star-stuff," and a recent account says a bit more prosaically that our planet and our bodies are composed of congealed cosmic dust. Such statements are reminders that, however conceptually far-out the new cosmology may be, in geographic terms it is not far-out at all. You don't need a telescope to look at the mysterious and still-evolving cosmos; you can try a mirror.

The Mysterious No-Nos

Two cosmological concepts are implicit in the weird reality that science is now constructing for us. Both have to do with what isn't as well as what is, and both are particularly awesome, worthy of our respectful attention. They are nonlocality and nothingness. The first is new, one of the many mind-scrambling gifts of quantum physics; the second is as old as the first stories about the creation of the world.

According to the concept of nonlocality, which is yet another step away from the Newtonian view of the solid and tangible universe, things aren't quite as concretely located in places as they might seem to us in everyday, commonsense perception. Locality is based on the assumption that no signal or energy transfer faster than the speed of light can take place between separated regions. This is also known in physics as the principle of "local causes," which holds that, in order to influence any physical event some signal must be sent, and that signal cannot travel faster than the speed of light. The principle holds even over great distances, such as when technicians on Earth send commands to a vehicle moving about on the surface of Mars. But it doesn't hold at the level of quantum physics, where nonlocality is a central theme—in fact, it could be argued, that's what quantum physics is really about.

A number of elegant experiments have proven conclusively over the past thirty years that nonlocality can be demonstrated and observed. The experiments typically involve pairs of photons linked in the same quantum state—"entangled" is the term commonly used by physicists—which are sent traveling in different directions over a considerable distance (about seven miles in one of the most impressive experiments) and then measured to see if distance has separated them for the extent that they cease to behave in unison. They do not; they continue to act simultaneously as a linked pair, with no time elapsed for any message to have passed between them.

Some of the news reports on these experiments have interpreted them to mean that the scientists caused information to travel more rapidly than the speed of light, which wasn't what happened. What happened was even stranger; the correlation occurred instantly, literally in no time at all. And in a sense, in no space, but in nonlocality. Nonlocality is now accepted as a fact of nature, and it may be, as one observer has suggested, "the most profound discovery in all of science."[15]

In the scale of quantum physics, a separation of seven miles is an immense distance, and the general scientific consensus is that distance has been shown to have no effect whatever. The effect would be the same if the two photons were on opposite sides of the universe. And the phenomenon of linked quanta—of nonlocality—is as much a part of the reality of the universe as space and time and gravity. As the authors of a book on nonlocality—one a physicist, the other a historian of science—point out, we now contemplate a universe much more richly interconnected than we might ordinarily imagine:

All particles in the history of the cosmos have interacted with other particles in the manner revealed by the Aspect experiments. Virtually everything in our immediate physical environment is made up of quanta that have been interacting with other quanta in this manner from the big bang to the present. Even the atoms in our bodies are made up of particles that were once in close proximity to the cosmic fireball, and other particles that interacted at that time in a single quantum state can be found in the most distant star. Also consider, as the physicist N. David Mermin has shown, that quantum entanglement grows exponentially with the number of particles involved in the original quantum state and that there is no theoretical limit to the number of these entangled particles. If this is the case, the universe on a very basic level could be a vast web of particles, which remain in contact with one another over any distance in "no time" in the absence of the transfer of energy or information.[16]

So you are not only a part of the universe, you are entangled with it, linked in a cosmic dance with everything everywhere, near and far. A strange scientific reality to contemplate, but certainly one that gives a new meaning to the ancient mystical assertion that we are all one.

No less strange is the concept of nothing, one that we contemplate whenever we think deeply about the fact that there is something—and yet really can't imagine. Some Eastern traditions speak mysteriously of the Void as the source of all that exists, a deep nothing which is as they say, "without attributes." Western science now speaks confidently about the big bang but has little to say about what caused the bang or what existed before it all happened. When a scientist does venture to answer the question that ordinary people like me want to ask, the answer is pretty much the same thing. Thus Heinz Pagels: "The answer to the question, 'Where did the universe come from?' is that it came out of the vacuum. The entire universe is a reexpression of sheer nothingness." And that is really about as good an answer as you're likely to get, because what anybody knows about that vacuum is—nothing. Creation myths that have fulsome answers to the question are really not explanations at all, only con-fabulations. All we have is a vast nonbeing that is somehow the ground of being, beyond everything we know, or think we know. It is a nothing but it is—as Alan Watts used to say—for a nothing, uncommonly frisky.

CHAPTER 7

The Mysterious Material Mind

The prevailing wisdom, variously expressed and argued for, is *materialism:* there is only one sort of stuff, namely *matter*—the physical stuff of physics, chemistry, and physiology—and the mind is somehow nothing but a physical phenomenon.
— DANIEL DENNETT[1]

The unconscious is not merely a morass of repressed sexual desires and forbidden hatred. The unconscious is an active, vital part of the human mind. — TOR NORRETRANDERS[2]

One of the perennial subjects of human philosophy, art, and science, a thing we seem never to tire of thinking about, is thought itself. It has always been one of the great mysteries, and it still is. Although it is the very stuff of our moment-to-moment existence, we remain baffled by the simplest of questions about it—such as what it is, and where it is.

Most people today believe as a matter of common sense that consciousness somehow happens in the brain, but there was a time when most people believed as a matter of common sense that it happened pretty much everywhere else. Scholars who have made a study of the Homeric epics and other surviving works of Greek antiquity point out that thoughts and feelings were often described as located in various noncerebral organs such as the heart or the lungs, sometimes in the general vicinity of the body but not necessarily inside it, and sometimes not in any location whatever.[3] And we have a legacy of words—spleen and bile and visceral and heartfelt—that put moods and emotions in the body.

The question of where consciousness is located, of course, begs another question—whether it is in some sense material, or whether it is of some other nonmaterial nature entirely. It might seem to a logical person (at least before people started talking about a nonlocal universe) that if consciousness is located some*place* then it must be some*thing*. It might seem that way, but, oddly enough, this was not the way educated people in the modern Western world saw the situation for several centuries. René Descartes' formulation is frequently quoted because he made a clear and persuasive case that consciousness was nonmaterial—a viewpoint acceptable from the point of view of Christian theology—while at the same time establishing the brain as its headquarters.

The key to this deft piece of reasoning was, of course, the pineal gland, which Descartes held to be the gateway between the physical body and the nonphysical mind/soul. In his version of cognition the brain—which is material—forms mental images of external objects—also material—and transmits those images to the gland (located more or less in the center of the brain) at which point the images are apprehended by the soul and translated into nonmaterial thought. This may seem a bit hard to swallow, but it was central to the mind-body dualism that comprised, along with Newtonian physics, the foundation of the Western worldview.

Descartes was a brilliant man—accomplished in several fields of scientific, mathematical, and philosophical inquiry, and deeply dedicated to the search for understanding. It's worth keeping that in mind because he has had the historical misfortune of being the person who most eloquently stated what contemporary thinkers about thought generally regard as dead wrong.

Dead wrong on two points: first, the question of whether consciousness is material; second, whether it occupies some central position in the brain. Let's look at each of these separately because they are more than just issues for philosophical nitpicking. They have to do with assumptions central to our experience of everyday life—assumptions we may not even recognize as such—about how we think, how we think we think, and what we think we are. First, the materialistic view of consciousness.

The Mind of Matter

The famous British biologist Francis Crick, now a resident of Southern California, recently wandered out of the boundaries of his academic discipline, as a Nobel laureate can freely do, and wrote a book about consciousness. The title of it was *The Astonishing Hypothesis,* and the astonishing hypothesis in question was that human consciousness is an activity of matter. " 'You,' your joys and your sorrows," he declared, "your memories and your ambitions, your sense of personal identity and free will, are in fact no more than the behavior of a vast assembly of nerve cells and their associated molecules. . . . This hypothesis is so alien to the ideas of most people alive today that it can truly be called astonishing."[4] I'm not altogether sure who Crick expected to be astonished by this, since (as Daniel Dennett puts it) the material view of consciousness is now "a received opinion, approaching unanimity."[5] Perhaps Crick was generalizing about nonscientific popular opinion, suggesting that, even though the materialistic view may be Brain Science 1A, ordinary people still think of consciousness as somehow nonmaterial. Even that is doubtful, however, since the modification of consciousness by means of chemical substances is a part of everyday life, and most people know something about how physical events such as surgery, senility, and inherited brain defects can affect thought—and all of that is based on materialistic assumptions. Scientists and laypeople alike now generally regard thought (both conscious and unconsciousness) as produced in the physical brain. If you fancy paradigms, there one is.

So the materialistic view of consciousness is not astonishing—at least not in the sense that Crick meant. Neither is it, as feared by some people with religious or spiritual axes to grind, a debasement of the grandeur and mystery of human thought. It grounds us in the physical world (now seen as much more than a lot of inert matter), reinforces the bridge between cosmology and psychology, and points the way toward a rich dialogue between the cognitive sciences and the enlightenment traditions—one that has already begun but still has far to go.

In and Out of the Rat Maze

A materialistic view of consciousness can be liberating—yes, enlightening—but Western science has wandered down some dark and unliberating alleys on the way to escaping from Cartesian mind-body duality. We have had various excessive statements of genetic determinism—attempts to explain our actions and thoughts as driven by biological inheritance—and we had that curious episode in psychology and the social sciences called behaviorism. Behaviorists attempted to explain our actions as responses to external stimuli and didn't want to pay much attention to thoughts at all.

The behaviorist movement was born out of a desire to found a more scientific approach to psychology—commendable in itself—that would employ the most rigorous methodology and stay free from the kind of psychologizing the behaviorists associated with Freud and his followers, which they thought to be somewhat on the flaky side. The behaviorists, mostly psychologists trained in U.S. universities, were highly suspicious of introspection as a method of scientific inquiry, and thought that most of the ideas produced by the philosophically oriented theorists were tainted by that method. Freud, Jung, and all their cohorts had generated a great number of propositions for which they claimed the status of scientific truth but were in fact damnably hard either to verify or to conclusively disprove through any known scientific method. The way the behaviorists proposed to overcome this fuzziness was to stay in the spectator role, stop chasing after thoughts, and pay attention only to observable behaviors. As J. B. Watson, one of the early cheerleaders of this movement, outlined its new approach:

> (Psychologists) reached the conclusion that they could no longer be content to work with the intangibles. They saw their brother scientists making progress in medicine, in chemistry, in physics. Every new discovery in those fields was of prime importance, every new element isolated in one laboratory could be isolated in some other laboratory; each new element was immediately

taken up in the warp and woof of science as a whole. . . . The behaviorist began his own formulation of the problem of psychology by sweeping aside all medieval subjective terms such as sensation, perception, image, desire, purpose, and even thinking and emotion as they were originally defined. . . . The behaviorist asks: why don't we make what we can observe the real field of psychology? Let us limit ourselves to things that can be observed and formulate laws concerning only the observable things.[6]

The behaviorist movement was a ham-handed way of getting toward a view of thought as essentially material: It simply abdicated many of the most important and interesting psychological issues and set forth to enforce methods of inquiry that resembled those of the physical sciences. The slavish imitation of "real science" was always palpable and sometimes ludicrous; the behaviorists wanted to do research on things that were measurable, to produce results that could be tested and replicated by other investigators, and that way build up, stone upon stone, a body of scientific knowledge. Their movement was immensely influential for several decades. It blew like a hurricane through the academic world and found strong support, particularly in the United States, with a science-admiring public. And it generated tons of data. Boy, did it generate data.

Behaviorism's most tangible accomplishments involved the study of the behavior patterns of various laboratory animals—all the business with rats in mazes and birds with food pellets. Its most dubious achievements involved applying similar behavior-modification methods and concepts to human beings. Behavior-modification approaches to psychotherapy—changing behavior thorough the controlled distribution of punishments or rewards—were sometimes effective, but they were regarded with considerable suspicion by critics who saw them as methods of control and coercion rather than any sort of healing or growth.

B. F. Skinner of Harvard, who became behaviorism's best-known spokesman, also happened to be the person who made the loftiest claims—presenting it as nothing less than the key to social progress. He proposed that we could achieve the ideal society through the widescale application of positive rather than negative reinforcement for desirable behaviors, thus getting away from the unsavory punishment aspects of stimulus-response methodology. This would make it possible to design culture and control people in such a way that they would be quite happy being controlled. In Skinner's utopian novel *Walden Two,* the social-engineer protagonist confidently announces:

> We can achieve a sort of control under which the controlled, though they are following a code much more scrupulously than was ever the case under the old system, nevertheless *feel free.* They are doing what they want to do, not what they are forced to do. That's the source of the tremendous power of positive reinforcement—there's no restraint and no revolt. By a careful cultural design we control not the final behavior, but the inclination to behave—the motives, the desires, the wishes.[7]

In a later book, provocatively titled *Beyond Freedom and Dignity,* Skinner further elaborated on his claim that behavioral science had reached the point of being ready to offer to the world a "technology of behavior" that could benevolently redesign the social order and solve through science and reason most of the world's major problems.

The humanist critics who denounced this as a manifesto for a coming techno-fascist social order really needn't have worried, since neither Skinner nor any of his colleagues had the vaguest notion of how to deliver on such grandiose promises. The glaring weaknesses of behaviorism were not so much in what it did but in what it did not do—indeed, could not even *study* within its self-imposed limitations, which ruled out most really important questions. As the sociologist Karl Mannheim pointed out:

> The carrying over of the methods of natural science to the social sciences gradually leads to a situation where one no longer asks

what one would like to know and what will be of decisive significance for the next step in social development, but attempts to
deal only with those complexes of facts which are measurable
according to a certain already existent method. Instead of
attempting to discover what is most significant with the highest
degree of precision possible under the existing circumstances,
one tends to be content to attribute importance to what is measurable merely because it happens to be measurable.[8]

Among the many subjects that the behaviorist approach to psychological research ruled off-limits are virtually all the ones we are
exploring in this book. You can't, for example measure or replicate
peak, mystical, or religious experiences—any kind of experience, in
fact—strictly on the basis of behavior because they involve states of
consciousness as well as visible behaviors. A person's worldview is
invisible to behaviorist methodology, as is the sense of personal identity, the extent of his or her maturity and moral development, and virtually anything having to do with meaning.

Well, revolutions come and go. The behavioral revolution has long
since peaked and gone into decline, and other revolutions—in the
brain sciences, in cognitive psychology—have unfolded. As they do, it
becomes apparent that it *is* possible to study cognitive processes scientifically, and to form robust concepts of how we make meaning—and
continually remake meaning—as we grow and mature. We now have
something more closely resembling what the behaviorists hoped to
achieve—a science of thought—and it is beginning to enable us to
look through Western eyes at some of the areas of human experience
that were once the exclusive province of Eastern mysticism.

The Distributed Self and the Third "C"

The contemporary cognitive sciences have no problem assigning the
brain a major role in the generation of thought, but they are not at all
inclined to locate consciousness as somehow centered in any part of it.
As Daniel Dennett puts it: "The pineal gland is not only not the fax

machine to the Soul, it is also not the Oval Office of the brain, and neither are any of the other portions of the brain."[9]

Many of the leading scientists in this field now seem reluctant even to view the brain as a single organ. They will talk about it that way because the language more or less requires it, but they will then go on to say that the brain is best described as a group or committee of organs, each developed at different stages in human evolution, each with different skills and predispositions. Thus Michael Gazzaniga entitles one of his books *The Social Brain,* and describes our mental functioning as "a reconstruction of the independent activities of the many brain systems we all possess. A confederation of mental systems resides within us. Metaphorically, we humans are more of a sociological entity than a single unified psychological entity."[10] Along the same lines, Steven Pinker of MIT describes the mind as "organized into modules or mental organs, each with a specialized design that makes it an expert in one arena of interaction with the world."[11]

And it turns out that the mind has still more players in the game of thought because all of the systems have subsystems, all of the modules contain vast and incredibly sophisticated networks, and the connections among the modules create still more networks that are continually being revised and reorganized. We have to add to the two key elements I mentioned in the previous chapter—continuity and change—a third element: complexity. Our minds are continuous with our bodies and with the material universe, they are engaged in a continuous process of change, never the same from one nanosecond to the next, and they are composed of a staggering number of parts.

This emerging mainstream view of the brain/mind is remarkably similar in important ways to the view of Buddhism and other enlightenment traditions. For a good summary of that mainstream let us turn to *Consilience,* by E. O. Wilson of Harvard. "Consilience" is a word that means jumping together, the unification of knowledge, particularly of biology with the social sciences and humanities, and Wilson is famous—in some circles infamous—as the father of sociobiology, a school of thought which to some (including me) often seemed to lean toward simplistic views of human behavior determined by the genes. But his summary of state-of-the-art research in the brain sciences is anything but simplistic: Wilson describes consciousness as the parallel processing of vast numbers of coding networks, many linked by the synchronized firing of the nerve cells, forming multiple maps or images based on sensory experience of the environment and information from the brain's memory banks. Together, he writes, these "create scenarios that flow realistically back and forth through time. The scenarios are a virtual reality. They can either closely match pieces of the external world or depart indefinitely far from it. They re-create the past and cast up alternative futures that serve as choices for future thought and bodily action."

Wilson's discussion of the contemporary scientific view of the brain grows particularly interesting when he turns to the question of who or what is in charge of this marvelously complex operation. It points toward one of the reasons why the concept of enlightenment seems so hard to grasp, so out of tune with our commonsense ideas about the mind:

Who or what within the brain monitors all this activity? No one. Nothing. The scenarios are not seen by some other part of the brain. They just are. Consciousness is the virtual world composed by the scenarios. There is . . . no single locus of the brain where the scenarios are played out in coherent form. Instead, there are interlacing patterns of neural activity within and among particular sites throughout the forebrain, from cerebral cortex to other specialized centers of cognition such as the thalamus, amygdala, and hippocampus. There is no single stream of consciousness in which all information is brought together by an executive ego.[12]

Impermanent aggregations, devoid of ego. The Buddha couldn't have said it better.

To see what I mean, let us revert to Buddhist basics for a minute and consider two short and simple statements that are central to *its* view of the human condition and human thought:

1. All aggregations—including people—are impermanent.
2. All things—including people—are devoid of ego. (The Sanskrit word for ego is *atman,* which can also be translated as "self" or "soul;" the Buddhist principle is *anatman*—no self, no soul.)

These statements are really two inseparable facets of a view that, while fairly common to Eastern esoteric traditions, is radically and profoundly different from the ideas that prevail in (1) all major theistic religions including Christianity, Judaism, Islam, and Hinduism; (2) Western Socratic/Platonic philosophy; (3) most New Age spirituality, which is saturated with soul-talk; and (4) the ordinary assumptions of more-or-less secular moderns. In the Buddhist view any human being is an aggregation of events—a whole lot of things happening—and not one single thing continuing over time. Each of us is not only unique, but unique in each instant of existence even though some parts of the pattern, of the sort that we can call character, personality, or habits, may be more or less persistent.

It follows that there is no identifying essence at the core of any human being—no eternal soul, no True Self. The assertion that there is no ego does not mean that there can be no experience of an "I" in consciousness—of course there is, or I would not be writing and you reading. Neither does it deny the existence of such drives as pride, ambition, greed, desire for status, and success—all the things that we in the West associate with the word "ego." But it denies that the "I" is either central to consciousness or custodian of an identity that continues more or less the same throughout our lives.

In the Buddhist view the "I" is only a part of the mind—a part that thinks it is the whole, an actor who thinks he or she is the whole play—and those ego drives are its activities. The whole is an aggregation of all its parts, and that aggregation is continually changing, and if you take away the parts there is nothing left.

Multiple Me

The internal soliloquy of Molly Bloom at the end of James Joyce's novel *Ulysses* is an imaginative and—even now, as I go back to read it—beautiful and moving representation in literary art of a human stream of consciousness, a woman reminiscing about her lives and loves as she drops off to sleep:

> . . . and Gibraltar as a girl where I was a Flower of the mountain yes when I put the rose in my hair like the Andalusian girls used or shall I wear a red yes and how he kissed me under the Moorish wall and I thought well as well him as another and then I asked him with my eyes to ask again yes and then he asked me would I yes to say yes my mountain flower and first I put my arms around him yes and drew him down to me so he could feel my breasts all perfume yes and his heart was going like mad and yes I said yes I will yes.

And because it was such a creative and daring piece of work we were prepared to believe yes that's the way we think in long sentences that sort of run together but can still be read from front to back and make perfect sense when you read them yes. But the written word is a limited and inescapably linear medium, even in the hands of the most daring experimental writers. It takes no more than a self-directed exercise in that ancient psychological research medium called introspection to observe that our streams of consciousness (if indeed we can call them that at all) don't really run so smoothly down the hill. Even when we are engaged in rigorous, rational thought, cognition tends to be rather more like what Asian traditions call the "monkey mind," sort of leaping about crazily from tree to tree, pursuing one line of action and then another, and periodically forgetting what it was up to a minute before.

This nonlinear, multiple-trajectory type of cognition is what Wilson described as the play of virtual-reality scenarios, and what Dennett describes with the editorial metaphor of "multiple drafts." He represents the processes of cognition as taking place in various parts of the brain, and then interpreted and reinterpreted indefinitely, so that you may well revise your story about something that happened (or didn't happen) in the remote past. This way of thinking about thought, he believes, "avoids the tempting mistake of supposing that there must be a single narrative (the "final" or "published" draft, you might say) that is canonical—the *actual* stream of consciousness of the subject, whether or not the experimenter (or even the subject) can gain access to it."[13]

This view of consciousness obviously has great relevance to psychotherapy—which is essentially an attempt to help the client edit his or her internal autobiography—and some contemporary schools of psychology are intensely interested in describing not only the personality but also the various *sub*personalities that also make themselves heard in our daily experience of life. They say you do not have to have a Jekyll-and-Hyde personality to be a different person at different times and places, to have varied voices that at different times speak internally with the authoritative voice of "I."

In some of my earlier books I have explored the notion that the growing openness to such concepts may relate to the conditions of life in mass-media, multicultural societies, which require us to form multidimensional structures of consciousness. This idea is developed more extensively in social-psychological studies such as Kenneth Gergen's *The Saturated Self,* which described an emerging syndrome Gergen calls "multiphrenia." He describes multiphrenia as the "populating of the self, the acquisition of multiple and disparate potentials for being." In premodern societies people might hear only one set of messages from their social environments about who they were, what was right and true, and how the world worked. But in a world of diversity, mobility, and rich media bombardment of the mind we encounter a different psychological milieu: "Social saturation furnishes us with a multiplicity of incoherent and unrelated languages of the self. For everything we 'know to be true' about ourselves, other voices within respond with doubt and even derision."[14]

I think Gergen's thesis about the tendency of multicultural life to favor multidimensional consciousness is highly persuasive, and yet I suspect that the internal consciousness of human beings has always been a babble of voices more than a single stream of consciousness, however casually punctuated. One of my favorite pieces of evidence in regard to this is a passage from a book by Alexandra David-Neel in which the author (who had spent many years traveling in Tibet) related an ancient parable that compares the workings of the mind to an unruly town meeting and sounds surprisingly like a popularized piece of postmodern psychology:

> A "person" resembles an assembly composed of a number of members. In this assembly discussion never ceases. Now and again one of the members rises, makes a speech, and suggests an action; his colleagues approve, and it is decided that what he has proposed shall be executed. Or now several members of the assembly rise at the same time and propose different things, and each of them, for private reasons, supports his own proposal. It may happen that these differences of opinion, and the passion which each of the orators bring into the debate, will provoke a quarrel, even a violent quarrel in the assembly. Fellow-members may even come to blows.
>
> It also happens that some members of the assembly leave it of their own accord; others are gradually pushed out, and others again are expelled by force, by their colleagues. All of this time newcomers introduce themselves into the assembly, either by gently sidling in or by forcing the doors.
>
> Again, one notes that certain members of the assembly are slowly perishing; their voices become feeble, and finally they are no longer heard. Others, on the contrary, who were weak and timid, become stronger and bolder; they become violent, shouting their proposals; they terrify their colleagues, and dominate them, and end by making themselves dictators.
>
> The members of this assembly are the physical and mental elements which constitute the "person"; they are our instincts, our tendencies, our ideas, our beliefs, our desires, etc. Through

the causes which engendered it, each of them is the descendant and heir of many lines of causes, of many series of phenomena, going back into the past, and whose traces are lost in the shadowy depths of eternity.[15]

Rethinking the Unconscious

So far in this chapter I have been using the terms "consciousness," "mind," and "brain" interchangeably, but from here onward I will have to be more precise in several ways: We need to remember that consciousness is far from being the totality of our mental activity, and in some ways looks more like the minority partner; that the brain and its mental processes are inseparable from the rest of the body; and that our minds are inseparable from the environments in which they were formed and in which they function.

The revised view of the unconscious is especially important: Influenced by Freud, or at least by a popular version of what Freud believed, modern Westerners tend to regard the unconscious as irrational and a bit of a troublemaker, while the conscious mind is viewed as the seat of rational cognition. Current research is revising this picture in a couple of important ways: The unconscious is now taken to be a much larger portion of our total mental activity, and it is not only larger but also in some ways smarter and more rational than Freud indicated.

Tor Norretranders, a prominent European science journalist, wrote a book subtitled *Cutting Consciousness Down to Size* that brilliantly summarized some of the main findings and conclusions that lead in this direction.

For example, it is generally agreed among contemporary brain researchers that the human computer receives and processes far more information than ever enters consciousness. The estimate for unconscious processing appears to be on the order of ten billion bits a second, whereas conscious experience processes something like ten to thirty bits a second.[16] A great majority of the raw data received by the sense organs is screened out; much of the editing work Dennett refers to has already been done before it lands on our desks. Also, vast amounts of information are in some way relayed to the body without our having to process it consciously. This is a good thing because it saves us from having to ponder a situation at great length before we drop a hot potato or get out of the way of an oncoming truck. The unconscious also sorts out—mostly during sleep, recent research indicates—what information is to be stored in long-term memory. And it takes part in higher order cognition, as anybody knows who has ever been suddenly awakened and discovers that his brain has been busily—and rationally—at work on some problem.

This process has implications for the subject that we'll take up in the next chapter—the construction of reality—because that is clearly not just something we do in the conscious brain. "We do not," Norretranders writes, "experience the world as raw data." We experience information that has already been selected, shaped, and interpreted. "What we experience has acquired meaning before we become conscious of it."[17]

CHAPTER 8

Being Constructive

About two hundred years ago, the idea that truth was made rather than found began to take hold on the imagination of Europe.
— RICHARD RORTY[1]

The phenomenon of knowing cannot be taken as though there were "facts" or objects out there that we grasp and store in our head. The experience of anything out there is validated in a special way by the human structure, which makes possible "the thing" that arises in the description. This circularity, this connection between action and experience, this inseparability between a particular way of being and how the world appears to us, tells us that *every act of knowing brings forth a world.*
— HUMBERTO MATURANA, FRANCISCO VARELA[2]

Transforming our epistemologies, liberating ourselves from that in which we were embedded, making what was subject into object so that we can "have it" rather than "be had" by it—this is the most powerful way I know to conceptualize the growth of the mind.
— ROBERT KEGAN[3]

There is a way of looking at the world—and of looking at how we look at the world—that stresses the active, creative aspects of perception and cognition. It's called constructivism. If you're not already acquainted with that term, you will probably have caught the flavor of it from some of the material in the foregoing chapter and the quotations at the beginning of this one.

It is arguably the most important—and probably the most controversial—new idea that has emerged in the realm of human relations over the past one hundred years. It has a longer history than that, but it was really only in the latter half of the twentieth century that constructivist ideas became a major force in psychotherapy and the social sciences, a cause of deep schisms in organized religion, and then, usually associated with postmodernism, a major theme of popular culture. It is a bit hard to wrap your mind around constructivist ways of thinking, partly because we have all been indoctrinated into a deliberate ignorance about that aspect of what our minds do, and partly because there are a lot of ways to construct—and misrepresent—constructivism itself: Some enthusiasts trivialize it into the silly belief that everybody can make and remake the universe at will. True believers of various persuasions demonize it into an insidious conspiracy against God and country. Many academics do their best to discuss it in ponderous and abstract language designed to make it minimally inaccessible to ordinary people.

Yet it can be grasped; people all over the world are doing so, more often than not without any sense of venturing into the higher realms of psychology or philosophy. They may do it in simple ways, merely by coming to accept that different people see things differently and that nobody—no faith, no ideology, no cult, no culture—has an absolute hold on the truth. There are a lot more de facto constructivists in the world today than there are people who have ever heard of the word or the concept.

However the change may come about, every step you take toward understanding how your mind takes an active part in the construction of reality is a step along the path of personal growth. And every step that every person takes advances the evolution of humanity as a whole beyond the grip of the unyielding doctrines that have caused untold suffering in the world. For individuals and societies, constructivism is liberation.

Human Truth

Constructive thought (for the rest of this chapter I'll drop the "ism") has been sneaking up on the Western world since the eighteenth century. It was foreshadowed in Immanuel Kant's distinction between noumena and phenomena, and—going back even further—by the Italian thinker Giambattista Vico's declaration that different peoples at different times and places had fundamentally different values and beliefs and worldviews, and furthermore, that it wasn't possible to stand completely outside of culture and pronounce one society's art or poetry to be better than another's. "As God's truth is what God comes to know as he creates and assembles it," Vico declared, "so human truth is what man comes to know as he builds it, shaping it by his actions."[4]

Constructives don't say that anything called a truth or a fact is *wrong* because it was constructed. But they do insist that any truth is the product of a specific human mind at a particular time and place. As Maturana and Varela put it, "Everything said is said by someone."[5] These two Chilean scientists, whose ideas I'll discuss further later in this chapter, believed that this seemingly obvious statement, grounding all human truth in human experience, has profound implications that are not always immediately grasped.

Constructive thinking comes in many varieties and has entered the world along several paths: history, anthropology, sociology, computer science, neurophysiology, and philosophy, to name some of the intellectual disciplines in which it has been developed. It is an important part of the "cognitive revolution," in which researchers and theorists from various disciplines challenged the behaviorist dogma that thought could not be an object of scientific investigation. Maturana and Varela were both trained in medicine and biology, and their main contribution to constructive thought is subtitled *The Biological Roots of Human Understanding*.

It may seem paradoxical that such ideas are so closely linked to scientific research, since they are likely to seem at first glance to be precisely the opposite of science: Isn't science about hard facts, objective truth untainted by human subjectivity? A lot of people still believe it is but, as we have already noted, some fields of science such as atomic physics and cosmology have been moving steadily away from the mechanistic worldview that once characterized them. And at the same time other scientists are making increasingly sophisticated and precise observations of the neurophysiology of thought. Electroencephalograms, positron emission (PET) scans, magnetic resonance imaging (MRI) scans and other wonders from the electronic toolbox are widely applied now in basic brain research as well as medical diagnosis.

With better understanding of that mysterious organ—or, as some prefer, group of interacting organs—it became increasingly clear that the brain isn't simply some kind of a mental camera automatically registering knowledge about its environment. Rather, it is—or they are—an amazingly active and creative set of systems for registering, processing, and interpreting information. Only a relatively small portion of the physical brain is devoted to receiving sense perceptions. Most of your gray cells at any given time are busy with internal communications, with signals racing about the neurons as the various parts do what the human brain does unlike no other organ of no other living creature: making sense, making meaning, trying to figure out and describe to itself what the hell is going on out there—an increasingly large "out there," a vast and expanding universe.

Although many people still want to argue about whether our thoughts accurately reflect the reality of the nonhuman environment, cognitive scientists generally see that debate as a waste of time, missing the whole point of what brains do. As one account puts it: "How can we ever know that the world inside the mind is a faithful representation of the one outside? It's irrelevant because it now seems clear that what is inside cannot be identical with what is outside; it is a selection and transformation into neural impulses, a *processed* version, of what is outside."[6] This is merely putting into cognitive-science terms the general semanticists' favorite dictum that the map is not the territory.

Our mental maps are living things—processed versions of the world that are continually being *re*processed. The cognitive systems are continually taking in new information, testing and revising assumptions, sometimes confirming pieces of their version of reality, sometimes discarding and replacing them. Most of the time we pay little conscious attention to this: The telephone rings, I reach out for it, my hand finds it where my eyes (and my memory) said it would be, an expectation is confirmed, and I go about my business. Another time I may reach for it in the dark, find it not there, and have to go through some more complex rethinking in order to form a more accurate idea of where it is located—or where *I'm* located, since I may have half-awakened from sleep and reached out from a bed in some hotel in another country. In such operations we continually seek feedback, testing the processed version against information from the environment.

And then there are times as we grow up when we do a massive restructuring of fundamental values and beliefs, fundamentally alter our concepts of who and what we are, what is real, and how the world works. Those transitions are the subject of an important area of cognitive science, development research, that we'll explore later in this chapter.

Anticonstructivisms

You can be constructive in many different ways: You can be a giddy solipsist persuaded that you create your own world. You can be a left-leaning follower of Michel Foucault and other theorists who see social constructions of reality as conspiracies of power. You can be an anthropologist in some university happily driving your colleagues in the science departments up the wall by telling them that their findings have no more claim to truth than the beliefs of primitive tribes. Or you can be a psychotherapist trying to help a client understand how great a role construction plays in her everyday experience of life.

And you can take up arms against such ideas in several different ways: You can be an old-fashioned "representationist" scientist, insisting that what you do is find objective truth about nature. You can be a religious fundamentalist believing that God's own truth is contained in the doctrines of your faith and infallibly written down in its scriptures. You can be a hard-line political ideologue dedicated to the certainty that some theorist or another (Marx is the favorite but there are other oracles, right and left) has discovered the laws of history. You can be a social conservative so tightly boxed into the traditions of your tribe, culture, or nation that you take them to be permanent truths. You can be an I-have-found-it spiritual seeker who is convinced that your guru, *satori,* or drug trip has revealed the final reality of the cosmos.

The most frequently (and angrily) voiced objection to constructive thought is that it holds no belief to be more correct than another, no value to be higher than another. Many scientists have these objections, although the philosophy of science—most famously but not exclusively in Thomas Kuhn's work on the structure of scientific revolutions—shows science as an open-ended quest for truth, continually constructing and reconstructing ideas about nature. You can't help noticing, if you pay any attention to progress in science, that its truths frequently get revised and discarded. Or you may note the more or less peaceful coexistence of different realities such as Newtonian physics, Einsteinian relativity, and quantum weirdness.

Constructives say there are many practical ways to test any claim to the truth—such as how well it works, what are the consequences of believing it, or how it fits with other things you believe to be true—and that nobody really thinks all beliefs are equal. The mind doesn't work that way; we are valuing animals, and evaluation is never absent from cognition, however devoutly fair-minded we may try to be.

Constructivism East and West

Eastern ideas about ego and enlightenment are inherently constructive. The Eastern traditions have a longer history than what Westerners call constructivism, and they don't use that terminology, but what they talk about is the discovery that matters people commonly take to be objective facts—such as the nature of the self—can be better understood as socially constructed realities. "Socially constructed reality" is of course a Western term. Buddhists talk about illusion.

Newcomers to Buddhism are sometimes confused and annoyed when they encounter the idea that the world the enlightened person sees is exactly the same as the world the *un*enlightened person sees. Yet this proposition, however paradoxical it might sound, has been stated again and again. "Dharma is the same as non-dharma," wrote

Saraha a thousand years ago. More recently D. T. Suzuki, author of the essays that helped familiarize modern Westerners with Zen Buddhism, said simply: "Zen is your everyday mind." Another Zen master declares:

If you understand, things are such as they are;
If you do not understand, things are such as they are[7]

It's hardly surprising that commonsense folks, even those open-minded enough to undertake some exploration of Buddhism, are put off by such statements. Nor is it surprising that people hankering for fancier flights of consciousness prefer Carlos Castaneda, with his morphing shamans and magical animals, to D. T. Suzuki contemplating the wonders of a flower.

But anybody who finds it difficult to believe that the same world can be understood differently by different people or by the same person at different times—and that the differences can be powerful and important—has not been paying much attention to the main currents of constructive thought over the past century. From gestalt psychology, general semantics, and the sociology of knowledge in the early 1930s through Jean Piaget's research on child development to contemporary moral development theory, postmodern philosophy, and cognitive science (from which the term "constructivism" emerged), it has become increasingly understood that human thought involves not just the passive perception of reality but the active construction of it.

Any psychotherapist can tell you that patients often have experiences of suddenly *getting it,* recognizing that they have been seeing themselves and their problems in a certain way and that there are entirely different ways. Indeed, those experiences are a large part of what psychotherapy is about—what it does when it's successful and what it doesn't do when it fails and the patient remains stuck in his box. Some of the literature calls them "aha" experiences, and compares them to the sudden awakenings, the *satori* or *kensho* of Zen, in which the student finally *sees* for herself what the master has been talking about. In such moments, she understands that the way she has been thinking about her life and her problems is not the only way at all, but rather a constructed reality. That can be a powerfully liberating discovery. And once that discovery is made by a patient in therapy, new possibilities for change emerge.

Early in the twentieth century, the gestalt psychologists studied how people organize the chaotic data of sensory experiences into *gestalten* or wholes. In the process they gave us some visual images that have become part of our common store of knowledge. We are all familiar with images such as the line drawing of two identical profiles facing one another, which can be seen also as the outline of a vase or goblet. Once you have discovered that there are two ways of looking at the drawing, you can then move back and forth between the two at will. Whether you fully appreciate the implications of such mental phenomena—and recognize that *everything you see* can be seen differently, even though it remains the same object—is another matter entirely.

The news that you actively construct reality and don't just take objective and neutral motion pictures of the world, is, like many other matters in this book, something you can regard either as a promotion or a demotion for the human species. It implies that all dogmas, ideologies, and belief systems are temporal social constructions rather than eternal truths, and some people get pretty huffy about that. But it also guides us into a new and liberating way of thinking about our own thinking. Constructive thought is not only a theory to be accepted or rejected; it is also a skill to be learned, and as you learn it you break out into far wider spaces of life than those occupied by people who believe there is only one correct description for any situation. The great sociologist Ernest Becker, in a passage that I included in my anthology *The Truth About The Truth,* exuberantly declared its appearance to be a monumental evolutionary achievement:

> The most astonishing thing of all, about man's fictions, is not that they have from prehistoric times hung like a flimsy canopy over his social world, but that he should have come to discover them at all. It is one of the most remarkable achievements of

thought, of self-scrutiny, that the most anxiety-prone animal of all should have come to see through himself and discover the fictional nature of his action world. Future historians will probably record it as one of the great, liberating breakthroughs of all time, and it happened in ours.[8]

I share Becker's estimate of the importance of the shift to constructive modes of understanding, but I think he paints a brighter picture than I would of how rapidly it is happening. I suspect it may take many years yet before we can say that the discovery has truly and finally happened. When that comes to pass we will be far more grown-up animals, and the world will be a very different place.

In the meanwhile, constructivist thought is especially helpful to understanding—in a contemporary way—what the esoteric traditions such as Buddhism have been trying for so long to tell us. Ego is not just illusion but a socially constructed reality, a way you learn to organize your thinking, your deepest sense of self. Enlightenment is a growth process—partaking of both conscious and unconscious changes—in which you learn to see ego-centered thought, perceive its socially constructed nature, and begin to organize your thinking in a different way.

But the growth process called enlightenment isn't simply a matter of giving up one way of being in favor of another. The liberated person can still think and function in an ego-centered way, just as you can switch back and forth between different ways of perceiving one of the famous gestalt drawings. In Zen they call this "big mind" and "little mind."

I have talked with a number of people who have had enlightenment experiences, and this comes across quite clearly in their comments. For example, there is Steve, a middle-aged physician who (with no particular exposure to any Asian discipline) suddenly Got It one day while walking in the woods with his dog. Steve is a quiet and unpretentious man whose case I will describe further in chapter 13. He says that, although the experience left him somewhat disoriented at first, he has gradually become quite comfortable with the feeling that life is a lot of things happening—but without an ever-present sense that they are happening to a Steve who is separate from everything around him. He says, "I'm as much me as I have ever been—more human, not afraid to feel. And I can construct myself as separate whenever it's appropriate to do so. If suddenly I have to do something like talk to a group, bang! there I am."

Steve has discovered not only that there are different modes of experiencing but also that they are not mutually exclusive, that enlightenment and nonenlightenment can be understood—and, much more important, lived—as a complementarity rather than a set of warring antagonists. Of course it's true that ego-based patterns of cognition are never quite the same after their existence has been discovered by the mind; they may change in many ways, and they may reassert themselves under certain conditions. But once you have recognized—even glimpsed—that the way you had been experiencing the world and had accepted as reality itself was rather a social construction of reality, nothing is ever quite the same. That recognition itself, the experience of looking at the world in a new way, is the essence of liberation.

Reconstructing Self and World

Constructive research on human development—on how we form new structures of understanding about ourselves and the nature of reality as we grow—has been going on since the first half of the twentieth century; the Swiss psychologist Jean Piaget (1896–1980) was the pioneer in the field.

Piaget got his academic training in biology and philosophy, and his main interest throughout his long career was epistemology—popularly defined as inquiry into *how* we know *what* we know. He thought epistemology should be a science, not a branch of philosophy, and should investigate how organisms develop new ways of knowing as they mature. He founded an "International Center of Genetic Epistemology" at Geneva, and he and his associates produced a formidable body of work showing how human beings grow and change by reconstructing their worlds—forming fundamentally new concepts of who and what they are. This, Piaget believed, is a process that can only be understood as happening in the context of a social environment. A person takes in information from her social context and periodically forms new concepts of how society works and how to go about living in it. As a student of Piaget's summarizes it, the theory can be called "interactionist" as well as "constructivist." Its core proposition is that: "The organism inherits a genetic program that gradually (through a process called 'maturation') provides the biological equipment necessary for constructing a stable internal structure out of its experiences with its environment. Paradoxically, that stable structure—that 'intelligence'—then helps the organism adapt to changes in that environment."[9]

Piaget's work focused on early childhood, and the essential feature of his thinking about infant development—the one that brought him the greatest admiration and the strongest criticism—was his assertion that there are certain stages a child *must* pass through as it learns its way into the world. He insisted that all children—regardless of the differences in intelligence and physical characteristics, regardless of what might happen to them, regardless of their cultural surroundings—must go through those stages in one way or another or fail to become psychologically an adult. And in one of his most influential works, Piaget asserted that the child's progress in forming concepts about the world is also progress in forming moral principles.[10]

Recent work influenced by Piaget has studied the psychosocial development of adults, the stages of moral understanding and behavior that emerge as people grow and change and think about their interactions with others. We are, after all, moral animals—even a sociopath has a certain sense of right and wrong—and we become significantly different moral animals as we mature. The moral-development theorists have in various ways elaborated on the basic Piagetian model. They all look at human beings as growing and changing through a process of reconstructing their epistemologies, and they all identify certain stages in this process—marked by the appearance of new central organizing concepts that hadn't formerly been part of the person's worldview.

And they all have something to say about what Freud called the superego, the famously oppressive stand-in for society that specializes in telling the naughty id that it can't have what it wants. They accept the basic idea that society's values and beliefs become parts of the structure of our personalities, but they are inclined to shy away from the garrison metaphor. Instead, they try to analyze and describe an ongoing process. They say you internalize different moral principles at different stages of growth, build them into your structure of understanding of how the world works, and then go on revising that structure—occasionally discarding some pieces that no longer seem as useful as they once did.

Lawrence Kohlberg, the godfather of adult moral-development theory, developed a system that showed the person growing as a moral actor by constructing and reconstructing principles of "reciprocity" between the self's actions toward others and those of others toward the self. He identified six stages of growth:

Stage 1: Obedience and punishment orientation. Egocentric deference to superior power or prestige. . . .
Stage 2: Naively egoistic orientation. Right action is that instrumentally satisfying the self's needs and occasionally others'. . . .
Stage 3: Good-boy orientation. Orientation to approval and to pleasing and helping others. Conformity to stereotypical images of majority or natural role behavior. . . .
Stage 4: Authority and social-order maintaining orientation. Orientation to "doing duty" and to showing respect for authority and maintaining the given social order for its own sake. . . .
Stage 5: Contractual legalistic orientation. Recognition of an arbitrary element or starting point in rules or expectations for the sake of agreement. Duty defined in terms of contract, general avoidance of violation of the will or rights of others. . . .
Stage 6: Conscience or principle orientation. Orientation not

only to actually ordained social rules but to principles of choice involving appeal to logical universality and consistency. . . .[11]

Kohlberg built this concept of ascending levels of moral development on the basis of research in which subjects talked about how they would behave in certain situations—and why. The best-known study used a story about a man whose wife needs a certain drug that will save her life, but the only supplier who has the drug demands an exorbitant price for it, far beyond what the man is able to pay. Question: If you were that man, would you steal the drug in such a case? People generally answered that they would, but that wasn't really what Kohlberg was after: He asked them how they would justify such an act and observed the process of moral reasoning at work. Some people (those he classified as operating at Stage 3) were worried about avoiding social disapproval for stealing the drug and wanted to be judged by their worthy intentions, which were to carry out a husband's proper function as his wife's protector. Stage 6 respondents, those of a more Gandhian turn of mind, denounced the drug supplier for placing the profit motive above human well-being, and said they would not only steal the drug but do so publicly in hopes that the act would be of service to others who might at some time be in a similar position.

Something like the Freudian superego was clearly on duty in Kohlberg's research subjects—particularly those at Stages 3 and 4— but the mind as Kohlberg described it is not quite the same as Freud's solid fortress. Instead, Kohlberg showed how people continually reconstruct their moral principles. The internal moral system is a work in progress. And Kohlberg, like most moral-development theorists, believed that most people never made it to the higher stages.

Kohlberg's work was enormously influential, and also widely criticized—particularly by some feminist psychologists who thought he had really only theorized about how *men* develop morally and had not considered the possibility that women might grow and shape their moral universes in quite different ways. Carol Gilligan opened a new line of moral-development theorizing with her book *In a Different*

Voice, which argued that women understood moral obligations in terms of relatedness to others.[12]

Some of the best work on moral development in women has been done by a team of researchers at the Stone Center at Wellesley College in Massachusetts. Going back to Piaget, they base their description of moral development on what they call "epistemological categories"—at each stage, the woman develops a new understanding of how reality is constructed and also learns how to play a more active role in the process. The researchers describe the steps along the path as follows:

- *Silence,* a position in which women experience themselves as mindless and voiceless and subject to the whim of external authority
- *Received knowledge,* a perspective from which women conceive of themselves as capable of receiving, even reproducing, knowledge from the all-knowing external authorities but not capable of creating knowledge on their own
- *Subjective knowledge,* a perspective from which truth and knowledge are conceived of as personal, private, and subjectively known or intuited
- *Procedural knowledge,* a position in which women are invested in learning and applying objective procedures for obtaining and communicating knowledge
- *Constructed knowledge,* a position in which women view all knowledge as contextual, experience themselves as creators of knowledge, and value both subjective and objective strategies for knowing[13]

I know "epistemology" isn't exactly a sexy word, and its very appearance on a page may be enough to send some readers into a light slumber. But, by whatever name, it is absolutely central to human life and human progress. It is the mechanism that is at work as you try to figure out what is true and real, who you are, how you should behave toward others, and how you deal with authority systems such as religions and laws. With a different epistemology—with different beliefs about belief—there is no more fundamentalism, no more racism, no more chauvinism, no cause for religious wars, and very little cause for any other kind of war.

In the view of Robert Kegan, another of the bigtime moral-development researchers, the key process in epistemological change is what he calls "objectification." That means as you grow, you periodically turn around and look at parts of your worldview—values, beliefs, ideas, ways of doing things—that you had experienced uncritically as *subject,* part of your self and the way things simply are, and begin to experience them in a new way, as *objects*—things whose origin you might wonder about and whose ultimate truth you might question. You might, as many people do, move from seeing your religion as the one true representation of how the universe works to seeing it as one of many such representations. And as a result of this objectification you might change churches, or convert to another religion, or believe in some parts of the religion but not others, or become a nonbeliever, or simply—without giving the matter a great deal of thought—keep going to the same church for personal reasons other than unquestioned belief. In any case, you are a quite different kind of person from the individual in a premodern, traditional society who did not have to make such decisions at all because he or she never began to *see* the society's beliefs as objects that could be thought about and questioned.

Knowing and Being

Homo sapiens grows by knowing—not only by knowing how to do things, such as build a car or fly to the moon, but also by knowing about knowing. People have always hungered for knowledge and also feared it, suspecting correctly that knowledge always brings change. The fear of knowledge is powerfully expressed in myths such as the story of Prometheus, punished for bringing humankind the gift of fire, and in the biblical account of Adam and Eve, punished for tasting the fruit of knowledge.

Knowing about knowing is the most threatening kind of knowledge because as you acquire it you inevitably become a different sort of person and find yourself in a different world, outside the garden of innocence. So Maturana and Varela titled their book *The Tree of Knowledge* as a deliberate allusion to Genesis, and said toward the end of it:

> We have invited the reader to eat of the fruit of that tree by offering a scientific study of cognition as a biological phenomenon. If we have followed its line of reasoning and imbibed its consequences, we realize that they are inescapable. The *knowledge of knowledge compels*. It compels us to adopt an attitude of permanent vigilance against the temptation of certainty. It compels us to recognize that certainty is not a proof of truth. It compels us to realize that the world everyone sees is not *the* world but *a* world which we bring forth with others. It compels us to see that the world will be different only if we live differently. It compels us because, when we know that we know, we cannot deny (to ourselves or to others) that we know.[14]

The fear of knowing appears to be a natural part of our makeup, always hand in hand with our hunger for knowledge. And to overcome it—and dare to know—may call for a certain leap of faith, a willingness to believe that life can be pretty good outside that garden, in the open space of liberation.

There's No Place Like Home

I doubt very much that anyone simply takes a transfer one day from a conventional way of seeing the world into a constructive one; rather, it is for most of us a slower unfolding, a gradual yet endlessly surprising series of little revolutions in which we come to new understanding of how we think—and, at the same time, a new understanding of what we are.

So it goes for me, anyway; I keep happening on new pieces of it, discovering new facets of something I thought I already understood. A few years ago, I made one of those discoveries in connection with the sense of place.

Now, place, as we all know, is one of the most profound and powerful dimensions of human experience. We form abiding emotional attachments to certain places, write poems and sing songs about them, fight wars over them, sometimes take our names from them—names that say, in essence, this place is who I am. And no place is more important than the one we knew in early childhood, the one in which we first discovered ourselves and the world—the place we loved and remember all our lives.

That place, for me, is a remote corner of northeastern Nevada, a region most people have never seen. It's cattle-ranching and hay-farming country, suitable for few other human purposes except perhaps trout fishing and deer hunting. It's a land of sagebrush hills above green river meadows, chilly streams that come down out of the mountains along the Idaho border, hot summers, and long, hard winters when the ranch families are snowed in until spring. I spent my first years in that place, happily prowling around the barns and corrals, pestering the cowboys, riding my old horse in the fields below the house, meditating on the exploits of Buck Rogers and the Lone Ranger, Superman and King of the Royal Mounties. That was my universe and then, rather abruptly, we left it when I was seven or eight, and I didn't see it again for over thirty years.

Then, one summer, my brother and I drove up that way, traveling over a few hundred miles of freeway and forty of dirt roads to visit the place.

It had changed, of course. Later owners had moved the ranch headquarters and cleared away all the barns, bunkhouses, outhouses, and sheds. Out of some mysterious urge at historical preservation, I guess, they had left only the main house, the one I had lived in, the original core built out of railroad ties as a homesteader's cabin. That one remaining building was smaller than I had remembered it, and it was slowly slipping into brown, weatherbeaten decay like some lonely old house you might see in a melancholy painting. Even the concrete sidewalk in front of the house had disappeared.

I've been back a couple of times since then and found it a little more eroded each time. The last time I went there I realized that it had not only changed, it had *moved*.

It had moved as the world moved, gone spinning around the sun thirty-odd times, while the sun moved around the galaxy, and the galaxy migrated around the universe. Every atom and molecule in that space had been changing, traveling, maintaining in all those journeys some semblance of the place my memory contained. A semblance, but not the same place. Because there is no place, only something like place—an aggregation of things that I made to seem the same place, as if it had stood still while all the rest of the cosmos went about its mobile business. Its identity as the same place was something I constructed.

A few hundred years ago, educated people could believe that there were actually places on the earth that did not move, that had fixed locations in the cosmos while the planets and stars moved around them. But we have inherited another universe from the twentieth century, that age of cosmological revolutions in which Einstein and the quantum physicists and the astronomers led us into a swirling cosmos of relativity and endless change. We retain our foothold in the old cosmos only by constructing fixed places, solid objects—and, for that matter, continuing selves.

Once in a while, because construction is an active process, we catch ourselves in the act of world-making. These can be disorienting experiences in which, for a time, the familiar phenomenal world seems to disappear. Such experiences are often reported in reports of psychedelic explorations, but they also happen in many other circumstances such as religious experiences, psychotherapy, or moments of profound discovery. The experience is well understood in Zen and summarized in one of its most famous koans:

> First there is a mountain, then there is no mountain,
> then there is.

So when you look up and contemplate This, consider this: Any object you see is a pattern of movement and change; it is also a mysterious play of nonhuman elements, forever beyond your knowing; and it is what you make of it. It is real, and it is constructed. Dare to know that.

CHAPTER 9

All the Things You Are

A single animal or plant is a vast community of communities
packed in interacting layers, like a rain forest.

— RICHARD DAWKINS[1]

I am large, I contain multitudes.　　— WALT WHITMAN[2]

And if place, with a bit of attention and thought, is seen to be
something other than what we might commonly assume it to be,
so is our self, our physical body, something other than the single and
neatly bounded entity we might assume it to be. As a step toward this
understanding, consider breath.

One of the most widely advocated meditation practices is simply to
pay attention to your breathing. It's restful, tends to quiet down
rowdy thoughts and—if you let it—teaches you something about the
porous boundary between self and other, organism and environment.
The atmosphere flows in and out of you and circulates continually
within you. You do not live for more than a few minutes without res-
piration, and you would not live for more than an instant without the
constant atmospheric pressure that holds your bodily structure
together. Without it you'd deconstruct, blow apart into what would
be—if the science-fiction writers are correct in their descriptions of
people ejected from space ships—a most unsightly and disorganized
mess of dying flesh.

There's another kind of practice along the same lines that I used to
invite people to try at environmental gatherings as a sort of thought
exercise. I would ask them to imagine themselves taking a drink of
water, and then to follow that water backward and think of where it

came from—out of the faucet, out of the public water system, out of a reservoir, and before that, out of some distant lake or river. Then I would ask them to imagine taking a pee, and similarly follow the course of the water through the pipes and sewers into the water purification systems and out to the rivers and oceans. And then, finally, to envision the whole cycle as the water is taken up into the atmosphere and brought back onto the land to feed the distant lakes and rivers again. It is the familiar water cycle we saw in our schoolbooks, but it includes our own bodies and the various mechanical arrangements of supply and sewage disposal that are also part of the larger system that maintains our organic lives. We usually have to guess at the details of the supply and disposal systems, of course, because most of us have only the dimmest notion of what they are or how they actually work.

So you not only are what you eat, as the old saying goes; you are also what you breathe and what you drink. And you are more than that.

The Buddhist claim that each of us is an impermanent aggregation of things and events holds up extremely well in the light of contemporary science—but it turns out there is a lot more to each one of us than the ancient philosophers suspected, and far more than any of us can see or contain in consciousness. So when we go to construct ourselves, we have a lot to work with.

All the Things That Are You

You are, for example, an astronomical number of cells—somewhere around ten trillion, with several million new ones created in your body each second while a comparable number die. Within the cells are various entities including the mitochondria, amazing little systems with a complex interior structure of membranes by which they perform a series of chemical operations that process energy from food molecules, store it, and release it when needed. Their service is microscopic, complicated, and absolutely necessary to our biological existence. If all the body's mitochondria went on strike at the same time, you would die immediately. And the most amazing thing about the mitochondria is that they were once separate microorganisms. At some point in the distant evolutionary past—probably some two billion years ago—their ancestors invaded single-celled organisms (our ancestors), most likely made them seriously ill, but then, like the man who came to dinner, settled in and became a part of their hosts. Such host-pathogen arrangements are not unusual in nature, but this particular one apparently had enormous consequences: Because the invaded cells were able to utilize their food so much more effectively and produce so much more energy, they could strike out along new pathways. A new stage of evolutionary exploration and innovation began, leading to the appearance of an enormous range of multicellular organisms—leading eventually to the clever bipeds who figured out they were part mitochondria.

The recognition by science of how the mitochondria got to be part of us and how they do their work is itself a remarkable piece of progress, with profound implications for our understanding of the separateness—or nonseparateness—of organism and environment, self and other. It was Lynn Margulis, a biologist at the University of Massachusetts at Amherst (also known for her work on the Gaia hypothesis), who first proposed that the remote ancestors of the mitochondria were free-living bacteria that at some point became stowaways within larger cells, setting in motion a symbiotic development that led to the appearance of higher forms of life. This idea went through the classic cycle of being regarded at first as rather outrageous and then gradually folded into the general understanding. As that happened, and as scientists contemplated the astonishing numbers of mitochondria, they also contemplated how awesomely populated we are. As Richard Dawkins notes:

> Each one of us is a community of a hundred million million mutually dependent eukaryotic cells. Each one of those cells is a community of thousands of specially-tamed bacteria, entirely enclosed within the cell, where they multiply as bacteria will. It has been calculated that if all the mitochondria in a single human body were laid end to end, they would girdle the Earth not once but two thousand times.[3]

Also within each cell are the chromosomes, containing the genes, which in turn are made up of yet smaller units, the nucleotides, about one thousand per gene. (And it is widely known now—a statistic quoted with a frequency that probably keeps Bishop Wilberforce spinning in his grave—that we share some 98 percent of our genome with the chimpanzees. We also have some genes quite similar to those of mushrooms—yet another blow to the Bishop. The reason is simple: evolution is kind of lazy, and when it figures out a good way to make a protein it does it over and over again.)

And in addition to the mitochondria, which are the distant descendants of free-living bacteria, you also contain an astronomical number of bacteria that are *still* free-living, peacefully (and sometimes not so peacefully) going about their specialized microscopic businesses in various parts of your body, and reproducing and dying by the millions.

Germs Good, Bad, and Indifferent

Life seems to be full of things that we have to learn and then either unlearn or relearn in a whole new context. The germ business is one, certainly for me.

In my early childhood I was frequently warned about avoiding contact with things that "had lots of germs on them" or were "full of germs." The reason for this, of course, was that germs were known to invade the body and cause disease. The warnings obviously made sense, since a number of diseases came our way. My older siblings had dealt with not only the usual colds and chicken pox and mumps but also with more serious ones like diphtheria and whooping cough. No wonder my mother was on guard against microbes, and no wonder I remain even now dependably programmed against eating food that has been dropped on the floor.

But then I went to school, where I was taught that there were also "good germs" that lived peacefully in the lining of my stomach and helped in the digestion of food. Most of us know about the good germs, but we are less likely to be clear about the endless varieties of these microorganisms in our bodies, or even their sheer mass—about 10 percent of our body weight. Each of us is not so much a separate organism as a walking ecosystem, teeming with life, inhabited the moment we enter the world. Science writer Jennifer Ackerman gives a wonderful description of her daughter's birth and colonization:

> While in the womb, her body was a pristine wilderness, essentially germ-free. But as soon as she began her short dark passage, she was no longer alone. Riding on the walls of my birth canal, on the sheets beneath my bare legs, on my hospital gown, in the air, nesting on the tips of my nipples, tucked in the creases of my husband's hands and lips, was an ark of tiny organisms, which jumped, catlike, into the cozy habitat of her body . . .
>
> Over the next few days, successive invasions of microbes quickly colonized my daughter, taking up residence in the crevices of her pudgy skin, in the toothless cavern of her mouth, in the tiny tunnels of her gut and vagina . . . Some of these creatures soon disappeared, but many pioneers took hold and multiplied until, a week later, they formed a community that would grow to be as rich and complex as any found in outdoor nature: four hundred species in the gut, six hundred in the mouth—all ensconced in special niches, inside the cheeks, on the top of the palate, on the back of the tongue, throughout the gut from esophagus to anus.[4]

And all of those various entities are of course made up of molecules, which are made up of atoms, and so on, down and down to the unimaginable reaches of submicroscopic inner space, where, perhaps, we and everything else are ultimately composed of dynamic strings, the essence of star-stuff.

In the language of complexity theory we (and all kinds of organizations, communities, and ecosystems) are described as "complex adaptive systems" made up of countless subunits, many of which are also complex adaptive systems. All these systems have certain key properties:

First, each is a network of many agents doing their own things but doing them in an environment produced by interaction with the other agents. They constantly seek information from this environment and adjust their behaviors accordingly. The agents may be the nerve cells in your brain, the competing (and cooperating) businesses in an economy, or the species in an ecosystem. In any case, they are not all acting in response to orders from a central command post, and the system as a whole is always changing.

Second, each has multiple layers of organization. The agents at one level become the building blocks for the agents at a higher level. A group of cells, for example, form a tissue, and then a group of tissues form an organ, and a group of organs forms an organism such as an individual human being, who may in turn become a part of some larger aggregation. And the system is continually reorganizing itself.

Third, all complex systems anticipate the future in various ways. Organizations construct forecasts and scenarios. Animals learn to do things that they anticipate will bring desirable results and not to do things that they anticipate will bring undesirable ones. A bird with any sense will not eat an insect that it knows has a yucky taste.

And finally, complex adaptive systems have many niches, and these may change as the larger system of which they are a part evolves and changes. New opportunities arise, new competitors emerge, old niches become unsatisfactory. And that, according to Mitchell Waldrop in his work on complexity theory, "means that it's essentially meaningless to talk about a complex adaptive system being in equilibrium: the system can never get there. It is always unfolding, always in transition. In fact, if the system ever does reach equilibrium, it isn't just stable. It's dead."[5]

As complex adaptive systems, then, we are composed of vast numbers of agents, structured in multiple layers, continually being reorganized, continually learning and changing, eternally in flux. And we are not simply decentralized, but decentralized millions of times over: the brain doesn't tell all the organs and cells what to do, and the organs and cells similarly lack any internal commander in chief to tell *their* subsystems what to do. To paraphrase the old saying, it's complex adaptive systems all the way down.

Of Genes and Egos

Of all the things you are, of all the strange, small entities that collectively constitute your biological being, none hold more fascination than the genes. At least according to the way they are popularly described, the genes seem to be nothing less than the instruction book that makes you what you are. That isn't quite the full story, of course, because we all know there are other factors that shape your makeup, but it's close. Your genes do form a sort of blueprint, a remarkably subtle and complex information system that encodes the instructions used by the cells to manufacture your bones, blood, muscles, hair, and all the myriad chemicals that regulate the functions of your body and brain.

And although we may blithely talk of genes as though they were individual entities with clearly defined powers—as happens when somebody claims to have discovered "the gene for homosexuality" or some other trait—each gene is actually an intricate chemical structure with thousands of parts, and may do different things under different conditions.

Your genes are echoes of the past, links to the beginnings of life and to its invention over time of increasingly more sophisticated means of reproduction. They are living links to your most remote bacterial ancestors and—much farther along the evolutionary path—to all your human grandparents, of whom you probably know very little, but one thing is certain: they lived long enough to engage in reproduction. There's nothing particularly special about this last fact, as Richard Dawkins observes:

> Not a single one of our ancestors died in infancy. They all reached adulthood, and every single one was capable of finding at least one heterosexual partner and of successfully copulating. Not a single one of our ancestors was felled by an enemy, or by

a virus, or by a misjudged footstep on a cliff edge, before bringing at least one child into the world. Thousands of our ancestors' contemporaries failed in all these respects, but not a single solitary one of our ancestors failed in any of them.[6]

This is a remarkable fact of life—even if quite obvious, when you think about it. But it's no longer quite the rock-solid certainty it was until just a few generations ago. In the era of in vitro fertilization, artificial insemination, surrogacy, and other new reproductive technologies, we can no longer assume that copulation is in all cases the process by which sperm cells connect with egg cells and pass along genetic information from one generation to the next. These new developments are all controversial, upsetting to many people who see in them violations of the laws of God or nature, and they all tend to dislodge certain traditional assumptions about self and identity. Ancestry has always been one of the dependable touchstones by which a person could say, "This is who I am," but that doesn't work so well for a person whose mother went shopping for genes at the local sperm bank.

Cloning—especially the prospect of human cloning—is the biggest troublemaker of all. Even though most reputable scientists insist that they are only interested in cloning human embryos in order to obtain stem cells for research, people seem utterly determined to fix on the possibility that some egotistical madman will one day succeed in hiring some unethical scientist and making a carbon copy of himself. It's an interesting example of how ego-centered thinking can frame a public debate.

The scenario is a fantasy about perpetuating an individual identity, a skin-encapsulated ego that is a true copy in all the details, from skin to ego, of another person.

And we really needn't worry, because it will never be done. No scientist will never be able to create a true copy of any human being—or indeed of any organism at all, but especially of a human being—for the simple reason that a genetic copy is not a true duplicate. A pair of identical twins, technically a clone, are never entirely identical. Any organism is the product of everything that happens to it in the womb and of all the biological events that take place after birth—nutrition, diseases, environmental conditions. And a human being is also the product of its society—family events, schools, peers, history. The fantasy of a copied human being is based on a view of the person as an entity bounded and distinct from its environment, rather than as an ever-changing organism/environment field.

This is not to say that genetic cloning of human beings will never happen. I expect that it will sooner or later, probably as another alternative method of reproduction, although it appears nowhere close to happening at the time of this writing. I don't see any reason why it shouldn't, and my reasons for not finding it a particularly horrendous prospect are roughly the same as my reasons for being convinced that nobody is ever going to be duplicated. We can't even duplicate ourselves from one minute to the next.

The Inner and Outer Self

As biological organisms we indeed contain multitudes, and our life processes are not so much internal activities as constant interaction with the environment. The idea of any organism existing apart from all the things that surround it is as meaningless as the sound of one hand clapping. There is no "you" apart from the ever-changing environment in which you live, no distinction between "in here" and "out there" that is anywhere near as clear as we commonly take it to be.

This is even more true in regard to consciousness. Most of us have little direct knowledge about what our nucleotides and mitochondria are up to at any given moment, yet we are continually drenched in sensory experience of the world around us. Human consciousness is much more composed of the "out there" than the "in here." It is hardly surprising that people who have had enlightenment experiences often report a deeply felt recognition that the inside-outside distinction, so central to commonsense understanding, misrepresents what we really are—all of us, all the time—which is a meaningful and ever-changing interaction between ourselves and our surrounding environment.

Neuroscientists such as Gerald M. Edelman and Giulio Tononi insist that consciousness arises not only out of the functioning of the brain but also out of *interaction*. As they put it, "We emphatically do not identify consciousness in its full range as arising solely in the brain, since we believe that higher brain functions require interactions both with the world and with other persons."[7] Society is always *within us* in a number of ways—not only in the stern voice of the Freudian superego but in many other voices that are heard in our internal thought processes. That was what psychologist Kenneth Gergen is getting at with his theory that contemporary life tends to generate a multiplicity of selves, and (as he summarizes here) what many other psychologists are discovering as well:

The populating of the self not only opens relationships to new ranges of possibility, but one's subjective life also becomes more fully laminated. Each of the selves we acquire from others can contribute to inner dialogues, private discussions we have with ourselves about all manner of persons, events, and issues. These internal voices, these vestiges of relationships both real and imagined, have been given different names: *invisible guests,* by Mary Watkins, *social imagery* by Eric Klinger, and *social ghosts* by Mary Gergen, who found in her research that virtually all the young people she sampled could discuss many such experiences with ease. Most of these ghosts were close friends, often from earlier periods of their lives. Family members were also frequent, with the father's voice predominating, but grandparents, uncles, aunts, and other relatives figured prominently . . . almost a quarter of the ghosts mentioned were individuals with whom the young people had never had any direct interchange. Most were entertainers: rock stars, actors and actresses, singers, and the like. Others were religious figures such as Jesus and Mary, fictitious characters such as James Bond and Sherlock Holmes, and celebrities such as Chris Evert, Joe Montana, Barbara Walters, and the president.[8]

And of course this internal dialogue changes, as suggested by the Tibetan parable of the noisy meeting in our heads. Some of the ghosts may disappear; for example, you may make the welcome discovery that you are no longer being interviewed by Barbara Walters. Conversely, new ghosts may make their entrance if you happen to encounter new individuals who have a strong impact on you, or if some powerful incident in your life creates a need for some new source of inner guidance.

This populating of the self with social ghosts is probably a universal characteristic of human cognition, although there is evidence that people in premodern societies had dramatically different ways of doing it—constructing the voices as real ghosts, or even as gods. But this internalization process becomes much different in contemporary social environments—media-saturated and polycultural—in which we may take in many new and divergent voices. In a traditional society you would hear the voices of people you knew, or of ancestors, or perhaps of tribal gods. In today's world you may seek out or be invaded by any number of divergent voices, some of whom may tell you things quite contrary to what you get from the village elders. And with their help we may construct a number of different subselves that we experience as "me" at different times and places.

Another aspect of the postmodern understanding of self is the concept of "context dependence." It also proceeds from the assumption that human beings are profoundly social creatures, shaping ourselves on the basis of what we learn from our societies through a million messages and interactions that implicitly or explicitly tell us what is true, who we are, and how we ought to behave. In addition, we now learn much more complex and conflicting messages, and as we go through our daily lives we are likely to move in and out of a number of different subcultures, each of which may have different values and beliefs, different folkways, different rituals, different languages. To succeed in these richer social environments, we need to learn new skills of adaptability and to define ourselves in new and more flexible ways: it becomes impossible to define any "me" apart from where I am, how I am, and who I am within the present moment.

The changing context of our social existences does indeed create a demand for new social skills, changing repertoires of behavior, redefinitions of what we mean by community, and creating an opportunity for a new and different understanding of the human individual. The definition of a person as a organism/environment field becomes somewhat more accessible when we can see people, and ourselves, if we pay attention at all, becoming different—sometimes just a little different and sometimes very different indeed—as we move back and forth through different social contexts. Like many aspects of life in the postmodern world, this can be painfully stressful for some, liberating for others, and for many of us a bit of both at the same time.

It takes us a step beyond the existentialists of the twentieth century, who wanted people to wake up and discover being. Now we discover that there is no being that is not also becoming. Becoming, in fact, is all there is.

PART THREE

DARING TO KNOW IN THE

TWENTY-FIRST CENTURY

Kant's *Sapere Aude* is even more applicable to our time than it was
to his. When he wrote his essay about enlightenment, he was concerned mainly with the courage to question religious doctrines. Today
we discover that we need the courage to question even the commonsense realities of society—basic assumptions about how the world
works, who we are, and what is truth.

When you consider what has been going on in the world over the
past few centuries—the emancipatory philosophical movements, the
biological discoveries, the advances in brain research, the growing
understanding of human learning and development over the life cycle,
the astonishing discovery of the evolving cosmos, the rich cross-
fertilization between Western psychology and Eastern schools of realization—you might easily conclude that our society stands on the
verge of universal enlightenment. We have pieces of something the
world has never seen before—a culture of liberation, encouraging us
all to grow up into the universe and let go of our idea of ourselves as
skin-encapsulated egos. But at the same time we have pieces of a cul-

ture of attachment that encourages us to stay stuck in ego and separateness, desperately holding onto our self-images, simultaneously grasping at life, yet afraid to awaken to it.

The attachments come in many forms. In the next two chapters we will look at some of the ways that the culture of attachment manifests itself in everyday life, in literature and pop culture, and in religion and spirituality. In chapters 12 and 13, we'll return again to the subject of liberation and the heartening evidence that, despite the rich feast of ego nourishment afforded us by the conditions of contemporary life, many people—ordinary people, more or less like you and me— manage to find it. And in the final chapter we will review some of the main features of the emerging enlightenment project.

Enlightenment is not absent from contemporary Western culture, either as concept or as experience. There is widening acceptance of the notion that such restructuring of cognition may indeed be within the scope of natural human development, and a rich cross-fertilization of disciplines and practices that are advancing its understanding. It's not a secret, and never was. But we still have a long, long way to go; the subject is still somewhere outside the mainstream of everyday thinking, and there are still many people who neither know how they are trapped nor suspect how they might be free.

CHAPTER 10

The Social Ramble of Ego and Identity

Practically every serious description of the "authentic person" extant implies that such a person, by virtue of what he has become, assumes a new relation to his society and indeed, to society in general. He not only transcends himself in various ways; he also transcends his culture. He resists enculturation. He becomes more detached from his culture and from his society. He becomes a little more a member of his species and a little less a member of his local group. —ABRAHAM MASLOW[1]

Under postmodern conditions, persons exist in a state of continuous construction and reconstruction; it is a world where anything goes that can be negotiated. Every reality of self gives way to reflexive questioning, irony, and ultimately the playful probing of yet another reality. The center fails to hold.
—KENNETH J. GERGEN[2]

The social ramble ain't restful. —SATCHEL PAIGE

We grow up by learning from our social environment; we also grow up, particularly at the higher stages of personal development, by un-learning from our social environment.

I think Alan Watts missed the mark with his charge that there is a social taboo against enlightenment or, as he put it, against knowing who you are. I certainly agree with him that "the prevalent sensation of oneself as a separate ego enclosed in a bag of skin is a hallucination which accords neither with Western science nor with the experimental philosophy-religions of the East." But there isn't any organized (or even unorganized) social conspiracy to prevent you from moving beyond that sensation. If you were to go out into the world tomorrow and proclaim yourself a fully enlightened human being, you might or might not incur some ridicule from those who don't hold with that sort of thing. Some folks will doubt your sanity, and it might not be a good career move in your place of work. On the other hand, you might just as easily find yourself with a thousand followers and a huge bank account. What is much more likely to happen, and happens much more frequently than we suspect, is that if you simply discover a new understanding of yourself and decide to keep your mouth shut about it, nobody is likely to know the difference.

Most social institutions are not dedicated to preventing people from becoming enlightened for the simple reason that most social institutions are not based on any clear concept of what enlightenment is. If it became more widely understood that the process of enlightenment involves recognizing that social truths are constructed and contingent—in other words, not taking your society too seriously—then there might be a lot more organized opposition to it. But we have instead something equally powerful, which is a series of incentives and pressures to support ego identity and ego-centered thinking.

To state the matter in behaviorist terms, there's not much negative reinforcement in the way of a taboo against enlightenment, but there is a lot of positive reinforcement—following each of us from the cradle to the grave—for constructing and maintaining the ego. In fact, most social structures are organizations of ego-identities, and they don't function so well when we cease to believe that we are in some essential and fundamental way how the organization defines us. When, for example, a religious identity ceases to be a part of your deepest sense of who and what you are, you are much more likely to wander from the faith in any of a number of ways that make it hard to hold a congregation together. And although most religious organizations no longer go in for the more violent forms of loyalty enforcement, you are likely to receive other, gentler kinds of social pressure to remain in the fold. The same process applies in relation to national, ethnic, class, and gender identity.

All societies, albeit in vastly different ways, are systems of illusion and attachment, and social customs of all kinds tend to perpetuate ego-based assumptions about the identity and continuity of the self.

Consider, for example, how we deal with death. When the skin-encapsulated ego dies, the customary practice in the Western world is to take whatever is left, beautify the remains, and then encapsulate *them* in high-priced containers meant to preserve them from decay. Or we may instead choose to have the remains cremated and store those in a columbarium. In either case we strive to keep the remains as separate as possible from the processes of nature, preserving our illusions through eternity. This practice is considered to be a proper expression of our respect and affection for the deceased person. How we die becomes a perfect expression of how we live.

Again, there really aren't a lot of overt pressures to make us preserve human remains, apart from some laws concerning how you are permitted to dispose of a body or scatter ashes. There are, of course, the commercial charms of the funeral industry that reinforce (and make a living from) our deep feeling that the remains of a deceased loved one are still in some sense a him or a her. But the real coercion is a much more subtle and powerful form of social pressure consisting of pervasive values and beliefs that we all internalize as we learn to deny that the dead are really dead—dead and gone—and what we the living do with the leftovers makes very little difference to the deceased.

Egos in Love

Then we have the matter of love, which in contemporary popular culture is another form of education in ego cognition. Romantic love is great fun, God bless it—a charming lunacy that helps to reproduce the species—but when taken as seriously as we do, institutionalized and commercialized, it becomes the foundation for a powerful set of social beliefs: in the one person who can make you happy, and in the love that will last forever. We grasp desperately at its blissful moments and blame ourselves and others when they end, which of course they always do because, like everything else, they are impermanent. And societies are not terribly good at teaching us about impermanence.

As a case history of romantic love carried to the level of psychopathology, consider F. Scott Fitzgerald's *The Great Gatsby,* which some critics have proclaimed the Great American Novel: Certainly it qualifies as one of the great American love stories—a fable of one man's heroic devotion to a romantic ideal and its tragic consequences. It's about something that Fitzgerald knew well. He was a romantic himself (his first novel was entitled *The Romantic Egoist*), passionately searching in his youth for love, fame, and success. But he was also a moralist in his own way as well as a great literary artist, and at the same time that he admired the Jay Gatsby character he also showed the sheer folly of Gatsby's struggle to hold onto a youthful passion.

There is a scene in which the narrator, Nick Carraway, tells Gatsby—who is at that point desperately engaged in his mad project to win back Daisy Buchanan, the beauty he had loved five years before, only to find upon his return from the war that she had married another man, that you can't repeat the past.

"Can't repeat the past?" Gatsby responds incredulously. "Why of course you can."

The narrator goes on: "He talked a lot about the past, and I gathered that he wanted to recover something, some idea of himself perhaps, that had gone into loving Daisy. His life had been confused and disordered since then, but if he could once return to a certain starting place and go over it all slowly, he could find out what that thing was. . . ."[3]

Some idea of himself. Gatsby had reinvented himself; he had once been James Gatz, a poor boy from the Midwest, and Fitzgerald clearly meant for the reader to see that loving Daisy—and being loved by her—was a part of that new self-image he had created, which definitely included an ascent to higher levels of socioeconomic status. In another often-quoted passage Carraway makes a casual remark to Gatsby about the quality of Daisy's voice:

"She's got an indiscreet voice," I remarked. "It's full of—" I hesitated.

"Her voice is full of money," he said suddenly.

That was it. I'd never understood before. It was full of money—that was the inexhaustible charm that rose and fell in it, the jingle of it, the cymbals' song of it. . . . High in a white palace the king's daughter, the golden girl. . . . [4]

Gatsby is not out for Daisy's money. He has his own money, tons of it, acquired in the bootlegging racket as part of his preparation for winning her back. He wants and desperately needs Daisy—rich Daisy—as a part of his new identity, a statement that he truly is Jay Gatsby and not Jimmy Gatz from Minnesota. His love for Daisy is passionate and sincere, but it springs from an ego-ideal, and consequently Daisy is part woman, part trophy. (Trophy collecting is an inseparable part of romantic love. Today we are all acquainted with the idea of the trophy wife as the beauteous bimbo acquired by some over-the-hill tycoon. But there is a trophy aspect to more relationships than you may suspect: not only trophy wives but trophy husbands, trophy boyfriends, trophy sexual conquests, trophy dates to the high school prom. Our love lives are always in part exercises in ego construction, and trophies—for those lucky enough to win them—can be of great value in such projects.)

Because he was deeply identified with Gatsby, Fitzgerald would never have pointed out that everyone concerned would have been a lot better off if Gatsby had accepted the loss of Daisy, looked for an honest job, found a new girlfriend, and gotten on with his life. Of course, it was not in Gatsby's driven character to do that, nor was it in the tradition of romantic fiction that is a part of our sentimental education. In novels, movies, and songs we learn to believe in the love that lasts forever and then go in search of it because it sounds like a pretty good thing. Unfortunately, there is no such thing. Love is an emotion, and emotions come and go like changing weather in the ever-shifting human mind, and to believe that any particular passion can or should last forever is another kind of denial of death.

I am not here to denounce all romantic love and am in no position to do so. I have been in it too many times myself, and done my share of dumb things in that connection. There is nothing particularly wrong with romance per se, but it has its dark sides, which are revealed in its exploitation, and in the pain that so many people feel when it dies its inevitable death after they had been led to believe that it would not. Perhaps its most serious offense is the tendency to blind us to other kinds of love: There is the selfless love called agape and the love of all humankind that Alfred Adler described with that heroic mouthful of a word, *Gemeinschaftsgefühl*. There is the quiet love of married couples who have survived the end of the honeymoon. There is the love of nature and the love of God and the love of children, and there is the all-pervasive feeling of love reported by people in moments of an enlightenment experience—a love that seems to have no object or agenda. All are well-known parts of the human repertoire of emotions, and that is something we might at least try to keep in mind while we are chasing one another around the love boat.

Famous Egos

Celebrity culture is another institution of ego-perpetuation. There have been societies structured on tradition, religious faith, and/or social class. Contemporary industrial societies often retain some traces of those, but social institutions are increasingly influenced by the contemporary obsession with fame. Celebrity—plain "well-knownness," regardless of the reason for being well-known—is now a value, conferring status in its own right. This celebrity culture is a hindrance to our prospects for psychological and social growth because fame is essentially the celebration of the ego, the organized public admiration of constructed and illusory selves.

I suppose you could be completely hung up on publicizing yourself in a primitive society or an isolated village, but the kind of fame we have become accustomed to in recent decades requires high technology, which makes it possible to project and enlarge individual egos to a scale beyond the wildest dreams of any conqueror or prima donna of ages past.

One historian calls Alexander the Great "the first famous person." Alexander certainly wasn't the first warrior to seek glory in war, but he was in it for personal glory rather than for perpetuating a dynasty, and he made maximum use of the technologies available at the time—sculpture and coins—to create heroic visual images of himself, usually in a Hollywood-style pose with flowing hair and eyes gazing majestically upward.[5]

Since then, many social changes and technological developments have helped to prepare the way for the contemporary obsession with celebrity. The growth of cities did its part by creating environments within which people interacted with greater numbers of other people, gossiped on a grander scale, and had the opportunity to make their mark through great deeds of one kind or another. So we find the appearance in Rome of words like *fama* and *celebritas,* and the appearance of world-class egos such as Caesar, Cleopatra, and Marc Anthony. The Romans also invented the concept of persona, a term that originally described the masks worn by theatrical performers, in recognition of the citizen's status as owner of a public self.

More recent technological advances in such areas as printing, photography, radio, and television have all contributed to the emergence of celebrity cultures, as have the breakdown of rigid class structures and the shift in so much of the world from monarchy to democratic government. Eminence is no longer monopolized by people of high birth; anybody can become famous. And fame isn't even linked all that closely with success, or with distinction through some laudable achievement. Merely having been in the news, seen on television, or talked about is enough to confer a certain magical aura. People become well known in curious ways and for odd reasons. In the 1990s the British teenager Louise Woodward became famous for having been convicted of manslaughter in the United States in a case involving charges that she had killed a baby while working as a nanny for an American family. Upon her return from England, she found herself barraged with requests for autographs and television interviews, hounded like a movie star by paparazzi. Seemingly aware of what a strange phenomenon it all was, she told a newspaper reporter that she was "not famous for anything good" and thought that the people who mobbed her for her autograph when she appeared in public were "not able to distinguish between notoriety and celebrity."[6] Clearly celebrity would have been okay with her.

In his book entitled *The Image: A Guide to Pseudo-Events,* historian Daniel Boorstin wrote about the celebrities who are not really identified with any achievement, either negatively or positively, but are, as he put it, "famous for being famous," well known for their well-knownness. John F. Kennedy Jr. has often been cited (not by Boorstin) as an example. Indelibly imprinted on the public mind by his image as a child saluting his father's coffin, Kennedy made no particular efforts as he grew up to seek attention. Nevertheless, he was avidly chronicled by the press in his romantic life, his brief career as publisher of the political magazine *George*, his marriage, and his early death in a plane crash.

Another often quoted remark is artist Andy Warhol's: "In the future, everybody will be world-famous for fifteen minutes." Frankly, I find it entirely meaningless as either a bon mot or a social forecast, but it seems to turn up everywhere, widely quoted for being widely quoted. Warhol himself was completely a creature of celebrity culture, famous for images of famous people—notably Marilyn Monroe—and adept at doing things that caught the attention of the media. And he was also a victim of one of the bizarre phenomena of the celebrity life, the attack by a would-be assassin. One way to become famous is to kill a famous person.

In somewhat the same way that institutionalized romantic love grows out of the simple emotional charge that accompanies our mating urges, celebrity culture grows—monstrously—out of basic human needs for approval and admiration and also out of an even deeper need, which is simply to have one's existence recognized and confirmed. We are social animals, and we create our selves out of social interactions. We also become trapped by those socially constructed selves, servants of the persona. Some people manage to an extent to free themselves from the trap by recognizing that they are not actually the names they go by, the roles they play, or the faces they present to the world. If they achieve some degree of fame in their lives, they either don't take it too seriously or actively avoid it. For a multitude of reasons, other people seek fame with a passionate determination; and still others seem to stumble into it. Whatever the reason or the degree, fame always requires a bit of plastic surgery on the persona, the creation of a new socially constructed self that may or may not have much in common with the person you were (the earlier social construction) before you became famous. Some newly famous people have a terribly hard time with this need, others come to understand clearly that they aren't the persona. One study of the psychology of fame includes a remarkable quotation from the movie star Myrna Loy, who said: "I daren't take any chances with Myrna Loy, for she isn't my property . . . I've got to be, on all public occasions, the personality they sell at the box office."[7]

You don't have to be famous to play the fame game. You can seek to allay whatever doubts you may have as to whether or not you really exist by knowing a famous person, having a famous relative or ancestor, even being present at a famous event. I have heard it said that Yankee Stadium would have had to have been a hundred times its size to contain all the old-timers who later claimed to have seen Don Larson pitch a perfect game in the 1956 World Series, and I have been sorely tempted a couple of times to say I was in the stadium when the famous last-minute victory in the 1982 Cal-Stanford Big Game took place instead of where I really was—in another part of Berkeley, watching my son in a soccer game.

Identity and Other Forms of Moderate-to-Severe Brain Damage

The thirteenth-century mystic Jalauddin Rumi once wrote a poem about identity that consisted primarily of declarations that he had none:

> I am neither Christian nor Jew nor Gabr nor Muslim.
> I am neither of the East, nor of the West,
> nor of the land, nor of the sea;
> I am not of India, nor of China, nor of Bulgaria,
> nor of Saqsin . . .

In the world's present state, limping along the road to liberation, people everywhere are suffering and confused—and sometimes driven to murderous violence—over matters of identity. Identity is the deepest and most universal social illusion; it is also humanity's number one problem, the thing we most need to figure out in order to get on with evolution.

I realize that describing identity as a problem is radically different from our usual tendency, which is to describe it as a fundamental human need, only problematic when absent. We generally assume—and are supported in the assumption by much of modern psychology—that in order to be real people we need to have a full complement of labels signifying our nationality, racial heritage, religious affiliation, political beliefs, occupation, position in society, gender, and sexual orientation. With all these in order we are in good shape. Without them we are nobody. And if we are somewhere in between, uncertain about which labels we should be wearing and when, we are diagnosed as sufferers from alienation, anomie, identity crisis, or other social diseases identified by modern theorists.

I'm quite sure that some people do suffer from those lack-of-identity concerns. Yet, if we look around the world, we can't fail to notice that most of the folks who are busily engaged in slaughtering their enemies, laying waste to the land, destroying the lives of innocent people, and turning cities to rubble have identities that are in robust health. They are nationalists busy with "ethnic cleansing" or fighting for statehood. They are religious fundamentalists doing the work of God. They are tribesmen gaining vengeance on their ancient enemies. They are the usual self-righteous "us" hacking away at the usual wrong-thinking "them."

What the human species has yet to understand fully is that you can be quite certain about your identity and still be confused, if not downright deluded, about what you are. Most identities are completely symbolic, including the ones we take most seriously, such as nationality and religious affiliation. There is much wisdom in the old European saying that defines a nation as a group of people united by a common hatred of their enemies and a common mistake about their own ancestry. Even race, one of the most troublesome of identities, is now recognized by science to be a social fiction, a set of procrustean categories that we impose on a huge spectrum of human variation.

And I propose that the path toward a more civilized world lies not in our deciding to be really good toward people of different groups—racial, religious, whatever—but in recognizing the trivial and arbitrary nature of all such identity categories. Once that is recognized, a change of behavior follows as the night the day.

And of course that recognition will be hard won. Although there is an emperor's-new-clothes quality to these social fictions, many people and groups around the world are fiercely dedicated to them. Respect for identity in various forms—as patriotism, religious faith, or racial solidarity—is widely taught, praised, and even enforced. These preservation efforts are becoming more strident because so many people are losing, changing, or rewriting their labels. The "culture wars" are in a sense identity wars. In religion they pit traditionalists, for whom it is inconceivable that one can be religious without membership in an organized faith, against those who insist that they can have religious feelings, experiences, beliefs, convictions, and ethics—and no particular religious identity. In the politics of many nations, they pit the defenders of the nation's historic culture and ethnic heritage against immigrants, deviates, cosmopolitans, and multiculturalists.

And there are good reasons for the traditionalists to feel alarmed: Many people now stir up their own combinations of religious beliefs and practices, or invent entirely new ones. This kind of experimentation is most prevalent in highly pluralistic societies. One scholar of religions recently pointed out that the United States "is transitioning from a Christian nation to a syncretistic, spiritually diverse society." At the core is a "new perception of religion: a personalized, customized form of faith views which meet personal needs, minimize rules and absolutes, and bear little resemblance to the 'pure' form of any of the world's major religions." National identity is also losing its power in an age of mass media and mass migrations; as people move around the world they start taking citizenship and patriotism a lot less seriously than many people in power would like.

The whole institution of identity is changing. Its theoretical foundations have been under attack for centuries—a stream of thought as old as David Hume and as recent as postmodern psychology—telling us that identity is a socially constructed reality. Whether this is trickling down to the masses, or whether the masses are figuring it out for themselves, it's obvious that a lot of people are dealing with identity in new and different ways.

CHAPTER II

Up and Down with Religion and Spirituality

Religions are divisive and quarrelsome. They are a form of one-upmanship because they depend upon separating the "saved" from the "damned," the true believers from the heretics, the in-group from the out-group. . . . Irrevocable commitment to any religion is not only intellectual suicide; it is positive unfaith because it closes the mind to any new vision of the world. Faith is, above all, open-ness—an act of trust in the unknown.

—ALAN WATTS[1]

The corruption of so-called spiritual power does not simply occur because the wrong person is in power. Rather, this occurs whenever a role or structure bestows power through images of infallibility or moral superiority. The fault then does not lie in a given leader's shortcomings, but rather in the structure itself, through defining one person as more pure and spiritual, and thus superior to others.

—JOEL KRAMER AND DIANA ALSTAD[2]

I maintain that Truth is a pathless land, and you cannot approach it by any path whatsoever, by any religion, by any sect. . . . If you first understand that, then you will see how impossible it is to organize a belief. . . . If you do it becomes dead, crystallized; it becomes a creed, a sect, a religion, to be imposed on others.

—JIDDU KRISHNAMURTI[3]

The human drive toward growth and transcendence is universal and also "religious," in the truest meaning of the word, expressing the deep desire—deeper than consciousness—to move beyond the lonely boundaries of the constructed self and become what you are.

[173]

The word "religion" is quite close in meaning to the Sanskrit word "yoga" (etymologically related to the English word "yoke"), which is used to describe a variety of paths toward transcendent unity: in the Hindu tradition, there are many yogas. The religious yearning may lead the seeker into spiritual explorations, to drugs, or psychotherapy. And of course it leads to organized religions: Churches. Mosques. Temples. Shrines.

And although most people in the worlds of evolutionary science, cosmology, brain research, and developmental psychology shy away from terms like "transcendant unity," we really can't help noticing that much of modern science, from Darwin and Freud through to the contemporary stargazers and gene decoders, are showing us linked and connected with the universe and all of organic life.

The trouble with organized religion—the religions of the churches and mosques—is that the believer is asked to connect and yoke to the belief system of the religion itself, including all of its dogmas, doctrines, hierarchies, traditions, symbols, and hatreds. Instead of fostering a sense of membership with all humanity, religions all too often foster a particularly pernicious form of the identity disease—a "them and us" mentality in which nonbelievers may be viewed not only as wrong on theological issues but also as evil and even less than human. The member is led to believe that salvation lies in uncritically swallowing all of the religion's official truths, passively surrendering to the spiritual authority of its leaders, and reverently conserving the relics—both material and symbolic—of its past. Buddha's tooth bites again.

Doubtless there have been many enlightened people among the saints and prophets and monks and nuns, possibly even among the bishops and popes, although that's reaching for it, but organized religions are not there to help you recognize the constructed nature of personal identity, and they do not encourage the relentless examination of all claims to truth that is essential to such a process. Liberation requires a willingness to live in a universe not fully explained—perhaps not even explainable. Traditional religious institutions *can* nourish that willingness, but seldom do. More frequently they suppress it because, after all, they have to push their own explanations. This doesn't mean that you may not find enlightenment by going to church—enlightenment is everywhere—but that's not what churches are about. On one level they are mainly about perpetuating their dogmas and reinforcing conventional social values and beliefs. On another level they are about much more human and likable things such as community, consolation, and getting dressed up on Sunday morning. I sometimes think that there is as imperfect a connection between theology and what people get out of going to church as there is between psychological theory and what people get out of therapy.

Going to Church, and Falling Away

For a while I used to attend a church regularly—even though I had long since ceased to have any belief in the literal truth of any such teachings—and then I gradually stopped. I discovered that I could meet my religious needs more satisfactorily on Sunday morning by taking a run in the hills, followed by a large breakfast. But I still like to drop in on a church service once in a while, especially when I'm traveling. If it's a church like the ones I attended as a child, there is a warm sense of familiarity and peace. The old hymns are comforting, the people are at their gentle best, and the sermons usually dull but sincere. And I like to attend services in foreign countries, for a different reason. It gives me a certain feeling for the life of the place, and of the people in that place, in a way that a stranger is not likely to find anywhere else.

I particularly remember going to a mass one Sunday at the cathedral in San Pedro Sula, a city on the eastern side of Honduras, when I was traveling through Central America on a journalistic assignment. To tell you the truth, there isn't much else to do in San Pedro Sula on a Sunday morning, and I had noted the location of the cathedral and the times of masses on previous sweaty strolls around the town.

Before the mass began that day I explored the inside of the cathedral, taking in the ambiance of candles and statues and stained glass. I noticed an elderly woman standing in front of a statue of the Virgin.

Paying no attention at all to anyone else in the building, she stood there weeping, with her hands on the statue's bare marble feet. I have no idea what her suffering was about; I only know that she had brought it there, and I suppose she had nowhere else to take it. I don't know what kind of surcease she drew there, either, and I don't consider it my business to judge, only to remind myself that, whatever my own personal misgivings about organized religion, it is still the only thing many people have.

There are all kinds of good reasons for going to church, or to a temple or a mosque or a shrine—certainly what brought that woman to the cathedral—but you should not expect more than it has to offer. In particular, you should not expect reliable inside information about how or by whom the universe was created, or infallible guidelines about how to conduct your life. Be on guard against any assumption that the people at the highest level of the organization are morally superior—or closer to God—than the people at the lowest. And don't let them take away the mystery.

We swim in a sea of mystery—the big mystery of how Being came to be, all the lesser ones of what we are, what consciousness is, where we're going, why. Organized religions try to dispel the mysteries by offering as literal truth the embalmed myths of various ancient civilizations and prescriptions for behavior handed down from the learning of past centuries—guidelines that may be useful in some cases, less so in others. The Bible really doesn't have much to tell us about stem cell research.

People all over the world have come to roughly similar conclusions about religious authority, and they have devised ways to participate in their religions that fall far short of uncritical acceptance of all beliefs and full obedience to temporal authorities. Among these wanderers from the path, of course, are active dissenters and revisionists such as the people in Christian churches who are struggling for ordainment of gays and women. But many more people come to terms with their religion in some other way, less contentious but equally troubling to the guardians of orthodoxy: They are secular Muslims or Hindus, "cafeteria Catholics" who accept some of the doctrines and pass on others; the freethinkers and liberals; the "sometimes on Sunday" folks who maintain a church membership for social or business reasons, or because they don't want their children to grow up heathens; the eclectics and shoppers who participate in more than one religion or spiritual school over time, or sometimes all at once. You also find people like Huston Smith—one of the most deeply religious people I know—who have a passionate reverence for all religions combined with a breadth of perspective that comes from having looked in at many doors and from a conviction that somewhere in the future of all religions lies the discovery of a way of being that transcends them all and "beats with the pulse of all mankind."[4]

In short, there are not only many religions in the world but many ways of being religious. If no one went to religious services except true believers, lots of churches and temples would be standing empty. Dismaying as this may be to those who cling to more traditional views, it comes with the territory of life in a fluid, information-rich, mobile, and ever-changing global civilization; it is simply a condition of freedom. And it means that there is far more religious diversity than you will see revealed in any list of creeds, sects, and denominations.

The Trouble with Religion

The trouble, as I suggested earlier, is that the seeker often becomes linked and yoked to the belief system of the religion itself, along with its occasionally fierce attitudes toward the belief systems of other religions. There are, to be sure, open-minded religions such as Baha'i and the Unitarian Universalist Church, and you can find freethinking groups or congregations within all of the major organized faiths, but all of the major organized faiths also have their fundamentalists and their own "culture wars" between orthodox and liberal wings.

Some observers say that the religious fundamentalism we see today is different from the religious conservatism of the past. Contemporary fundamentalists are mobilized against what they perceive as the evils of a global information society, hoping to reverse the course of history or, failing that, to maintain strict adherence to the faith within bor-

dered communities of true believers. This kind of fundamentalism—
and the political agenda that goes with it—made its unforgettable
mark on September 11, 2001.

After that fateful day the whole world became acquainted with
Osama bin Laden and his militant Al Queda network, and also with
the Taliban, the devoutly rearward-looking political group that for a
time ruled Afghanistan. And we learned about the ideology that drove
them: Bin Laden had launched his terrorist holy war with the stated
objective of returning the Muslim world to a pure Islam untainted by
secularism, deviance, internal dissent, or foreign influence. The obstacle in the way of its achievement was the United States and, to a lesser
extent, Israel. And the logical solution: Kill Americans and Jews. In its
childish reasoning and mad objective, his quest was quite similar to
Adolph Hitler's goal of creating a racially pure Germany.

Taliban leaders professed to believe that the Koran contained the
rules for how to behave in the twenty-first century (thus applying the
same epistemology as the "infallibalist" Christians who believe such
guidelines are to be found in the Bible), but at the same time they
managed to create new rules for behavior that a Koranic scholar
would be hard put to find in scripture. The penal code put forth by
the Taliban's Ministry for the Promotion of Virtue and Prevention of
Vice was noticeably on guard against excessive pleasures, influences
from the outside world, and practically anything having to do with
sex. It included prohibitions against women appearing in public without the proper covering of head and body, videotapes or cassette tapes
of music, shaving or shortening of beards, keeping pigeons, kite-
flying, displaying photographs, "un-Islamic" hairstyles, and singing
or dancing by women in weddings or other celebrations.

Another edict, one of the letters from then-ruler Mulla Omar to
customs officials, banned for import a number of items including
satellite dishes, cinematographic or sound-projecting equipment, "any
equipment that produces joyful music," and anything provoking sex
or nudity, as well as neckties, necktie pins, and sewing catalogues
with pictures.[5] Yet, this curious collection of prohibitions and Thou
Shalt Nots has a certain lunatic logic, rooted in the agenda of shutting

out all the temptations of the world in order to maintain the Pure Land within.

Pitfalls on the Spiritual Path

People turn away from organized religion and toward various other pursuits commonly called spiritual for many reasons: reaction against the manifold rigidities, geriatric dogmas, and fundamentalist tendencies within organized religions; attraction toward the mysterious promise of enlightenment; the sheer appeal of the new and/or exotic; the yearning for community. By "spiritual" I mean pretty much everything outside of the more orthodox varieties of major organized religions. There really isn't a clear boundary between religion and spirituality: New spiritual movements tend to solidify into religions, and organized religions tend to give birth to esoteric movements from within. Besides, different people seem to have quite different meanings in mind when they use those words.

Spirituality is strongly associated with the amorphous subculture called the New Age, an important force in the postmodern world. You can't adequately deal with it simply by taking sides for or against— although many people are energetically doing one or the other. Some believe that the New Agers are the "cultural creatives" who are the keepers of the future, others join the good fun of ridiculing the whole scene of goofy cults and fuzzy spirituality. But it can't really be so easily dismissed, in part because it is a diffuse array of cultural phenomena and personal sensibility that extends far beyond the people who consciously identify with it or go shopping for healing crystals or Deepak Chopra books.

On the positive side, the New Age includes a great openness to ideas about growth and consciousness change, an interest in all religious and spiritual lore, and a general recognition that the Newtonian/Cartesian mindset is neither the only nor the best way of looking at the world. It has led many people into a sustained and disciplined study of Asian enlightenment traditions. It is a vital and important part of the emerging enlightenment project.

On the negative side, it has been a vast fountain of trivialization, commercialization, sloppy thinking, and general smarminess.

I am inclined to think its contributions are more positive than negative, but in this chapter I plan to deal chiefly with the shortcomings because each is a problem to be understood by the person who undertakes a serious exploration of consciousness. Among the main ones:

- A tendency toward narcissism, logically resulting from the popularity of the romantic notion of an idealized inner "true self"
- A bias against rationality, especially unfortunate when coupled with an affection for Big Ideas
- A *kitsch* constructivism that fails to respect the limits of our ability to create reality and degenerates into little more than a belief that wishing will make it so
- A lack of ability—or even desire—to evaluate critically the various beliefs, practices, and ideas imported wholesale from other cultures and other ages
- A chronic susceptibility to cults and cult leaders

This last shortcoming—the tendency of so many people to swoon in the presence of anybody who claims to be the keeper of spiritual insight—has led to some of the darkest moments of the New Age. There is a grim record of economic, sexual, and psychological exploitations of the followers of celebrities such as the California promoter Werner Erhard, who built his est teachings into an international business empire that was prodigiously successful until it collapsed under the weight of its founder's ego. The est saga offers an excellent example not only of how such movements go wrong but also the really remarkable willingness of otherwise intelligent people to turn off their shit detectors.

The Rise and Fall of Werner Erhard

Werner Hans Erhard had been Jack Rosenberg, a car salesman in Philadelphia, before he picked his new name out of a magazine article about the leaders of Germany's postwar economic and political rebirth. At the time of this rebirth he was on an airplane headed west, having just abandoned his wife and four children, and he needed to adopt a new name to avoid getting tracked down by his wife's relatives. He was traveling with his pregnant girlfriend, who changed her name to Ellen Erhard.[6]

The young couple eventually settled near San Francisco, where Erhard built up a new career, first as a door-to-door book salesman and then as sales manager for an encyclopedia company. He was a dynamite salesman and a great reader of self-help books such as Napoleon Hill's *Think and Grow Rich* and Maxwell Maltz's *Psycho-Cybernetics*. He also explored various offerings of the human potential movement and attended some of the lectures that Alan Watts gave at his houseboat in Sausalito. For a while he was a committed follower of Scientology, and it did not escape his attention that its peculiar psychological/spiritual beliefs were not merely taught but vigorously marketed. He studied a transformational program called Mind Dynamics and by this time was obviously thinking about making another career change.

These events occured over the period of time—mid-1960s to early 1970s—when the human potential movement was riding high. Everybody wanted to get some kind of therapy or become a therapist—or both; I knew any number of people who changed occupations, studying to become Rolfers or gestalt therapists. Erhard happened to occupy a more commercially oriented wing of the *Zeitgeist*. The people selling programs such as Mind Dynamics weren't necessarily more interested in money than the people who were trying to build up therapy practices or write self-help books—but they were a lot better at getting it. They understood advertising, marketing, and sales promotion, and always viewed the teachings they offered as products to be packaged and sold.

Erhard purchased the San Francisco franchise of Mind Dynamics and began teaching its course to groups of people who would gather for intense weekend sessions in hotel conference rooms. And he became very good at it, a charismatic showman who dazzled his students with his energy and his powerful assurance that they could do great things in their lives by following the precepts of the training. He also developed some of his own sales methods, such as using attractive female assistants to sign up customers and recruiting his students to serve as unpaid volunteers who brought more new participants into the program. This unpaid activity, they were given to understand, was to help them learn more deeply how to apply the principles of Mind Dynamics.

In 1971 Erhard left Mind Dynamics and launched his own product, which he called Erhard Seminars Training, est for short.

There was a lot of buzz about est in the early 1970s. The reports weren't always favorable, but most people I talked to seemed to be quite impressed with the training and I couldn't resist the temptation to check it out for myself. So I paid my $250 and on the appointed day (the seminars covered two weekends, four days in all), I joined several hundred other people—mostly white, but a mix of ages, genders, and types—in a ballroom at the Sheraton Palace Hotel. I can't remember over this gap of years precisely what my expectations were. I knew that the trainings were intense, that they went on for a long time, and that participants were not allowed to leave and go to the bathroom except during the official breaks. But I didn't know much about the details of the training because participants were sworn not to talk about it to others—one of Erhard's many good marketing touches.

The training turned out to be a loosely assembled smorgasbord of many different methods and techniques. There were "processes," exercises somewhat resembling psychodrama or role-playing, long lectures, periods of "sharing" when participants talked about their personal problems, occasional confrontations when a participant was mercilessly browbeaten by the trainer for saying something unacceptable such as: "Why don't we take a break and go have a cup of coffee?" I recognized elements of many approaches that I was familiar with, ideas and even mannerisms obviously borrowed from Alan Watts, and other bits I wasn't familiar with at all but which I'm told had roots in Mind Dynamics and Scientology. I found the experience in some ways to be similar to that of attending one of those psychology conferences at which different people put on demonstrations of various styles of group therapy. In this case, however, all the demonstrations were guided by one person, a man named Ted Long, formerly an attorney and a politician in a suburb of San Francisco, who explained to us rather proudly that he had been personally chosen to become a "copy" of Erhard. (I learned later that the people Erhard selected to lead trainings in his place were literally instructed to think of themselves as copies of himself—the word "clone" hadn't come into common use then—and they were meticulously schooled to conduct the trainings precisely as he had done, word for word and step by step. In the process, Erhard's odd jumble of techniques, ideas, and exercises took on an almost scriptural mystique of its own.) Insofar as there was a general theme tying the various pieces together, it was that you alone create your own reality, are personally responsible for everything that happens in your life, and if you successfully "got it"—that is, absorbed the message of the training—you would be able to do damn near anything you wanted.

On the whole, I thought the content was unimpressive—some good ideas intermixed with a lot of baloney, not an unusual thing in any body of doctrine—but nevertheless enjoyed the experience, and I had no particular problem with it until the very end. At the close of the training we were informed that we were all now enlightened, then instructed in how to sign up for further "advanced" trainings. There seemed to be no question about this obligation; we were simply expected to do it, then and there. So, hundreds of people who were supposed to have just become totally in charge of their lives obediently lined up with checkbooks and credit cards in hand to take more trainings. I declined, and suddenly found myself on the receiving end of a somewhat contemptuous hard sell, the general message of which was that my life was going to be a total mess if I didn't get a further fix of est. I declined anyway, went home, and then started getting telephone calls from other est volunteers who were similarly dedicated to saving me from the horrors of a life without Werner Erhard. Eventually I became sufficiently rude and vulgar in my responses to these sales pitches to convince the head office that I really and truly did not want to receive any more of their phone calls.

I was left with the conviction that the value of the est training was in itself nothing much, but that the sales machinery around it was the most formidable I had ever seen. I mean, not only forceful but effective. Est was submediocre psychotherapy and brilliant marketing. And in the years that followed, as the movement continued to expand, I found myself constantly in contact with people who had bought the whole package—the superhuman character of Werner Erhard, the wisdom of the teachings, the belief that everybody is totally responsible for everything that happens to them (mere vapid hubris in most cases, but occasionally ugly as on the occasion when an est devotee lectured a woman I knew who was dying of breast cancer), and the remaking of their vocabularies to include heavy use of est jargon. People were constantly talking about "creating a space" for something to happen, or beginning sentences with: "What comes up for me is . . ." (A friend of mine once remarked that what came up for him when he got around a bunch of est people was his lunch.)

I took a dislike to est for reasons like that—the shabbiness of its product, the silliness of its jargon, the hard-sell glitz of its packaging, the exploitation of its participants, the cult of personality around Erhard. My objections for some time were mainly what you could classify as matters of taste. Later I began to hear some darker allegations about the financial structure of est, Erhard's personal behavior, and the suicides and emotional collapses of people who found that they weren't as firmly in control of the universe as they had been led to believe. There were more lawsuits and adverse news reports and in 1991 a devastating *60 Minutes* television report that accused Erhard of beating his son, sexually molesting his daughters, having his ex-wife beaten and nearly strangled, tyrannizing his staff, and occasionally declaring himself to be God. There were also allegations about the financial structure of est. And then came the Internal Revenue Service, seeking millions of dollars in taxes that had been evaded through an incredible structure of offshore corporations and hidden bank accounts. Erhard sold his share in what remained of the business and left the country; the last I heard, he was reported to be living in exile and masterminding from afar several est spinoffs that run corporate training practices.

The est episode was different in some ways from the rise and fall of other cults and masters of the universe; its content had stronger links to the peculiarly American success themes of Dale Carnegie and Napoleon Hill, and it had a uniquely relentless sales-promotion struc- ture. But regardless of the content—which in some ways wasn't really that important—the dynamics that made it so successful, and eventu- ally destroyed it, were universal. It is not enough merely to wallow in disapproval of the sins of Jack Rosenberg; what we need to do is understand why and how such things happen—and keep happening.

Particularly remarkable about the est episode, as I look back on it, is its similarity to fundamentalist religious cults. I'm sure the hip young people who became Erhard's followers didn't see it that way. After all, they were being taught that they created whatever happened to them. But they became slavishly devoted to the man they called "the source" (some people even worked as unpaid house servants) and displayed an astonishing readiness to follow his rules, parrot his words, and, if possible, think his thoughts. It was a brilliantly pack- aged escape from freedom, but it was an escape from freedom nonetheless.

The Dynamics of Spiritual Tyranny

Other spiritual empires—quite different in some ways but strikingly similar in others—arose and fell over that same period of time.

One was led by Frederick Lenz, also known as Atmananda and Zen Master Rama. I first learned about Lenz through full-page news- paper advertisements in which he not only represented himself as a spiritual leader but—taking the idea of reincarnation beyond any- thing I had experienced in all my hot-tub years of listening to people gossip about their past lives—included a resume of his previous incar- nations: Among other things he claimed to have been a temple priest in ancient Atlantis, the head of a Zen order in Japan in the seventeenth century, and a Tibetan Lama just prior to his own birth in the twentieth century. It was a really outstanding piece of spiritual chutzpah, and while some of us who saw the ads got a hearty laugh about it, others swallowed it whole and joined the ranks of his followers. Lenz built up a business entitled Rama Seminars, Inc., wrote a bestselling book entitled *Surfing in the Himalayas* about his apocryphal spiritual adventures in Tibet, amassed a sizable personal fortune, sexually exploited many of his female followers, and died in 1998. His body was found in the water near his Long Island estate, and the death was ruled a suicide by drowning, with drugs a contributing factor. An employee said that Rama Lenz was depressed because of the many lawsuits being filed against him by families of followers who had committed suicide.

And there was Bhagwan Shree Rajneesh, a former Indian philosophy professor who became the leader of an international spiritual movement that at its peak in the 1970s and 1980s had thousands of followers and hundreds of meditation centers. Born Rajneesh Chandra Mohan in 1931, he took on the titles "Bhagwan" (the blessed one) and "Shree" (master) when he became a full-time spiritual teacher. He had an ashram in an upscale suburb of Poona in southern India and, later, a much larger one near Antelope, Oregon, purchased by his followers for approximately $6 million. It was there that Rajneesh and his followers attained their greatest notoriety: Rajneesh for amassing a fleet of twenty-nine Rolls Royces for his personal use and his followers for various escapades, including the first documented U.S. case of bioterrorism when they used salmonella bacteria to poison a salad bar. The salmonella incident was a part of a political conflict between Rajneesh followers and local townspeople; apparently the objective was to reduce the voter turnout on a local measure that would have placed new restrictions on the ashram's activities. Soon after that incident, Rajneesh ran into troubles with U.S. immigration officials on charges of arranging phony marriages in order to enable some of his Indian followers to remain in the United States, and of lying on his own immigration papers. He was given a suspended sentence and returned to India, where he died in 1990. In his last years he changed his name again, this time to "Osho," derived from the term "oceanic experience."[7]

For all the differences among these and other spiritual cults, there are certain striking similarities. These include:

1. A charismatic leader, not noticeably devoid of ego.
2. An authoritarian structure, generally pyramidal and hierarchical.
3. A central body of teaching and beliefs. The teaching may be a loose anthology of material from many sources, but, whether it takes the form of the Holy Bible or the seminar scripts of Werner Erhard, it comes to be regarded as a coherent whole, infallible, and not subject to revision—except, of course, from above.
4. A strong sense of community and group loyalty among the followers. This may be encouraged (or enforced) in any number of ways: In the case of est, it was nurtured by continued participation in trainings and occasional big social events attended by est luminaries such as folksinger John Denver. Lenz ordered his followers to socialize only with one another and make themselves "inaccessible" to outsiders. Rajneesh encouraged strong in-group identification by giving his followers new names and instructing them to wear only orange clothing.
5. A grandiose agenda or myth of destiny. At an important stage in the history of Synanon, as it began to degenerate from an innovative drug-treatment program to a full-blown cult, the term "Synanon is the future" became an oft-repeated motto of the organization. In the Arica movement, a spiritual group based on Sufi teachings that flourished in the United States for some time under the leadership of a Chilean named Oscar Ichazo, followers were instructed that a "wave," a major upheaval, was imminent and they should be prepared to take on roles of leadership when society collapsed. In the Maharishi Mahesh Yogi's transcendental meditation movement, his followers also were encouraged to prepare themselves for roles of leadership in the world and at the end of their training period, teachers were given diplomas certifying them

as Governors of the Age of Enlightenment. Werner Erhard had the Hunger Project, and at several different gatherings I heard his copies proclaim, usually to thunderous applause, that they would end world hunger by the end of the twentieth century. At about the same time, in 1979, Rajneesh announced his plan to lead the way to the creation of a "new man" within the next twenty years.

Becoming Enlightened about Enlightenment

There are two things that I need to say in qualification of the general theme of spiritual tyranny. One is that many spiritual teachers and seekers manage to go quietly about their business without getting into any such cultish craziness. Another is that the cult dynamic is not exclusive to spiritual movements. Cults spring up within organized religions as well, and there are secular cults of terrorism and revolution that exhibit all the usual symptoms. But the fact remains—and it's a sobering one that needs to be taken seriously—that the *folie a deux* of ego-tripping leader and true-believing follower occurs frequently. Part of it is inherent in old and deep-seated human tendencies, the dynamic of tribes and chieftains. Part of it has to do with transplanting into Western culture the unquestioning submission to the guru that is common in Eastern spiritual traditions. And it seems obvious that partly to blame is the heady impact of commercialism and celebrity, so that the spiritual teacher gets to be not only venerated but—twin glories of achievement in the Western world—rich and famous.

It is important that we try to gain a contemporary understanding of enlightenment, and no less important that we try to understand how the search for it can go so terribly wrong. Although there are no reliable statistics on such matters, I suspect that more people today are actively engaged in such pursuits than at any previous time in history. Unfortunately, it is inevitable that this situation becomes a rich hunting ground for spiritual predators.

The process of personal evolution may indeed require some letting go of ideas, opinions, self-concepts. It also requires—especially in today's world with its vast bazaar of religions and spiritual schools old and new—some rational thought and critical judgment. Preachers and gurus often deride critical thought as the work of the devil or the ego, but it has an ancient and respectable place in enlightenment lore, as in the following piece of advice from the Buddha himself:

> Do not put faith in traditions, even though they have been accepted for long generations and in many countries. Do not believe a thing because many repeat it. Do not accept a thing on the authority of one or another of the Sages of old, nor on the ground that a statement is found in the books. Never believe anything because probability is in its favor. Do not believe in that which you have yourself imagined, thinking that a god has inspired it. Believe nothing merely on the authority of your teachers or of the priests. After examination, believe that which you have tested for yourselves and found reasonable, which is in conformity with your well-being and that of others.[8]

The passage quoted above is from the Kalama Sutra, one of the scriptures of Buddhism, and it will not have escaped the attention of the alert reader that there's something inherently contradictory about my quoting scriptural authority in support of a skeptical attitude toward scriptural authority. So don't take it as one of the commandments—just a suggestion from a recognized authority in the field that unquestioning submission to a teacher, a denomination, or a spiritual school is not the only way to learn about yourself, and probably never was. As a general guideline for the spiritual seeker, I would suggest avoiding any teacher who does not publicly and frequently acknowledge being a learner as well.

With regard to organized religions, I suggest a critical stance, evaluating them as to the degree to which they are actually religious—

that is, dedicated to connection. The evolutionary challenge—upon which the future of the species may well depend—is for all people to discover their real and present connection with organic life, the biosphere, the cosmos, and being itself. Any religious organization not actively serving that objective is not worthy of the name.

CHAPTER 12

Real People, Transcendent Moments

My findings indicate that in the normal perceptions of self-actualizing people and in the more occasional peak experiences of average people, *perception can be relatively ego-transcending, self-forgetful, egoless.*   —ABRAHAM MASLOW[1]

Perhaps, one hopes, the day is not far off when the phenomena of Enlightenment and Liberation may be found included in the standard medical texts of psychology—and a Liberated or Enlightened person is seen not as a freak of Nature, but as the most normal, sane, uncomplicated human being that there can be.

—NITIN TRASI[2]

In the course of their association with a teacher, or in the context of a spiritual tradition, people often have transcendent experiences of one sort or another—moments of expanded understanding, of seeing self and the world in a new way. When they do, they are likely to conclude, logically enough, that the experience was the product of contact with the teacher or tradition and should be taken as confirming proof of his/her/its wisdom. And they may be right. But even when they are, no enlightenment experience or understanding is ever simply given, sold, or in any way *done to* someone by someone else. Whatever form it may take—and the possibilities appear to be enormous—it is something that grows out of the individual. This may sound paradoxical when what individuals discover is that they are *not* individuals in the usual meaning of that word. The feeling of doing something is often replaced by a sense of the thing doing itself, or being done by a larger entity that some people describe as the universe, others as God. But even that discovery expresses something that was always latent in the individual, something that may be brought out by the teaching experience but is not simply produced by it. As yet there are no recorded cases of enlightenment transplants.

You may have heard the saying, popular in Zen circles, that all of Zen is nothing more than a finger pointing the way. It's meant to remind you that, whatever you may gain from practice and instruction, the ultimate result will be something that you yourself have discovered, experienced, or figured out. Zen gets more than its share of true believers despite such warnings, but, nevertheless, the saying is laudably honest, certainly preferable to the uncritically reverent mentality that is fostered in spiritual cults and commercial operations such as est. In est the only fingers I saw were pointing to the dotted line where you signed up for more trainings.

However, the subject matter in this chapter is not cults and gurus—we just did that—but something bearing on the absence of any real reason for becoming dependent upon them. The subject is the *naturalness* of enlightenment. I contend that enlightenment—the liberation from the illusion of separateness, the deeply felt sense of being an integral part of the workings of the cosmos—is inherent in human consciousness and never far from the daily experience of every one of us, however well we may conceal it from ourselves. And one evidence of that is the remarkable number of transcendent experiences that people have without ever having received any formal spiritual instruction.

Needed: A Wider View of Normality

The view that enlightenment comes from somewhere beyond the boundaries of "normal" human life is held by true believers as well as hard-nosed skeptics, but of course in different versions: If you are one of the faithful, it takes the form of a conviction that the person who has learned to experience the world in a way different from ego-centered consciousness must be a heavy-duty spiritual being, possessed of infinite wisdom and having the right answers on any number of subjects. If you are a skeptic, it takes the form of conviction that ego-centered consciousness is the equivalent of sanity and good sense, and that any deviation from it must be either a symptom of psychopathology or a weird state of *un*consciousness achieved off there in the East someplace by skinny old men in loincloths.

Yet that assumption is no longer quite as widely held as it once was. The change is evident in popular culture and the social sciences. We are closer to having a scientifically definable and even measurable understanding of enlightenment than you might suspect. Researchers of various persuasions have been circling around this and related subjects for decades, and it is now thinkable that we might arrive at a Western-style description of enlightenment—perhaps not using that term, but as clear as any of the descriptions of pathologies that are found in the Diagnostic and Statistical Manuals, or of the various psychological traits that are measured by tests such as the Minnesota Multiphasic Personality Inventory.

An important piece is the research on experiences that happen in the lives of people more or less like you and me, but largely overlooked by conventional psychology.

The Varieties of Transcendent Experience

One of the pioneering works in this neglected area of psychology was William James' remarkable book *The Varieties of Religious Experience,* subtitled *A Study in Human Nature* and first published in 1902. James' study had its origins in his invitation to deliver the Gifford Lectures on Natural Religion at Edinburgh University, a highly prestigious assignment and a recognition of his international stature as psychologist and philosopher. The lectures he gave were a survey of recorded religious experiences, probably the most exhaustive and rigorous work of that nature that had ever been undertaken. He described such experiences in great detail; he classified, compared, and analyzed them. The conclusions he came to were in some ways congenial to conventional religious thought and in other ways they were not. He did state his conviction that religious experiences are a central, persistent, and normal element of human life, and that they have to do with a sense of being a part of a larger reality. But he could not decide whether they are a "gift of God's grace" or "a gift of the organism," nor would he describe them as in any way proving the existence of God—or even proving that belief in God is essential to religious experience. In a postscript to his study he wrote: "I feel bound to say that religious experience, as we have studied it, cannot be cited as unequivocally supporting the infinitist belief. The only thing that it unequivocally testifies to is that we can experience union with *something* larger than ourselves and in that union find our greatest peace."[3]

James' ideas were influential in the worlds of philosophy and theology, but marginalized by the psychological movements that took the high ground in the early twentieth century: The Freudians regarded anything religious with great distrust, and the behaviorists had no time for experiences that couldn't be verified in the laboratory. Then in the 1960s we began to hear about Abraham Maslow's work. In addition to believing that mainstream psychology was failing to pay sufficient attention to healthy "self-actualizing" human beings, Maslow also accused his academic colleagues of having a blind spot regarding the important (and not at all uncommon) events in human life he called "peak experiences."

Maslow deliberately chose that term to avoid the trouble a mid-twentieth-century social scientist was likely to get himself into by talking about *religious* experience. He acknowledged his debt to James' groundbreaking work but wanted to go beyond it: to expand the boundaries of academic psychology and bring the subject of transcendent experience even further into the domain of "normality" than it had been brought by James. In *Motivation and Personality* he ventured that that might be accomplished by recognizing not only the variety but the degree of such experiences:

> We may also learn from our subjects that such experiences can occur in a lesser degree of intensity. The theological literature has generally assumed an absolute, qualitative difference between the mystic experience and all others. As soon as it is divorced from supernatural reference and studied as a natural

phenomenon, it becomes possible to place the mystic experience on a quantitative continuum from intense to mild. We discover that the mild mystic experience occurs in many, perhaps even most individuals, and that in the favored individual it occurs often, perhaps even daily.[4]

More recently, University of Chicago psychologist Mihaly Csik-szentmihalyi undertook a systematic study of a different but still closely related subject area he calls "optimal experience" or "flow." These are the moments when, without sacrificing our individuality, we nevertheless lose ourselves completely in an activity—in the *doing* of it rather than in the *purpose* of doing it. Flow, he writes, "is the way people describe their state of mind when consciousness is harmoniously ordered, and they want to pursue whatever they are doing for their own sake."[5]

Csikszentmihalyi's concept of flow experiences is even wider and less explicitly religious or mystical than Maslow's peak experiences. It includes any moment when attention is concentrated, when inner conflict and self-consciousness are swept away by immersion in an activity—working, dancing, climbing a mountain, playing a game, tending a garden. In such experiences, he believes, many people bring about a temporary restructuring of their consciousness—not a loss of self or consciousness, only a loss of consciousness of the self: "What slips below the threshold of awareness is the *concept* of self, the information we use to represent to ourselves who we are." Like James' accounts of religious experiences, these moments of flow involve a sense of merging with some larger entity:

During the long watches of the night the solitary sailor begins to feel that the boat is an extension of himself, moving to the same rhythms toward a common goal. The violinist, wrapped in the stream of sound she helps to create, feels as if she is part of the "harmony of the spheres." The climber, focusing all her attention on the small irregularities of the rock wall that will have to support her weight safely, speaks of the sense of kinship that develops between fingers and rock, between the frail body and the context of stone, sky, and wind. In a chess tournament, players whose attention has been riveted, for hours, to the logical battle on the board claim that they feel as if they have been merged into a powerful "field of force" clashing with other forces in some nonmaterial dimension of existence. Surgeons say that during a difficult operation they have the sensation that the entire operating team is a single organism, moved by the same purpose; they describe it as a "ballet" in which the individual is subordinated to the group performance, and all involved share in a feeling of harmony and power.[6]

At this point you might reasonably wonder, if there are so many degrees and varieties of self-transcendent experience, and—if transcendence does indeed wander so easily in and out of the lives of violinists and surgeons and chess players, whether the word means anything at all. Is there any clear boundary separating, say, what you are doing right now from a moment of powerful insight? I would have to say in reply that, (a) there is no such clear boundary, and (b) the more pronounced transcendent experiences are nevertheless real and quite different from ego-centered consciousness, even though the two modes of being may interpenetrate or coexist. But even the more powerful and unmistakable experiences come in many shapes and sizes, as I am going to show with a few examples.

When Life Is Not Elsewhere

In this chapter we will look at three accounts of powerful enlightenment experiences, one taken from published works and the others adapted from talks with people I know. You'll note that along with the common themes there is a variety in how these experiences come about, what form they take, and how they affect the person. One of the common themes is a sense of being part of and continuous with a larger entity. Another is a sense of discovery, of *difference:* the world is the same, yet it is seen and understood in an entirely new way. A third is a rush of feeling; enlightenment experiences definitely have an emotional component, difficult to describe but unmistakably a part of what happens. And a fourth theme—often overlooked in accounts of such experiences—is simply presence: The person is not thinking about being anywhere else, or doing anything else. He or she is fully in that moment.

The novelist Milan Kundera must know something about enlightenment, or he would not write books with titles like *The Incredible Lightness of Being* and *Life Is Elsewhere*. It is remarkable, if you stop to think about it, how much of life *is* elsewhere—how little time we really spend in the here and now and how much of our cognition is highjacked by anticipations, recollections, regrets, and fantasies about other things that we think we should or might like to be doing instead. But the experiences we somewhat inappropriately call "transcendent" are the times when the person is fully engaged in what is happening; they are in a way more "real" than the experiences we customarily think of as normal and realistic.

The Man Who Lost His Head

Enlightenment experiences come in many flavors, and I know of none that seems more peculiar, at least when you first encounter it, than that related by an elderly Englishman named Douglas Harding.

I first heard about Harding and the followers of his rather curious teachings at a psychology conference in Miami in the early 1970s. The intelligence came not in one of the formal presentations but in an evening gathering in the hotel's cocktail lounge, where a woman was regaling us with accounts of a recent trip she had taken to Europe to visit some of the British and Continental manifestations of the human potential movement. She talked about meeting a group of people in England who believed they had no heads.

No heads! It was wonderful, 1970s spiritual goofiness at its finest.

After that, I heard about Douglas Harding from time to time, and in the late 1990s I went to a lecture in San Francisco to see and hear the headless man in person. From my point of view he had a head, complete with white hair, beard, and smiling face. But that, of course, was the subject of the lecture. Because, as he explained to us, he had no head for himself.

Harding's first encounter with this strange experience had taken place during World War II, when he was a British soldier stationed in India and an invasion from the east by Japanese forces seemed imminent. As soldiers commonly do in such situations, he found it necessary to contemplate the possibility that he might die in battle. This led him to intense questioning: Who was this person that might die, anyway? He writes that he was deeply engaged for several months with asking himself "Who am I?" and that one day in the course of a solitary walk, while taking stock of his own experience of himself, he suddenly underwent a profound cognitive reorganization, and he looked at everything around him in a new way:

What actually happened (he writes in his memoir) was something absurdly simple and unspectacular: just for the moment I stopped thinking. Reason and emotion and all mental chatter died down. For once, words really failed me. I forgot my name, my humanness, my thingness, all that could be called me or mine. Past and future dropped away. It was as if I had been born that instant, brand new, mindless, innocent of all memories. There existed only the Now, that present moment and what was clearly given in it. To look was enough. And what I found was khaki trouserlegs terminating downwards in a pair of brown shoes, khaki sleeves terminating sideways in a pair of pink hands, and a khaki shirtfront terminating upwards in— absolutely nothing whatever! Certainly not in a head.

It took me no time at all to notice that this hole where a head should have been, was no ordinary vacancy, no mere nothing. On the contrary, it was very much occupied. It was a vast emptiness vastly filled, a nothing that found room for everything— room for grass, trees, shadowy distant hills, and far above them snow-peaks like a row of angular clouds riding in the blue sky. I had lost a head and gained a world.[7]

Harding excitedly told his fellow soldiers about having no head, and of course they thought he had gone 'round the bend. He writes that he felt a great loneliness and frustration, even while he remained convinced that what he had experienced was not an hallucination but a correct, realistic, and important description of the way all people see the world: You know you have a head, of course, but you do not have a head *for yourself,* in your own field of vision. Harding survived the war and went on to write books, to become an acclaimed teacher, and to gain a wide circle of admirers and followers, including the headless people my friend met in London.

The experience he describes certainly includes the basic elements common to transcendent experiences: the sense of being continuous with the "world outside," the changed sense of self, the complete immersion in the moment. And the funny thing about the part that seems most bizarre—the sense of not having a head—is that it's exactly the way we all see the world; we just don't think we see it that way, or that it's anything worth noticing. It happened that Harding's spontaneous shift of perspective opened the door for him (and, I'm told, by others who deliberately adopted the practice) to a realization that the way of looking most of us favor all the time is a constructed worldview. Our moment-to-moment experience is filtered through the continuing sense of persona, of the face that the world sees looking back.

Abe's Group

Over a period of several years, during which I was thinking about and writing this book, I was in intermittent contact with a few people who met periodically in the office of a psychotherapist to discuss, in the most informal way you could imagine, the subject of enlightenment.

Abe Levitsky is a psychologist of the gestalt school, trained first in psychoanalysis and later as a student and personal friend of Fritz Perls. Abe has long been interested in Eastern philosophy, and he has gone about it with a combination of open-mindedness and skepticism that I have never encountered among all the other seekers I have known over the years. I particularly remember a time when the two of us had been granted a private audience with an eminent Tibetan lama who was passing through the Bay Area. When we met with him in person we were invited to ask questions, and Abe posed one that I thought was devastatingly direct. He said: "Is your life any better than mine, and if so, how?"

Oddly enough, although I remember the question vividly, I don't recall the answer—or even whether there was one. The lama had a bad cold at the time, had just sent somebody to buy him some medicine, and was heavily occupied with blowing his nose. It was fairly apparent that, although his life was different from Abe's, it wasn't much better at that particular moment. However, my sense of the occasion was not so much that the psychologist had one-upped the lama; rather it was that Abe had posed the right question, the one that probably lurks somewhere in the minds of most people who explore such matters: everything you wanted to know about enlightenment but were afraid to ask.

A couple of decades later, Abe was inviting some people to meet once a week or so to consider the implications of the experiences reported by two of his former clients, experiences that sounded rather more Eastern than Western, somewhat like those described by Herbert Fingarette in his research with people who had been through psychoanalysis. One was Steve Berkov, a physician; the other was Linda Brandon, a graphic designer. What follows is a brief summary of their own reports on these experiences. I don't offer these as case studies. These are merely informal accounts of moments in the lives of two people I know:

Steve Berkov and Luminous Nonbeing

Steve is an M.D. who had spent some twenty-odd years as an emergency room doctor by the time he came to Abe. He had recently been diagnosed as having an inoperable brain tumor and given a short while to live. He sought counseling to help him deal with this and get his affairs in order—and then the medical diagnosis was revised; he was told he had only suffered a stroke, did not have a brain tumor after all, and was not about to die.

Sudden release from a death sentence seems in its own way to have been as traumatic as the first diagnosis. As Steve was in the process of adjusting to his new life situation, he had two profound experiences, about a week apart, each while walking in the woods with his dog Sadie. The first could perhaps be best described as a flow or peak experience; the second was an enlightenment. The following is edited from tapes of several different sessions and conversations in which he describes them:

> After coming out of this illness and feeling good, there was this sense of suddenly realizing that I didn't have to have things be the way they were before. There was nothing I needed to do. I didn't understand what that meant, but I wasn't doing anything. I was just feeling good about life. And I also had this profound sense that just walking in the woods and being aware of the beauty of it was the whole purpose of life. I had never been somebody to think there were purposes in the universe, that sort of thing, but I had this clear sense that if you *could* define a purpose it was that I was there to appreciate the beauty of life. That made sense to me, but it was still Steve Berkov's eyes that were being opened.
>
> About a week later I was walking in the woods again. I looked up at the sky, and then something happened that to this day is very difficult for me to describe. You know how if you just stare into space for a while, things will lose their definition, get washed out? That happened, and all of a sudden I sort of spaced out, and then found myself with an awareness of coming back from someplace. The only way I can describe it is a place of luminous nonbeing. There was nothing and then everything was back, and back like a thunderclap. And in that moment I absolutely understood that it was not my consciousness that was

there. What I had thought was *my* consciousness was *all* consciousness, universal consciousness in which Steve Berkov was one of the many elements.

That experience was so powerful it damn near knocked me off my feet. I stopped, and Sadie, who had been running ahead, came back wondering what I was doing. She wasn't the only one.

I felt shaken and weak, kind of disoriented. I was so fatigued, I was concerned about whether I could handle the 45 minute walk back to my house. It was not a jaunty walk, I was dragging. I made it, and slept about an hour after I got home, and then when I woke up everything was different. The disorientation and the confusion were gone. I had this absolute clarity about the origin of my being of who I am—not as Steve Berkov, but as *all*. I knew it like I've never known anything in my life.

Steve is no longer a client of Abe's, more of a friend and collaborator. The two sometimes appear together on panel discussions about the psychology of enlightenment, and in these sessions Steve is frequently quizzed by the audience about the details of his experience. He is often asked why he talks about "luminous nonbeing," a term nobody seems to have heard before. Steve simply answers that he doesn't know why the term applies, but it does and it is in some way inseparable from his ongoing consciousness of being himself. He is still Steve Berkov and feeling more alive and human than before the experience, but somewhere in the background is the knowledge of the luminous nonbeing, the frisky nothing. They ask how he can go about the business of acting like an ordinary person, and he says:

When I'm sitting around talking with people I feel as separate as anybody else but on another level I know it's the universe that's doing it. We're not separate and we're not doing it. What I now experience more or less continuously, is this sense of non-separateness, and also the socially constructed self, Steve Berkov running around living his life. Those two things I experience simultaneously. They're only different when I choose to see them that way, but it's all one. It's what we all are, that's what there is.

Steve lives a quiet life, appearing on panels when Abe organizes them. He recently remarried (he was divorced at the time of the experiences described above), and he and his wife are building a new house. He drives around in a red sports car and looks like an ordinary doctor—and perhaps he is; he recently referred me to a Web site entirely about scientists, including a number of M.D.s, who have had transcendent experiences.[8]

Linda Brandon and Infinite Compassion

Linda Brandon is an attractive woman in her fifties—brown hair, a quick smile, a certain mix of warmth and shyness. Like Steve, she had sought counseling to help her get through some difficult times. "Difficult times" is a wimpy phrase for the series of events that hammered her life in the mid-1990s:

First she was evicted from her home, a rented house she had grown to love, after the owner died. She moved in with her boyfriend Karl, with whom she had had a close (and she believed exclusive) relationship for over ten years, only to find soon afterward that he was having an affair with another woman. That was a heartbreaker, she says, and she and Karl went into therapy together. The affair ended, but then Karl developed lymphoma. Around that time, she had had to leave the company where she had been working for some twenty years, and she had started her own graphic design business. But as Karl's condition worsened and he became unable to work, caring for him took more and more of her time and energy. She lost her main client and was slowly using up her life savings. Karl was hospitalized and near death, but he wanted to die at home. They persuaded Karl's landlord to give him his wish, although he was clearly furious about it.

Three days after Karl died, the landlord gave Linda an eviction notice. In the next few months she was hit by two lawsuits. The first plaintiff was a woman with whom she had been involved in a minor auto accident two years before and who apparently had been advised to go after some money from her insurance company. The second was Karl's landlord, who claimed deferred maintenance damages from the years Karl had lived in the house. Meanwhile, her father died of a heart attack and her remaining family broke apart as siblings and in-laws squabbled bitterly with one another about distribution of inherited property. Her cat died. With all the stresses in her life, it was an almost unbearable loss.

I have left out a few details, but you get the general idea: dislocations, losses, disasters, and betrayals, people being avaricious and cruel. Enough to turn anyone into a misanthrope, but what happened was almost the exact opposite: One morning she woke up feeling an enormous sense of joy and compassion that extended to everything. Afterward, that feeling came and went many times:

> Frequently it would happen when I would walk through a doorway. One time I walked into the Safeway—I remember that there was a man in front of me pushing a shopping cart and he was limping, a crippled man, and I felt such love for him. This is not normal for me. This store is not in a very safe part of town and usually when I went there I had my armor up. I was feeling the goodness of every soul and pushing my shopping cart down the aisle and saying, "What is going on here?" It was so amazing.
>
> As I had more experiences and started to have some insight into them, my whole sense of my self as being separate from everything out there changed. One time I was getting a massage: I put some music on and, where in the past it would have been very clear that I was on the massage table and the masseuse was giving me a massage, and the music was over there, that changed and I didn't have a sense of myself on the table listening to music. There was just music, and I was wrapped around every note and not different from it. And there was no differ-

ence between the getting and the giving of the massage—there was just the massage.

Those first experiences were just lovely experiences, unusual and strange. The one I think the most significant and really pivotal happened one evening when I was chopping vegetables. I happened to look out the window and I watched a blue jay just through swallowing some water. Time stood still and I saw into the heart of things. I experienced a golden glow and a presence of such great magnitude that nothing in my life prepared me for what I experienced. I understood in those moments that this living presence is everywhere and everything, indivisible and beyond measure. Birth and death, time and space do not apply. The experience of it was boundless love and the knowledge that there is nothing that is not this. The somatic experience was like being crushed with love. I felt like a glass vessel holding something that it couldn't possible hold, and about to break.

All I could do was cry. Then the phone rang and the world came back again. I answered the phone. It was a friend, and I told her that I didn't know what was happening to me and I would just have to talk to her later. I hung up and I was sitting there for 10 or 15 minutes, and then Abe called. It's not like Abe calls a lot, because Abe doesn't like to talk on the phone. He wanted to ask me to do something, I think tape a football game. I said I was ok. I was in the process of covering this up, of telling myself that nothing had happened, if you can believe that. But there must have been something peculiar in the way I was acting. Abe said something like, "So how are you?" I was quiet and he said, "You can tell the truth." So I told him what had just happened, and practically in the same breath I started making excuses for it, covering it up, and he said: "Wait a minute. I think you have just had a very important experience."

After that, she had many more experiences of suddenly shifting into an expanded consciousness. She was also aware that her senses were becoming more acute. Using a graphic-design metaphor, she says it felt as though she had been seeing the world all her life as a coarse black-and-white newspaper photograph and was now seeing it in full color. Her sense of hearing changed in the same way. All this felt exhilarating but also frightening at times, and she experienced a good deal of anxiety as she went through the process of becoming a different person than she had been before. She is still assimilating the change and getting used to living with what she calls "unitive consciousness." She is also doing well in her work and has recently purchased a house.

I would describe both Steve and Linda as happier and healthier than average. Both have done some reading and exploring into Eastern enlightenment traditions since their experiences, but neither seems inclined to become actively involved with any spiritual group or movement. Both are willing to talk openly about their experiences, but neither shows the slightest hint of guru aspirations. Abe refuses the guru role even more vigorously, and at the various occasions where he has spoken publicly along with Steve, and, more recently, Linda, about their experiences, he hastens to make it clear to the audience that he has never had any such experience himself.

You undoubtedly will have noticed that in addition to the commonalties I mentioned earlier, the experiences of Douglas Harding, Steve Berkov, and Linda Brandon shared a close encounter with matters of life and death. For Harding it was the prospect of dying some time soon in military action; for Steve, the recent shattering experience of believing that death was imminent and then learning it was not; for Linda, a devastating series of personal misfortunes, including the death of a lover and a parent. Such brushes with tragedy are not reported as factors in all transcendent experiences, but they seem to be highly common, particularly in proximity to the more powerful ones. Huston Smith observes: "The most emphatic epiphanies are those that arrive in times of darkness and despair."[9] Dr. Samuel Johnson, a man of a more secular turn of mind, once remarked that the prospect of imminent death clears the mind wonderfully.

Yet another commonality is that none of the three was in search of

enlightenment or actively involved with any practice or spiritual tradition. Neither Steve nor Linda had any particular interest in such
matters. Steve, who has a Ph.D. in pharmacology as well as an M.D.,
regarded himself as primarily a scientist and still does; Linda says she
always "ran away from spiritual things." Both live in the San Francisco Bay area where spirituality is part of the cultural furniture, but
the concept of enlightenment has been much more of a factor in how
they made sense of the peak experience *after it occurred* than in how
they came to arrive at it. Similarly, Douglas Harding had his moment
of powerful insight in India, world capital of matters mystical, but he
did not undertake to explore those traditions until later.

Throwing Some Light on Enlightenment

In the course of becoming acquainted with Steve and Linda and
learning about what has been going on in their lives, what I have
found amazing is that two people out of a fairly small statistical sam-
ple group—Abe's clients—happened to have experiences and arrive at
insights that match so closely those you frequently encounter in books
about enlightenment traditions, even though they had had no immersion in them. And the question that comes to haunt me is: How many
others, in or out of those traditions, have had similar experiences and
arrived at similar insights? I am coming to suspect that many, perhaps
even most people have had experiences somewhere along the flow-
peak-transcendence spectrum and simply didn't know how to talk
about them, or feared talking about them, or sought psychological
counseling and had them diagnosed away as pathological. Is there
another silent majority out there? Any answer would depend on how
generously you set the boundaries, what experiences you choose to
accept as in some degree transcendent.

Neurologist James Austin, in his book *Zen and the Brain,* reviews
the findings of several different surveys that attempted to arrive at
some numbers: One found that 31 percent of the adult population
reported having a sudden or dramatic religious or mystical experience
at some time in their lives; another found that between 33 and 43 per-

cent answered affirmatively to a question of whether they had ever been very close to a powerful spiritual force that seemed to lift them outside of themselves; and in a survey done in Great Britain, 35 percent of the respondents said they had been affected by a power different from their everyday selves. A significant number who responded in the affirmative associated the experiences with nonreligious contexts such as nature or art.[10]

The findings are interesting but don't really answer my question. We don't have enough information of that sort to do what needs to be done—bring the whole subject of enlightenment into the mainstream of Western thought so that people can understand it and relate it to their own life experience in whatever way makes sense for them.

It has been over a hundred years since Western researchers began undertaking scientific studies of enlightenment; William James' *Varieties of Religious Experience* was published in 1902, Bucke's *Cosmic Consciousness* a year earlier. We have made a lot of progress since then, with wider acceptance by psychologists of ideas such as peak and flow experience, but still not enough. We should have more surveys—more rigorous and in greater depth—and extensive longitudinal studies of people who have had or think they have had major transcendent experiences.

We also need better understanding of the cognitive structures of such people—how they think, how they do or do not revise their values and beliefs: How do these experiences and the insights generated by them relate to the developmental stages studied by such researchers as Piaget, Kohlberg, Gilligan, and Kegan? How can the reports or the results of transcendent experiences be tested or verified? How do or do not the reported cognitive changes fit into all the research on brain waves and the physiology of meditation? This investigation should be explored with the attitude that characterizes scientific research at its best, when it combines a healthy skepticism with openness and creativity.

Some people fear that such a barrage of investigation—with statistics on peak experiences piling up in the data banks and white-coated scientists poking into the lives of people who have had transcendent experiences—would sort of take the mystery out of it. I don't worry about that at all. The physicists and astronomers have not succeeded in making the cosmos any less weird, and I don't think we are in any imminent danger of taking the mystery out of human being, life, or consciousness.

This investigation should become a part—perhaps the central and integrative part—of the next Enlightenment. It would give a new coherence to the various cosmological, psychological, and epistemological explorations that are already under way as we move toward an understanding of the human being as an organism that is not only growing up in society but growing up in the world, and in the universe.

CHAPTER 13

Personal Evolution:
Becoming Who You Are

Ask, and it shall be given you; seek, and ye shall find; knock, and
it shall be opened unto you.   — MATTHEW 7:7

And over time, and with repeated cautioning by the roshi, the aspi-
rant realizes the deeper level of wisdom in Dogen's old statement:
"Cut off the mind that seeks, and do not cherish a desire to gain
the fruits of Buddhahood." The hot pursuit of enlightenment is
seen to be but another form of grasping, spiritual materialism.
                                        — JAMES H. AUSTIN[1]

Enlightenment doesn't care how you get there.
                                        — THADDEUS GOLAS[2]

The stronger the case becomes for the kind of personal development variously called enlightenment, liberation, or awakening
being a real and natural part of human adult development, the more
people are likely to wonder how they might make some progress in
that direction themselves. What do you do? What do you need?

Today, all over the world, tens of thousands are already looking for
answers to these questions—in the traditional spiritual disciplines, in
cults, and in all manner of practices and exercises. Some of the practices are expensive, some are highly demanding—marathon meditation sessions, strenuous yogas. People sometimes sacrifice money and
time to follow them, making drastic changes in their personal lives
and placing themselves completely under the authority of teachers
who profess to have the answer.

They also buy things: I used to have a friend who frequently developed new enthusiasms, mostly having to do with self-improvement.

That in itself is not peculiar. What was peculiar—and peculiarly American, I suspect—was the way he went about it. His first step was always in the direction of a shopping mall, where he would acquire as many objects relevant to the new project as he could manage to purchase. Since his enthusiasms came and went, his house was an elephant's graveyard of things left over from previous ones—exercising machines, tape recorders and lesson materials, musical instruments, self-help books, martial arts uniforms. When he decided to take up meditation he of course purchased the official Japanese *zafu* pillow and *zabuton* mat and set up a little shrine to the Buddha with several different varieties of incense.

I often think of old Ed on the days when the mailman brings me—as he periodically does—beautiful catalogs of material designed to help me unlock the mysteries of my mind. One offers recorded material such as the nine-CD "Transcendental Mind Library," which includes "Zen Healing Chants," "Amazon Shaman," "Voodoo Mating Ritual," "Eskimo Spirits," and "Aboriginal Dreamtime." Another sells books on similar subjects; yet another features a luxurious array of meditation pillows in various shapes and colors. How about a Zen alarm clock? It not only wakes you up in the morning, it has chimes that can be used to "enhance dream memories, use self-suggestion while your brain is in its alpha stage, and achieve more satisfying meditation." It costs $106.

So what do you really need? Well, nothing: no *thing*, at all. No harm in having a Japanese meditation pillow around the house, but don't expect it to do anything special for you. Might come in handy to throw at the cat.

The Open Toolbox

Most if not all of the countless methods and techniques aimed at restructuring consciousness are in the public domain; there really aren't any secrets. All of them are essentially ways of investigating your own conscious experience, most are things that you might do well to explore and/or add to your life, and there is not a single one that you should expect to lead you straight to enlightenment of any degree or kind. Despite this, many spiritual leaders have yielded to the temptation to guarantee results to those who would follow their path: The Maharishi Mahesh Yogi, for example, used to assure his students that they would definitely attain enlightenment through six to eight years of Transcendental Meditation.[3] Other students of such matters such as Nitin Trasi, the Indian physician and author of *The Science of Enlightenment,* declare with equal certainty that "there is no particular regime of activity, or technique, or type of meditation, which will result in enlightenment." Trasi contends instead that enlightenment is a "natural tendency," which is obstructed by fixed ideas and beliefs. The only practice, then, is to seek understanding—especially of your own fixed ideas and beliefs—and then get the hell out of the way:

> Our volitional spiritual "effort" can only reach as far as trying to understand the situation intellectually. . . . Any other (apparently) volitional activity on our part aimed at the achievement of Enlightenment, being me-based, is bound to strengthen the me-illusion, making us go round in circles, like a dog chasing its tail, or like a man trying to kick himself in the rear. But intellectual understanding, even though initially occurring as a result of me-based effort, makes us aware of this very fact, and when this fact is clearly seen the effort (even further effort at intellectual understanding), eventually ceases to be me-based.[4]

In this chapter I am going to discuss some practices that can profitably be used as ways of "understanding the situation." And, more or less in the spirit of Dr. Trasi's remarks, I suggest that they *not* be pursued as efforts to achieve enlightenment. Do not approach them with the mindset in which you might set forth to lose weight, improve your salesmanship skills, or build up your abdominal muscles. Think of them instead as experiments—ways that you might investigate this subject without waiting for the definitive academic research project.

This approach is quite similar to what a gestalt therapist some years ago described as "the paradoxical theory of change," in which the emphasis is not to instruct the patient in what she should do, but rather to increase her awareness of what she is currently doing: *"Change occurs when one becomes what he is, not when he tries to become what he is not.* Change does not take place through a coercive attempt by the individual or another person to change him, but it does take place if one takes the time and effort to be what he is—fully invested in his current positions. By rejecting the role of change agent, we make meaningful and orderly change possible."[5]

The emphasis on investigation, becoming aware of what you are already doing and how you are now being, has to do with the proposition that our everyday consciousness is crowded with assumptions that we do not recognize as assumptions; interpretations and constructions of reality that we take to be reality itself; cognitive actions—such as reification, the game of turning processes into people, places, or things—that we do not normally see or understand, even though we are doing them. These shape our way of organizing experience, structure our ideas about who and what we are, and set the boundaries that separate us from the surrounding world. The act of investigation, however you might carry it out, tends to have an effect somewhat comparable to what happens when your eyes adjust to a darkened room; you begin to notice things you had never noticed before and reorganize your understanding accordingly.

The Sitting Brain

Seated meditation is easily the best-known practice of this sort, so much that many people regard it as the definitive mark of Eastern enlightenment traditions. It isn't; there are many such traditions whose methods of self-investigation don't involve sitting cross-legged on a mat, and the practice is not even universal in all of Buddhism. It is mainly associated with Zen Buddhism, "Zen" being a word handed down from Sanskrit by way of Chinese that roughly means "meditation."

In addition to being the best-known form of practice, sitting meditation also has been the one most extensively studied by scientists. For over a half-century, researchers in numerous countries have conducted experiments with Zen monks and other advanced meditators. They have established conclusively that brain wave changes do take place during meditation, and also that there are differences between the brain patterns of Zen meditators and Yogis. Joe Kamiya at the Langley Porter Neuropsychiatric Institute in San Francisco also showed that other people could be trained through feedback techniques to control their brain waves and achieve patterns somewhat similar to those of the meditators. Physiological changes of various kinds—involving blood pressure and heart rate, for example—are well documented also, and explain why meditation is often recommended by physicians.[6]

What you do while you are sitting there on your cushion or in your chair will, of course, depend on what kind of instruction you may have received or heard about: being aware of the breath, counting exhalations, focusing your vision on an object in front of you, repeating a mantra. Students of Zen are often encouraged to pay attention to the flow of thoughts, not to force them in any direction but simply to watch them come and go, and to observe that there is a silent observer, a cognitive process that stands somewhat apart from the verbalized thoughts.

The research tells you a lot about what happens in your brain and body during meditation, but it does not tell you which approach is the best. Meditation teachers sometimes act as though there *is* a best way, and that you are in big spiritual trouble if you don't sit, breathe, or direct your thoughts according to a certain set of instructions. And there may well be some value in the discipline of learning a specific method and practicing it the traditional way. Just remember that the method is not the point. The point is This.

Meditation is also about unconscious processes. Although it is not in itself a state of unconsciousness, it is aimed at producing states of relaxation—and perhaps some form of cognition—in the two-thirds of your brain that are not your ordinary conscious mind. Researchers can tell clearly with their instruments that such states are being produced, but they cannot tell why or what is actually going on.

However esoteric meditation may be, it is solidly grounded in the unastonishing hypothesis that mental activity is *material* activity. The mind is not separate from the body. As they say in Zen: When the body sits, the mind sits. In the process of sitting, relaxing the body, and slowing down breath and metabolism, meditation puts the mind into a receptive state for observing thoughts, or perhaps for entertaining some new ones.

Meditation is not for everyone. I like it because I like silence. But I used to know an intelligent and rather verbal woman from New York City who said she had tried it several times, and it always gave her a headache.

Thought Experiments

Albert Einstein and his colleagues used to engage in "thought experiments" as a way of investigating scientific propositions that could not always be tested in the laboratory, and I will describe five exercises that can be used as experiments in consciousness. All are derived from various enlightenment traditions and/or schools of psychotherapy; all are, in a sense, exercises in phenomenology, ways of exploring your own human being-in-the-world:

1. "I AM"

In some spiritual schools the core practice, which may be carried on for long, long stretches of time, is a dialogue in which the teacher asks the question: "Who are you?" over and over until the student either runs out of answers, or perceives that all social definitions are illusory and that who he or she truly is, in a sense, is nobody. Douglas Harding was unwittingly following that practice when he pondered the question of who the man was who might not survive World War II.

Along the same lines, the late Indian teacher Nisargadatta—a man who had achieved a reputation for enlightenment, and whose crowded rooms in Bombay were visited by seekers from all over the world—offered a very simple prescription: "Refuse all thoughts except one: the thought 'I am.' The mind will rebel in the beginning, but with patience and perseverance it will yield and keep quiet. Once you are quiet, things will begin to happen spontaneously and quite naturally, without any interference on your part."7

This relates to the proposition, a thread running through all enlightenment traditions, that we don't really know who and what we are. But it also relates to the belief of existential psychotherapists such as Rollo May that we repress our own sense of existence, and that the recovery of mental health involves a "discovery of being" in which we find—usually to our pleasant surprise—that we're really here.

2. DROPPING IT

In an earlier chapter I mentioned the famous Zen parable about a student who comes to a master in search of enlightenment. The master tells him to drop what he holds in his right hand. The student obligingly drops the object. The master then tells him to drop what he holds in his left hand, and another object hits the floor. Then the master asks him what he still holds in his hands.

"Nothing," replies the student.

"Drop it," commands the master. And the student is immediately enlightened (the happy ending that frequently comes at the conclusion of Zen parables).

The parable is easily taken as a command, like those so frequently found in religious and spiritual traditions, to give away all your personal possessions and go naked in the world. This is the course pursued by people who have taken religious vows, by the Buddhist monks who go about with nothing but a begging bowl for their daily rice, and perhaps most thoroughly, by the Jain holy men of India who go about naked—a spiritual discipline best pursued in a warm climate.

But it can also be interpreted as the token for a thought experiment, one that can be practiced at any time and place, an exercise in deliberately constructing reality differently without attempting to alter what is actually taking place. The exercise is to simply let go of one's sense of the self as present in the experience. Drop it, so to speak.

If you can perform that cognitive maneuver, you find yourself taking a brief stroll through the state of mind that is commonly described in accounts of enlightenment experiences, and it is a recurrent theme of Zen literature:

> Thoughts without a thinker
> Sounds, but no one who hears

Like so many aspects of Zen, such an idea seems quite goofy when first encountered, and completely sensible when experienced. It is simply a matter of being awake and alive without processing all of experience through the ego, and, of course, of discovering that particular viewpoint on life is not the totality of your consciousness.

3. THOU ART THAT

This experiment is really a variation on the "I am" exercise, but approaches the question of who and what you are along a somewhat different path. It involves an application of the ancient motto *tat twam asi*—thou art that—and a deliberate shift of perspective.

Ordinary ego-centered consciousness, the way most of us think most of the time, proceeds from the unquestioned assumption that what you are is an entity surrounded by an environment of things that are separate and distinct from yourself. The essence of this experiment is to look about and imagine that *all the things you are seeing and experiencing at the moment* are what you are. And what you are changes as you move, as the environment changes, and as other things are felt, smelled, heard, tasted, seen; instead of a skin-encapsulated ego, you are an ever-shifting kaleidoscope of consciousness.

This experiment can lead easily into the kind of flow experience described by Csikszentmihalyi; it is also one of the most common phenomena in recorded accounts of enlightenment or mystical experience—a sudden, unsolicited sense of unity with some object in the field of vision—sometimes a single object, other times the entire environment.

The experiment can be nothing more than a pleasant diversion on a hike, a morning run, or (my favorite time for this particular practice) a long drive. It can also be a powerful introduction to the reality (rather than the concept) of the construction of thought as you switch back and forth from one mode to another.

4 . SILENCE

Ego-based consciousness—the whole business of structuring the world in a certain way—swims along on a river of words, and it can be a most interesting insight into your own thought process simply to shut up inside for a second or two: not just stop talking but stop verbalizing.

I say "a second or two" because that is quite likely as long as you will be able to do it when you first try the experiment. But with a bit of practice you may find it possible, interesting, and surprisingly pleasant to cease the internal monologue and either focus without that distraction on what you see and hear, or to close the eyes and merely experience consciousness in deep silence and discover that there can be such a thing.

This is a commonly taught meditative practice, and it is also an exercise recommended as a way of recovering personal awareness in one of the key works of gestalt therapy—that school founded by the eminently unspiritual Fritz Perls:

> Try to keep internally silent, to refrain from subvocal talking—yet remain awake and aware. At first you will be able to do this for no more than a few seconds at a time, for the thinking will obsessively start up again. So, to begin with, be content simply to notice the difference between internal silence and talking, but let them alternate. . . . If you persist in your performance of this experiment, what you visualize will become brighter, your body-sensations more definite, your emotions clearer, for the attention and energy used up in pointless talking will now be invested in these simpler and more basic functions.[8]

5 . BRUSHING YOUR TEETH IN THE UNIVERSE

Let us assume, for the purposes of this thought experiment, that you are in general agreement with the big bang theory of the origins of the universe and contemporary thinking about its evolution—the explosion out of nothing; the conversion of gases to matter; the formation of stars and planets; the appearance of life on earth, and then of consciousness, and then of symbol-using, self-reflective human consciousness. If you do see things this way, and if you don't believe yourself to be somehow separate from this series of events, you might try sometime—say, when you are brushing your teeth in the morning—contemplating the eminently rational proposition that what you are doing and seeing is an integral part of those processes: The universe is not only going about its mysterious business with quarks and black holes and supernovae; it is also brushing its (your) teeth.

Try it and see where it leads you. Where it leads me is into a sense of wonder, a new discovery of being akin to some of the fresh experiences so commonly recorded in the various enlightenment texts.

"What miracle is this!" goes a Zen saying. "I draw water and I carry wood."

What miracle is this: Something emerges out of nothing and, fourteen billion years later, takes the form of words being written on a computer screen. Molecules spinning about the galaxy settle into the more or less stable forms of pine trees outside my window, an expanse of blue water, the Golden Gate Bridge. Others take the form of a woman in a gray pith helmet delivering the mail.

What miracle is this: The debris settled out of long-dead stars takes the form of you reading a book.

All of the above thought experiments are offered as a means to give some intellectual understanding of enlightenment states and, perhaps, an enhanced acquaintance with your own cognitive processes. I do not promise that, in exploring them, you will get swept away on a wave of transcendent experience. They happen, but they seem to have a volition of their own.

The Drug Problem(s)

Psychoactive chemicals are the most problematic, the most pervasive, and quite possibly the most powerful of all the methods for the exploration of consciousness, the things that modern societies can't live with but don't seem to be able to live without.

Today there is much talk about the drug problem, meaning the global trade in illicit substances, the overuse of hard drugs such as cocaine and heroin, and the attendant crimes and degradation of human life. That's the official drug problem. Actually we have a number of drug problems in the world today. Listed, but not in order of importance, they are:

1. **The official drug problem** as described above. However much it may be overblown by our political leaders, it is a real problem: There really is a vast international network of illegal transport and sale of narcotics, much of it conducted by vicious criminals. There really are tragic effects on people's lives as a result of addiction, adverse physical and mental effects of drug abuse, and crimes committed by addicts.
2. **Overuse and misuse** of psychoactive drugs in treatment of emotional disorders. Drugs are often rather promiscuously prescribed by doctors and relentlessly hyped by the companies that manufacture them. Sometimes they are inappropriate substitutes for other modes of therapy or other health practices. People often become addicted to "legal" drugs. There is a vast shadow land of prescription drugs that are smuggled across borders, sold, or stolen for personal use having little connection with what may be printed on the label. Psychoactive drugs are massively used in mental hospital and penal institutions, at least as frequently for purposes of control as for therapy.
3. **Inequitable access** to drugs. To cite only one of many examples: Antidepressants are widely used in rich countries, but are rarely available to poor people who suffer just as much, if not more, from illnesses such as chronic depression.
4. **Prohibitions** against use of drugs such as Ecstasy, LSD, marijuana, and mescaline, which have well-documented effectiveness in psychotherapy as well as the ability to produce a wide range of peak/enlightenment experiences. When and if the nations of the

world become truly civilized, they will have laws, regulations, and educational institutions to permit and actively encourage the use of such chemicals in psychological research and in responsible settings by religious, spiritual, or secular groups that use them for the enhancement of personal development. Today, most people are so paralyzed by the official drug problem that they recoil in horror from this prospect.

The attempt to make some sense of the transcendent capabilities of psychoactive chemicals has been a consistent minor theme in Western science and philosophy. Go back a hundred years and you find William James in the *Varieties of Religious Experience* describing his own experience with nitrous oxide, and writing the often-quoted speculation that "our normal waking consciousness, rational consciousness as we call it, is but one special type of consciousness whilst all about it, parted by the filmiest of screens, there lie potential forms of consciousness entirely different."[9] In the 1950s, when Aldous Huxley began campaigning for a new project of exploring "human potentialities," he was most explicit in his expectation that mind-altering chemicals would play a major role in the endeavor. He had already opened up that subject with his book *The Doors of Perception,* an important prelude to the psychedelic 1960s in which Timothy Leary, Alan Watts, and others popularized the idea that drugs could generate authentic enlightenment experiences. Watts was a good deal more moderate than Leary on this subject, but he did go on record about the value of drugs such as mescaline, LSD, and psilocybin:

Despite the widespread and undiscriminating prejudice against drugs as such, and despite the claims of certain religious disciplines to be the sole means to genuine mystical insight, I can find no essential difference between the experiences induced, under favorable conditions, by these chemicals and the states of "cosmic consciousness" recorded by R. M. Bucke, William James . . . and other investigators of mysticism.[10]

More recently, Huston Smith, our most eminent philosopher-theologian, has entered the dialogue, modifying it somewhat by using the term, "entheogenic," roughly meaning "God-containing," or "God-enabling," as an alternative to the more common modifiers such as "psychedelic" and "hallucinogenic." He also regards these chemicals as paths to authentic sacramental experience, and he reviews some of the arguments that they have not only played a part in many religious traditions but also in the origin of most major mythological and theological systems—perhaps even of religion itself. He quotes anthropologist Mary Barnard's provocative question: "Which was more likely to happen first, the spontaneously generated idea of an afterlife in which the disembodied soul, liberated from the restrictions of time and space, experiences eternal bliss, or the accidental discovery of hallucinogenic plants that give a sense of euphoria, dislocate the center of consciousness, and distort time and space, making them balloon outward in greatly expanded vistas?"[11]

It follows from my proposal for accelerated research into all subjects related to enlightenment that we need to move—and not too slowly, either—toward a wider understanding and a public acceptance of drug experiences. This understanding should be more mature than the Tim Leary version, aware of the dangers, yet more permissive than what we get from the drug czars. "Drug-free America" is one of the most ludicrous public slogans ever coined, hardly compatible with the facts of life in a society that has its children on Ritalin, its adults on Prozac and its old men on Viagra.

Other societies of the past have learned about the properties of the chemicals available in their environments—for example, that some kinds of mushrooms can give you religious experiences under the proper conditions and that others will kill you—and devised over time the appropriate practices, policies, and rituals to apply that knowledge. The problem today is that our environment is the whole world, so the learning challenge is huge and daunting, made more so by the fact that transcendent experiences (even if many people have them) are still somewhere off on the margins of respectable public dialogue.

It's always easier to talk about things than processes, especially transcendent experiences that are difficult to describe, so difficult that the people who experience them sometimes have a hard time describing it even to themselves. So we argue about which chemicals should be legal, and the authorities duly make their lists of "controlled substances"—none of them actually under control.

Perhaps, when the processes of enlightenment becomes better understood, people will become more willing to relax some of the prohibitions against substances that can facilitate them. On the other hand, perhaps if it were easier to experiment with these substances, public understanding would arrive a lot more quickly.

I suspect that the most important value of psychoactive drugs may turn out to be as aids to learning. One of the things that comes through clearly in all the literature about psychedelic experiences is that drugs often have the effect of opening up the subject to integrative processes, to assimilating things already known. That kind of learning becomes an essential part in our next evolutionary step.

CHAPTER 14

The Emerging Enlightenment Project

There is no reason to think that the evolutionary process has
stopped. Man is a transitional animal . . . not the climax of
creation.   — CARL SAGAN [1]

We will continue to change physically, probably at roughly the
same rate that our species has always changed. But our biggest
changes will undoubtedly come about because of our growing
ability to explore the potentials of (the) human brain. . . . These
capabilities of our brains have been building for millions of years.
Harnessing them more fully will actually accelerate our evolution,
though not necessarily in the directions that we might expect.
                              — CHRISTOPHER WILLS [2]

Is the claim of humanity to uniqueness disappearing along with
the claim of each human to a separate identity shaped by a local
habitation and a name? Is the idea of what it is to be human disappearing, along with so many other ideas, through the modern
skylight?   — O. B. HARDISON, JR. [3]

Since the dawn of the modern era some centuries ago, human history has been a feast of horizon-expansion—explorers extended
the boundaries of the known world while scientists redefined the cosmos and philosophers questioned the basic premises of all knowledge. And it became evident as modernity unfolded that this wasn't
just a one-time change of perspectives but an ongoing process. That
recognition was what prompted Oliver Wendell Holmes in the
nineteenth century to write his poem about the chambered nautilus
with its successive moves into new and larger habitations, and it
prompted Thomas Kuhn in the twentieth century to picture science
as a series of intellectual revolutions in which new paradigms
replaced old ones.

Now we ride the crest of yet another wave of exploration and rede-finition, carrying us into a place that promises to be as different from the world of the late twentieth century as that age was from the pre-Darwin, pre-Freud, pre-Einstein, pre-quantum, pre-nuclear, pre-genetic, pre-electronic age of the European Enlightenment. This is a situation that makes a new enlightenment project not just possible but necessary.

Everything in this project relates in one way or another to what I have called the Big Three: cosmology, identity, and epistemology. By cosmology I mean our understanding of the universe; by identity, who and what we think we are; by epistemology, what we believe about belief and the nature of truth (and, today, what we understand about how our brains work). In regard to each, many familiar pieces of last century's worldview are disappearing through Professor Hardison's skylight; it's a veritable traffic jam up there.

The most mind-boggling changes are taking place in cosmology. Talk about expanding horizons: Only a century ago—an instant in the time scale of evolution—leading scientists still believed that the universe consisted of our galaxy with perhaps a few nebulae or minor galaxies floating around in the suburbs. Then, with the help of new instruments and new theories, they revised their views and gave us not one galaxy but a hundred billion of them, each with billions of stars. Now the cosmologists are pushing their envelope again to consider the possibility of multiple universes, and some say that the concept of a multitude of them may be the only way to make sense of this one. I'm not qualified to say whether the multiple-universe concept will become mainstream science in our time, but the mere fact that it is a legitimate item on the research agenda is in itself an astonishing development. Dr. Martin Rees, the British astronomer royal, neatly summed up the situation in a *New York Times* interview in which he was quoted as saying that the task of science in the twenty-first cen-tury is to seek answers to such questions. As to whether he believed in the multiple-universe hypothesis, he stated: "I don't believe, but I think it's part of science to find out."[4]

We have another difficult piece of cosmological work to complete regarding "the death of the spectator," the shift in perspective from looking at a universe "out there" to being a part of the universe looking at another part of itself. This shift is best known in relation to quantum physics, but it relates to all science. It is less remote from everyday life than is the multiple-universe question since it has to do with what is right in your own field of vision. It is often spontaneously discovered in peak or flow experiences. And it is closely linked to the second item in my big-three list: identity.

In the classic Western view, the self is an individual consciousness with clear boundaries that separate it from its environment. But the boundaries fade with the demise of the spectator stance toward the universe, and they fade in another way as we come to understand more about the complex and numerous ways that self and environment interpenetrate. The idea of individuality changes as researchers move away from the Cartesian notion of a single central observer toward the view of the brain as a committee of organs working together (and sometimes separately) to process and reprocess myriad versions of reality. Similarly, in the social sciences the constructive psychologists insist that, in a multicultural world people can and do create multiple selves, with changing personalities and different faces to present to the world on different occasions.

Closely paralleling this thinking is the notion of multiple epistemologies. Once it was assumed that the goal of rational thought was to find the one right way to ask the one right question and get the one right answer, the one right belief about belief. We now find that there are many ways, and that the search for truth requires some understanding of the knower—how he or she goes about the business of knowing—as well as of the thing known. Some think this undermines science; others think it takes science a great step forward. I am inclined to nominate Jean Piaget—with his audacious assertion that epistemology should be a branch of science rather than a branch of philosophy—to membership along with Freud, Einstein, and the rest in the pantheon of foundational twentieth-century thinkers. He insisted that epistemology itself can be studied concretely and empirically—not just argued about in the abstract—and that by doing so we can begin to understand how different people, as they mature, form different ways of understanding truth.

Changes in all three of these categories are the subject of bitter controversy, epistemological change most of all. All over the world you find a polarization between the purists, who hold to a more absolutist or traditionalist view of truth, and the revisionists, who see all manner of truths—religious, scientific, ideological, social—as human constructions subject to *re*construction when the times demand it.

The Evolution Express

The next enlightenment project has to do its work within an era of exponential change, regarding it not only as context but also as object of investigation, a part of what we have to try to understand.

The Asian enlightenment traditions come to us out of an age in which the prevailing concept of time was circular—the eternal turning of the wheel, everything coming around again and again like horses on a cosmic carousel. The European Enlightenment, already pregnant with evolutionary ideas, was fired with a different vision: *linear* change, an onward-and-upward course of progress. Today, with the theories of an evolving Earth and cosmos only scarcely installed as the prevailing worldview, we have to deal with a still newer and more disturbing idea: accelerating evolutionary processes, change in the rates of change. These changes come so fast that "progress" for some becomes a word used with a certain distaste, signifying a rueful wish that things would regress, remain the same, or at least move ahead in a more orderly fashion.

Exponential curves pop out of all kinds of data: world population growth, species extinction, the number of nongovernmental organizations, the quantity of genomic information, the speed of computer chips. They are traceable in the records of the past, and they figure heavily in scenarios of the future. We know that some of the exponential curves, world population growth, for example, will have to level off; but in relation to science and technology we have to be prepared for still more upward changes in the speed of change.

Lester Thurow of MIT wrote a summary of likely future developments that I often quote from because it puts the pieces together neatly and points out the power of convergence. In it he heralds the coming of a "third industrial revolution (the steam engine being the first and electrification the second) . . . based upon technical breakthroughs in computers, telecommunications, microelectronics, robots, new materials, and biotechnology." He believes that the interactions among the six breakthroughs are just beginning and are likely to have wide-ranging impacts—"changing not just business but warfare, culture, government, and religion."[5] Even the U.S. National Science Foundation, hardly a hotbed of giddy futurists, declared in a recent report that we "stand at the threshold of a New Renaissance in science and technology."[6]

Biotechnology, the most problematic part of this new Renaissance, is rolling along on its own upward curve. Over half a century elapsed between the birth of genetic science and the discovery of the structure of DNA, and in only a couple more decades the first products of recombinant DNA technology were on the market. Now we have an explosion of microbiological data, born of the convergence of biology and computer technology, and with it come troublesome new wonders such as cloned sheep, mammals producing spider silk, fruits and vegetables that double as edible vaccines, and bioengineered pigs bred to be organ donors for human beings.

The inevitable controversies about such innovations are generally described as questions of ethics, or stated in terms of risks to human health or ecological stability. These may be valid ways of framing the issues, but the emotional heat generated by some of the debates reveals deeper psychological currents flowing just beneath the surface, hints that even now—a century and a half after *The Origin of Species* was first published—we are still uncomfortable about our relationship to Cousin Mushroom. We tend to think of species as separate and distinct entities rather than as manifestations of the same evolutionary processes (one anti-biotech crusader actually proposed a federal law protecting the sanctity of all species) and we are especially fretful about developments that appear to violate the boundary between humans and other living things. Such boundary-maintenance worries can have a religious basis—as they did back in the early days of vaccination, when English clergymen protested that it was a violation of God's will to give a cow disease to human beings—but they also arise out of a more secular queasiness linked to a reified view of the whole human species as something that is, or should be, fenced off from the rest of organic life.

The whole biological revolution becomes part of the emerging enlightenment project, because we are obligated not only to regulate it and ensure reasonably fair access to its benefits, but also to think about what it *means*—what it tells us about who and what we are, and what we may become.

Other curves of accelerating change that raise similar questions about human identity and species boundaries are unfolding in the field of computer technology. Consider, for example, the prediction of computer whiz Ray Kurzweil that machines will have evolved in twenty years to the point of being equal in computational ability to the human brain, and that in the process they will become integrated into our own cognitive equipment. In a recent television interview he said: "We're going to be placing intelligent machines in our own brains. . . . So if you encounter somebody in 2030 or 2035, they're really a hybrid of biological and non-biological intelligence."[7] What kind of a somebody, with what kind of a self? That is a valid question to ask about a biocomputer hybrid, and even more so about a person who has taken leave of his old biological body and is walking around in an entirely new medium. Kurzweil talks about "downloading" the contents of a human mind into some kind of a nanoengineered body, considers the question of whether a person would be the same after such a transfer, and concludes that, "once over the divide, the new person will certainly think that he was the original person."[8] The assumption is that the ego may cease to be skin-encapsulated but will still be its old familiar self in a new container. This also appears to be the hope of Danny Hillis, whom Kurzweil quotes as saying: "I'm as fond of my body as anyone else, but if I can be two hundred with a body of silicon, I'll take it."[9]

I'm highly skeptical about the prospects of downloading human consciousness into other containers—not because I doubt that the mind has a material basis but because I doubt that the human personality is separate from the biological container, brain from body. I suspect that anybody downloaded into a silicon body would be somebody else, literally. But that cavil doesn't mean we get to dismiss the whole prospect of human-computer symbiosis. On the contrary, it is an important and immediate part of the emerging enlightenment project; it suggests that, even before we finish breaking down the conceptual partitions that separated us from the mushrooms and the stars, we will have to start getting chummy with Cousin Robot.

Yet another exponential curve traces the arc of increasingly speedy communications systems and the corresponding proliferation of communications technologies. Divided though we may remain in many ways, we are becoming electronically interconnected—not only people with people but people with data banks and Web sites and global positioning systems. And as that happens, some visionaries begin to sketch scenarios of a vast and majestic union—perhaps of all humanity, perhaps of all information systems, perhaps of all humanity *and* all information systems as well as all organic life and all mechanical constructions. In these scenarios, such terms as "global brain" or "global superorganism" are frequently employed, and the growth of the various planetwide communications systems is compared to the development of an infant's brain. Two members of the Global Brain Group, a university research consortium located in Brussels, propose this scenario not only as a metaphor but also as the model for a new development project aimed at deliberately turning the global network into a global thinking machine.[10]

And again the question arises: What becomes of the individual consciousness? Will our minds all flow together, submerged in (or subordinated to) the superbrain? This question is closely linked to present-day anxieties about the loss of privacy, and it is raised in various critiques warning about possible collectivist, totalitarian, even fascistic tendencies that might be implicit in such a future development.[11]

The spokesmen for the Global Brain Group respond that, although some people may see the superorganism philosophy as a collectivist ideology, "the opposite is true: further integration will basically increase individual freedom and diversity."[12] A similar scenario from another organization, looking ahead a thousand years, envisions a world in which, with the "continual intensity of complex interactivities with so many people and artificial intelligences," human intelligences continue to differentiate. With each person's subjectivity becoming "far more unique than our ancestors' of thousands of years ago . . . humanity has become a richer diversity of minds, while reinforcing much of the underlying spiritual commonality."[13]

This is an attractive vision, but meanwhile the dominant image of human minds linked together in a large entity probably comes from the movie *Star Trek: First Contact*. The film's collective bad guy is the Borg (obviously short for "cyborg"), a nasty biorobotic entity that captures human beings into its network, robbing them of their individual identities and transforming them into soulless automata that march about in space suits and funny eyeglasses while carrying out the hive's dastardly intentions.

All of these visions—both the pessimistic warnings and the more optimistic reassurances—indicate that people are thinking about something more than the oft-cited ethical and ecological concerns related to technological progress. They are wondering whether humanity might not evolve into something far different and scarcely recognizable. What I think will prove to be by far the most significant aspect of all these scenarios is that they are also wondering where to draw the lines between self and other, human and nonhuman. This is one of the central challenges of the twenty-first century's enlightenment project—and it's not just a matter of peering into scenarios of the distant future.

The Moving Boundaries of the Self

In a recent journal article, I surveyed some of the specific predictions of new developments in science and technology that will in some way affect the course of human evolution—things that people hope will happen, or fear will happen—and sorted them out into three categories: augmentation, symbiosis, and transcendence.[14] Augmentation has to do with creating abilities not biologically inherent in the organism. Symbiosis, which until recently meant only cooperative interaction between two organisms, now also means interaction between organisms and machines. Transcendence refers to various scenarios in which individuals go beyond their familiar boundaries to become parts of a larger, even global, entity.

Today's science news (and of course science fiction) are full of predictions of such things to come: augmentations of the human body and mind, new kinds of symbiosis, and even the drawing together of humanity into a transcendent global entity.

Not all those things will come to pass, of course. As some wise person has pointed out, there are no facts about the future. But something else is going on that I find no less fascinating and important than the proliferation of visions of the future—a rethinking of the past and present, based on the proposition that augmentations, symbiosis, and transcendence are and have always been integral and defining elements of human evolution.

One well-known treatment of the augmentation theme was Marshall McLuhan's popular 1960s book *Understanding Media,* subtitled *The Extensions of Man.* In it he suggested that clothing can be regarded as a heat-conserving extension of human skin, that houses are also a type of skin or garment, and that cities provide other extensions of bodily organs such as water supplies and sewage systems.[15] Richard Dawkins, in a more recent exploration of this theme, coined the term "extended phenotype" to describe all additions or improvements to the biological organism—augmentations that animals create instinctively and human beings create through technology.[16]

Regarding symbiosis, psychologist Merlin Donald sees the human-computer interaction as already something more than augmentation: "The growth of the external memory system," he writes in his impressive study *The Making of the Modern Mind,* "has now so far outpaced biological memory that it is no exaggeration to say that we are permanently wedded to our great invention, in a cognitive symbiosis unique in nature."[17] Historian Bruce Mazlish, whom I mentioned in chapter 3, also argues that human beings have never been discontinuous from their machines, and that human evolution has always been simultaneously and inseparably biological, cultural, and technological.[18]

Computer scientist Alexander Chislenko thinks the augmentation-symbiosis distinction is completely irrelevant, that we are better described as "functional cyborgs," biological organisms functionally supplemented with technological extensions, and that functional cyborgation is nothing new at all.[19] In his Web paper on this subject he includes a drawing of a knight in armor as an example of a cyborg; he could as easily shown a caveman with a club.

Regarding transcendence, several people have offered alternatives to the conventional distinction between humanity and the Earth. As candidates to replace the metaphor of "spaceship Earth," with humanity as passengers on a somewhat overbooked flight through the solar system, we have visions such as Theodore Roszak's *Person/Planet,* with the individual and Earth seen as two faces of the same reality.[20] Gregory Stock, in his book *Metaman,* contends that we need to reframe our thinking about human evolution and instead contemplate the evolution of a larger entity, the whole community of Earth's organisms and artifacts. Metaman is humanity and its environment and also "the crops, livestock, machines, buildings, communications transmissions, and other nonhuman elements and structures that are part of the human experience." This "thin planetary patina of humanity and its creations is truly a living entity . . . a 'superorganism.' "[21] Even James Lovelock, famed as coauthor of the Gaia hypothesis, speculates (in a passage echoing Julian Huxley's idea of humanity as evolution becoming conscious of itself) that Homo sapiens, "with his technological inventiveness and his increasingly subtle communications network, has vastly increased Gaia's range of perception. She is now through us awake and aware of herself."[22]

So far, most people seem to have managed to skim past the evidence of already present forms of augmentation, symbiosis, and transcendence, and continue to think of themselves as clever skin-encapsulated egos who just happen to have a few tools to use from time to time, perhaps a pair of glasses and a hearing aid and a pacemaker, maybe a television and a computer and a cell phone. And in the blood a few billion antibodies generated by vaccines. Oh yes, and a bunch of satellites out there monitoring all the planet's ecosystems while we argue about scenarios of anthropogenic global climate change. Nothing out of the ordinary, nothing to force any revision of our self-images. But unless all the exponential curves turn around and head the other way, we are in for some deep rethinking. The times are like a relentless guru asking again and again: Who are you? Who are you? Who are you? One challenge of growing up in the twenty-first century will be to acquire a self-definition that can encompass person and planet, socially constructed self and transcendent being, organism and machine.

Are We In over Our Heads?

Even if we could avoid contemplating the prospect of accelerating scientific and technological progress and what it may do for us or to us, and to our central beliefs about who and what we are, we face other cognitive challenges as old assumptions disappear through the skylight and new concerns, having to do with life in a rapidly changing, multicultural, globalizing, politically explosive and ecologically threatened world, force their way into our consciousness.

Robert Kegan, one of the best of the contemporary developmental psychologists, fears that we may be in over our heads, faced with a world that has rendered familiar cosmologies, identities, and epistemologies maladaptive, requiring us to master new cognitive skills. The most important of these skills is what he calls the ability to "objectify"—to recognize as socially constructed and contingent rather than as God-given and eternal fundamental concepts such as selfhood, nationality, or religion. That doesn't mean rejecting them, only seeing them as matters about which some sort of a *decision* can be made. Without developing such an ability we remain trapped in our social structures.

Kegan calls this ability the key to the fifth, or postmodern, level of cognitive development. This is a level that most people have not achieved—they're still trying to make sense of an emerging postmodern world with ways of thinking learned in the institutions of modernity—sort of like trying to build a computer with a monkey wrench. Even the transition from premodern, traditionalist mindsets, the consciousness of village or tribe, into the fourth-level cognitive world of twentieth-century modernity is one that many people haven't managed, and they are now trying to do it in one generation.

Yet there's ample evidence that many people *are* making such developmental transitions, probably more than have ever undergone such changes in any single period of human history. Political scientist James Rosenau, in one of the better attempts to describe this transformation, calls it a global "skill revolution" that often takes the form of political action but is fundamentally psychological: people, he says, are developing new capacities to *analyze* their social, political and economic situations and, equally important, to *imagine* different lifestyles, futures, and circumstances for themselves and others.[23]

In trying to think about such heady matters as cognitive development, we need to pay attention to easily overlooked factors such as health and longevity. People who are reasonably well nourished and free of debilitating disease have a far greater chance to develop their thinking capabilities, and Kegan believes that the promise of longer lifespans offers great hope for accelerated cognitive development:

> What might the individual generate given an additional generation to live? My candidate: a qualitatively new order of consciousness. I suggest that we are gradually seeing more adults working on a qualitatively different order of consciousness than did adults one hundred years ago, because we live twenty or more years longer than we used to.
>
> In our longitudinal study it is rare to see people moving

beyond the fourth [modern] order, but when they do, it is never before their forties, the very age when life ended for most people at the turn of the [twentieth] century. Highly evolved people do not mate and create highly evolved children. The evolution of consciousness requires long preparation. We may gradually become ever more ready to engage the curriculum of the fifth order because we have found ways to increase the number of years we live. And why are we increasing the number of years we live? Are we living longer as a species precisely so that we might evolve to the fifth order? Who knows?[24]

Who knows, indeed? Kegan doesn't attempt to answer those questions, or even to say exactly what he means by them—they are the last words in the book. He seems to be suggesting some evolutionary design or intention that is operating in or through people without their being fully aware of why they are doing what they are doing. Clearly the whole subject of cognitive development in individuals leads inevitably to the larger subject of cognitive *evolution* in societies and in the human species.

I think it's entirely reasonable—as reasonable as, say, talking about minisupercomputers in our brains—to propose that the fifth level of cognitive development is closely related to the transition described as enlightenment or liberation, and that within the ranks of those who, as Kegan puts it, are working on the curriculum of the fifth level will be found people who are breaking through into levels of experience and understanding equivalent to those described by the literature of Eastern mysticism. To put the matter in slightly different terms—and to restate the main argument of this book—enlightenment *is* cognitive development, and the various approaches to that development, whether we call them spirituality or psychology, are just different ways of groping the same elephant.

So are we in over our heads? I don't think so. Despite all the wisdom of psychologies ancient, modern, and postmodern, we still don't really know that much about what's *in* our heads—what possibilities of adaptation, imagination, and creativity may come with human intelligence. But there is no higher priority on the human agenda than learning more about those possibilities.

Toward a New Human Nature

Human cognitive development, an academically enhanced way of saying "growing up," lies at the heart of the emerging enlightenment project. Regardless of what path you may choose to travel—art, spirituality, science, psychotherapy, developmental psychology—you must deal along the way with questions about how the human mind matures in individuals and how it evolves in Homo sapiens, the species that defines itself by its wisdom. The limits of human cognitive capability are the limits of our potential for comprehending new cosmologies, identities, and epistemologies, reconciling science and mysticism, and inhabiting wider spaces of thought and experience. And our work will be to test, understand, and, wherever possible, transcend those limits.

Summarizing some of the major points in this book, I offer a brief list of propositions that a new enlightenment project might engage, refine, revise, refute, or expand into a new view of human nature:

- Enlightenment, however unique as a phenomenon of human development, is nevertheless a continuation of "normal" maturation and growth, inherent in all people.
- Progress toward enlightenment involves a "constructive way of knowing" in which the individual develops an understanding of the socially constructed nature of human institutions and a consequent ability to deal with them in many different ways.
- It also involves an engagement with the cognitive process called reification, the tendency to turn processes into things.
- Human development, especially at the higher levels, involves a number of transcendent "aha!" experiences of different kinds and degrees in which the individual reorganizes his or her sense of self and structure of consciousness.

- Although an enlightenment experience may be (as is often argued) universal and "beyond culture," the person's integration of it draws on sources available in the cultural environment; some people may describe it as a unity with God; others may use spiritual or secular terms.
- Many or most (possibly all) people have transcendent experiences in their lives that they do not understand or satisfactorily integrate. In some cases, these experiences may be regarded by the individual (or by others) as pathological.
- Enlightenment experiences may be precipitated or enabled by a variety of practices or processes including meditation, personal tragedy, psychoactive chemicals, or deep philosophical reflection.
- Enlightenment may fairly be described as knowledge or wisdom, but it does not confer superior knowledge on all subjects. The enlightened person is capable of being uninformed or "wrong" about many things, including the subject of enlightenment itself beyond his or her personal experience of it.
- Higher levels of cognitive development are accompanied by a high level of moral development based on compassion and regard for others, and not necessarily congruent with prevailing social moral codes.
- Eastern spiritual traditions are a rich body of wisdom about enlightenment. However, no such tradition has an infallible capacity to guide all individuals in that direction or to produce higher levels of understanding. All enlightenment traditions are a part of the evolutionary process, and are themselves in the process of evolution.
- The term "ego," as used in English to describe the psychological pattern to be transcended by enlightenment, is best understood in terms of habits of reification—including the construction of an image of the separate self—rather than the various character traits, such as arrogance or selfishness, that also are described by that word. You can be a very humble person and still be completely in thrall to ego-based thinking.

These are some issues that can be pursued as part of the process of "investigating the situation" on a larger scale. As I've already indicated, this project can be regarded as an agenda for interdisciplinary research, and some people in the academic world are already on that track, but these are matters for consideration by people and organizations of all sorts. The implications are enormous, especially if, as I contend, enlightenment is the human birthright, the still-mysterious manifestation of dimensions, however natural they may be, that we have not yet learned how to develop.

Aldous Huxley had some good ideas in his "human potentialities" proposal, but he seems to have been thinking about a centralized, directed program. And, although you could argue that intellectual, artistic, scientific, and political movements need a critical mass of people working together, they also have a need for real vitality to be scattered and multicentric. In the five movements we surveyed in Part One you will find as much divergence as central control. Only two of the five can be identified with one man's name, and both of those are famous for their divergence and dissent. Today the world of Darwinian-based evolutionary theory is anything but a centralized command—what with the debates about such matters as punctuated evolution—and neither is the world of psychotherapy. They are, as they should be, open systems rich with both common purpose and spirited disagreements, and thus good models for the larger project.

We live in the age of networks, and we are now technologically empowered to commence a decentralized conversation about our own evolutionary future on a scale beyond anything we have known before. Participation does not require blind faith—we have had enough of that—but rather a critical yet open stance toward the ideas and explorations I have described in these pages. It doesn't require an advanced degree, either; it is everybody's business.

About Time

In some ways the agenda I describe is the same one that Dr. Bucke offered a hundred years ago in *Cosmic Consciousness*—universal enlightenment as the next step in human evolution. I am quite confident that it *is* the next step, a natural maturation of the species toward knowing its inseparability from the planet out of which it grows and the universe it seeks to explore and understand. I am also confident that we have the intellectual tools at our disposal to undertake such a project, make it widely understandable, and explore all its implications and dimensions more systematically than people have ever done before.

However, I have no certainty at all that such an evolutionary project will be completed soon—or ever. Dr. Bucke, Aldous Huxley, and the human-potential writers who followed in their footsteps had a touching belief in the imminence of large-scale transformation, combined with a tendency to underestimate the depth and tenacity of ego-based cognition and the institutions that maintain it. They also failed to take into account the power of militant reactionary and fundamentalist belief. I don't look for a quantum leap to a new level of human evolution the day after tomorrow, and I don't discount the various conceivable disasters on a global scale that could stop all terrestrial evolution in its tracks.

It's easy to understand why some people leap so readily into the conviction that a great transformation is imminent—particularly understandable in the present time, with exponential curves running in all directions. But the fact of the matter is that evolutionary change of the sort we are experiencing now has never happened before, and we have no basis for laying out a timetable—optimistic, pessimistic, or somewhere in the moderate middle—about how well or how rapidly it may proceed. We would do better to take up the work of the twenty-first century, consider ourselves in it for the long haul, and be prepared for surprises.

In the essay I quoted in chapter 1 Immanuel Kant declared his era to be an age of enlightenment but not yet an enlightened age. That declaration, like his proposed motto, "dare to know," applies admirably to the twenty-first century, which is giving birth to a new enlightenment project, grander in scope than any that has gone before. I can't imagine anything better than living in such an age and taking a part in such a project.

The human species—sometimes called the symbolic animal—is in the process of breaking through the web of illusion that it has been constructing around itself ever since it developed the capacity to speak and write. It is in the process of making the fundamental discovery that identities, beliefs, and social institutions are symbolic structures, built by human beings. As this discovery seeps into public consciousness, we do not cease to be symbolic animals—we still have identities, beliefs, and social institutions—but we occupy those structures in much different ways, and we live more lightly amid our cultures. I have no idea of how long it may take for this process to unfold. We do know now, from the lessons of history and anthropology, that different societies have had entirely different ideas of what constitutes common sense. In time, the way of being in the world known as enlightenment will become the new common sense. We will not know this has happened—that we have proceeded from an age of enlightenment into an enlightened age—until we see that people have ceased beating one another to death over stale dogmas and fictitious identities.

You Are Never Alone,
You Are Always Home

One evening a couple of years ago, while sitting in a garden and admiring the evening sky, I pulled an index card from my pocket and wrote two lines that had suddenly entered my mind:

You are never alone.

You are always home.

I wrote these lines as descriptions of my own condition at that moment. This is curious in a way, because to an objective observer they would have appeared to contradict the facts of the matter. I was geographically far from home, sipping a martini and waiting to be called to dinner in a Cuernavaca restaurant. I was technically alone except for a pushy peacock who was trying to steal salted nuts from a bowl on the table before me, and whose immediate company I could have done without. Yet, however contradictory the lines may have seemed to someone else, I knew I was simply recording the truth—not only about the way I felt then but about the way I am, and we all are, always. Loneliness comes out of the delusion of separateness; home is wherever you are because it is *what* you are at that moment.

This truth revisits me from time to time; it descends gently, like a friendly hand resting on my shoulder, and when it does it dissolves not only boundaries but also demands. I know I don't really have to do anything in particular. I enjoy the feeling for a while, and then I go about my business anyway.

When those moments occur, I think I understand something that is so often reported in accounts of enlightenment experiences—a perception that somehow everything is as it should be and there is nothing that needs to be done. This is one of the seeming paradoxes connected with this subject because the people who report these feelings do not lose their sense of concern about the injustices of the world—quite the opposite, in fact—and they usually go about their business. I say usually, because often they begin to go about some other business; but they do not retreat from everyday life.

I mention this here, in closing, because it touches on a question that sensible people often ask me when they examine the proposition that enlightenment is the future of the species. Good God, what will people *do?* Won't they just sit around and contemplate their navels? A fair question, and one for which no absolute answer exists. I think they will do a lot, especially the explorers: the individual seekers and thinkers, the artists and philosophers, the psychologists and brain scientists, the stargazers and physicists and biologists and computer geeks. But I also think that everybody gets to be an explorer. I mean that learning is close to the heart of what it means to be human. If we don't learn, and keep learning, we start dying. And so I expect that, if and when the species grows up, there will be plenty to do: draw water, carry wood, brush your teeth, contemplate the wonder of being, and learn. We have not evolved out of a steady-state universe, and we are not steady-state creatures. Being is always becoming.

There is so much to learn, and there is also something to learn about learning. People have known for a long time that knowledge is power, and a lucky few have always understood that knowledge is joy. Now as we begin to understand that exploration is not only what we do but what we are, we find that knowledge—the search for knowledge, the daring to know—is also peace. Who would have thought it?

NOTES

INTRODUCTION: PULLING BUDDHA'S TOOTH.

1. "Saraha's Treasury of Songs," in ed. Edward Conze et al, *Buddhist Texts Through the Ages* (New York: Harper Torchbooks, 1964), 226.
2. Quoted in Herbert Fingarette, "The Ego and Mystic Selflessness," *Psychoanalysis and Psychoanalytic Review* no. 1 (1948), 5–41.
3. ALEXANDRA DAVID-NEEL and LAMA YONGDEN, *The Secret Oral Teachings in Tibetan Buddhist Sects* (San Francisco: City Lights, 1967), 3.
4. RICHARD MAURICE BUCKE, *Cosmic Consciousness: A Study in the Evolution of the Human Mind* (New Hyde Park, N.Y.: University Books, 1961), 318.
5. OLIVER WENDELL HOLMES, "The Chambered Nautilus," Stanza 5 (1858).

PART ONE:
FIVE MODERN LIBERATION MOVEMENTS.

CHAPTER 1. ENLIGHTENMENT, EUROPEAN STYLE.

1. DAVID HUME, *Treatise of Human Understanding* (1740).
2. IMMANUEL KANT, *Critique of Pure Reason*, trans. Norman Kemp Smith (Boston/New York: Bedford/St. Martin's, 1965), 82. (First published 1781.)
3. GORAN THERBORN, "Routes to/through Modernity," in *Global Modernities*, ed. Mike Featherstone, Scott Lash, and Roland Robertson (Thousand Oaks, Calif.: Sage, 1995), 126.
4. DENIS DIDEROT, quoted in Peter Gay, *The Enlightenment: An Interpretation* (New York: W. W. Norton, 1977), 71.
5. PAUL HEINRICH DIETRICH, Baron d'Holbach, *Common-Sense, or, Natural Ideas Opposed to Supernatural* (1795), quoted in Frank Manuel, *The Enlightenment* (Englewood Cliffs, NJ: Prentice-Hall, 1965) 62.
6. ROBERT NISBET, *History of the Idea of Progress* (New York: Basic Books, 1980), 171.

7. Anne-Robert Turgot, *A Philosophical Review of the Successive Advances of the Human Mind* (1750), quoted in Nisbet, 180.

8. Marquis de Condorcet, *Sketch for an Historical Picture of the Progress of the Human Mind* (1795), quoted in Nisbet, 207.

9. Abbé Pluché, *Histoire du Ciel* (1759), quoted in Arthur Lovejoy, *The Great Chain of Being* (Cambridge, Mass.: Harvard University Press, 1953).

10. Erasmus Darwin, *The Temple of Nature* (1803), quoted in Ronald W. Clark, *The Survival of Charles Darwin: A Biography of a Man and an Idea* (New York: Random House, 1984), 25.

11. Allen W. Wood, introduction to *Basic Writings of Kant* (New York: Modern Library, 2001), vii.

12. David Harvey, *The Condition of Postmodernity: An Enquiry into the Origins of Cultural Change* (Cambridge, U.K.: Basil Blackwell, 1989), 27–28.

13. Immanuel Kant, "Answer to the Question: What Is Enlightenment" (1784), *Basic Writings of Kant*, ed. Allen W. Wood (New York: The Modern Library, 2001), 133–141.

CHAPTER 2. MEETING COUSIN MUSHROOM.

1. Julian Huxley, introduction to Mentor edition of *Charles Darwin, The Origin of Species by Means of Natural Selection or the Preservation of Favoured Races in the Struggle for Life* (New York: New American Library, 1958), xv.

2. Samuel Wilberforce, review of *Origin of Species* (1860) in *The Quarterly Review* 108, no. 215 (July 1860): 231.

3. Aristotle, *De anima*, quoted in Thomas Lovejoy, *The Great Chain of Being* (Cambridge, Mass.: Harvard University Press, 1936), 58–59.

4. Lovejoy, 242.

5. Joseph Clarke (1734), quoted in Lovejoy, 242.

6. Lovejoy, 244.

7. Gottfried von Leibnitz, "On the Ultimate Origination of Things," in *The Monadology and Other Philosophical Writings*, trans. Robert Latta (London: Oxford University Press, 1925), 350.

8. Ronald W. Clark, *The Survival of Charles Darwin: A Biography of a Man and an Idea* (New York: Random House, 1984), 13.

9. This subject is discussed at greater length in my previous book *To Gov-*

ern Evolution: Further Adventures of the Political Animal (Boston: Harcourt Brace Jovanovich, 1987), 39–61.

10. GERTRUDE HIMMELFARB, *Darwin and the Darwinian Revolution* (New York: Doubleday, 1959), 423.

11. EDMUND LAW, notes to *An Essay on the Origins of Evil* (1732) by William King, quoted in Lovejoy, 206.

12. SOAME JENYNS, *A Free Inquiry into the Nature and Origin of Evil* (1757), quoted in Lovejoy, 207.

13. KARL MARX, letter to Ferdinand Lassalle, Jan. 16, 1861, quoted in Clark, 212.

14. Both quotations from Clark, 139.

15. CLARK, 143.

16. Wilberforce review, 239.

17. THOMAS H. HUXLEY, *Evidence as to Man's Place in Nature* (London: Williams and Norgate, 1863).

18. CHARLES LYELL, *The Geological Evidences of the Antiquity of Man, with Remarks on the Origin of Species by Variation* (London: John Murray, 1863).

19. ALFRED WALLACE, "The Origin of Human Races and the Antiquity of Man Deduced from the Theory of 'Natural Selection' ", in *The Anthropological Review and Journal of the Anthropological Society of London* (May 1864): clvii–clxx.

20. O. B. HARDISON JR., *Disappearing Through the Skylight: Culture and Technology in the Twentieth Century* (New York: Viking, 1989), 28.

CHAPTER 3. THE DARK MATTER OF THE MIND.

1. *The Standard Edition of the Complete Psychological Works of Sigmund Freud*, ed. and trans. James Strachey (London: Hogarth Press, 1953–1974), Vol. 15, 22.

2. CARL G. JUNG, *Memories, Dreams, Reflections*, ed. Aniela Jaffe; trans. Richard and Clara Winston (New York: Vintage, 1963), 340.

3. FREUD, *Standard Edition*, Vol. 16, 285.

4. JOHN H. ENGLER, "Becoming Somebody and Nobody: Psychoanalysis and Buddhism," in *Paths Beyond Ego: The Transpersonal Vision*, eds. Roger Walsh and Frances Vaughn (Los Angeles: Tarcher/Perigee, 1993), 118–121.

5. FREUD, *An Outline of Psychoanalysis* (1940), trans. James Strachey (New York: W. W. Norton, 1949), 14.

6. FREUD, *New Introductory Lectures on Psychoanalysis* (1933), trans. James Strachey (New York: W. W. Norton, 1965), 73.

7. FREUD, *Civilization and Its Discontents* (1930), trans. James Strachey (New York: W. W. Norton, 1951), 44.

8. JEROME BRUNER, "Freud and the Image of Man," *Partisan Review* (Summer 1956): 340–347.

9. BRUCE MAZLISH, *The Fourth Discontinuity: The Co-evolution of Humans and Machines.* (New York: Yale University Press, 1993), 4.

10. JUNG, 138.

11. JUNG, 337.

12. HERBERT FINGARETTE, "The Ego and Mystic Selflessness," *Psychoanalysis and Psychoanalytic Review* XLV, No. 1 (1948): 5–41.

CHAPTER 4. EXISTENCE LOST AND FOUND.

1. SØREN KIERKEGAARD, "An Existential System Is Impossible," from *Concluding Unscientific Postscript* (1846), quoted in *Reality, Man and Existence: Essential Works of Existentialism*, ed. H. J. Blackham (New York: Bantam, 1965), 18.

2. FRIEDRICH NIETZSCHE, *The Gay Science* (1882), quoted in Walter Kaufmann, *Nietzsche: Philosopher, Psychologist, Antichrist* (Princeton: Princeton University Press, 1974), 159.

3. SARTRE, "Existentialism Is a Humanism," *Existentialism from Dostoevsky to Sartre*, ed. Walter Kaufmann (New York: Meridian Books, 1956), 290–291.

4. KARL JASPERS, "First Lecture: The Origin of the Contemporary Philosophical Situation" (1935) in Blackham, 125.

5. WALTER KAUFMANN, introduction to *Existentialism from Dostoevsky to Sartre*, 12.

6. GABRIEL MARCEL, "Outline of an Essay on the Position of the Ontological Mystery and the Concrete Approaches to It" (1933), in Blackham, 166–167.

7. WALTER KAUFMANN, *From Shakespeare to Existentialism* (New York: Anchor, 1960), 365.

8. MARTIN BUBER, *I and Thou*, trans. Walter Kaufmann (New York: Scribner's, 1970), 127.

9. KAUFMANN, introduction to Buber, *I and Thou*, 30.

10. BUBER, 62–63.

11. BUBER, 85.

12. BUBER, 82.

13. BUBER, 136–37.

14. I have written about Moreno and the history of psychodrama in two other books: *The Upstart Spring* (1983) and *Reality Isn't What It Used To Be* (1991).

15. J. L. MORENO, *Who Shall Survive?* (Beacon, N.Y.: Beacon House, 1953), xix.

16. ROLLO MAY, *The Discovery of Being: Writings in Existential Psychology* (New York: W. W. Norton, 1983), 98–99.

17. MAY, 100.

18. MAY, 171.

CHAPTER 5. EAST MEETS WEST IN THE HOT TUBS.

1. FREDERICK S. PERLS, "Workshop vs. Individual Therapy," paper delivered at American Psychological Association Convention, New York City, September 1966.

2. ALAN WATTS, *The Book: On the Taboo Against Knowing Who You Are* (New York: Vintage, 1989), 12.

3. "Human Potentialities," lecture delivered at the University of California, San Francisco Medical Center, 1960.

4. The history of Esalen and the human potential movement is chronicled in greater detail in my earlier book *The Upstart Spring* (Reading, Mass.: Addison-Wesley, 1983).

5. ABRAHAM MASLOW, *Motivation and Personality* (New York: Harper and Row, 1954), 180.

6. MASLOW, *Motivation and Personality*, 200–201.

7. MASLOW, *Toward a Psychology of Being* (New York: Van Nostrand, 1962), 4.

8. MASLOW, *Toward a Psychology of Being*, 68–69.

9. JOEN FAGAN and IRMA LEE SHEPHERD, eds., *Gestalt Therapy Now* (Palo Alto, Calif.: Science and Behavior Books, 1970), 1.

10. THEODORE ROSZAK, "Counter Culture IV: The Future as Community," *The Nation* 206 (15 April 1968): 502. These articles formed the basis of Roszak's book *The Making of a Counter Culture* (New York: Doubleday Anchor, 1969).

11. FREDERICK S. PERLS, *In and Out the Garbage Pail* (Lafayette, Calif.: Real People Press, 1969), pages not numbered.
12. CLAUDIO NARANJO, *The One Quest* (New York: Ballantine, 1972), 102.
13. NARANJO, 127.
14. ALAN WATTS, *In My Own Way* (New York: Pantheon, 1972).
15. ALAN WATTS, *The Book . . .* , x.
16. ALAN WATTS, *The Book . . .* , 12.
17. GEORGE B. LEONARD, *The Transformation: A Guide to the Inevitable Changes in Humankind* (New York: Delacorte Press, 1972).
18. MARILYN FERGUSON, *The Aquarian Conspiracy: Personal and Social Transformation in the 1980s* (Los Angeles: J. P. Tarcher, 1980).

PART TWO:

THE NEW MIRROR OF SCIENCE.

1. STEPHEN TOULMIN, *The Return to Cosmology: Postmodern Science and the Theology of Nature* (Berkeley: University of California Press, 1985).

CHAPTER 6. MEETING COUSIN SIRIUS.

1. TOULMIN, *The Return to Cosmology.*
2. FRITJOF CAPRA, *The Tao of Physics* (New York: Bantam, 1976), 57.
3. ALBERT EINSTEIN, quoted in *The New York Post,* Nov. 28, 1972, 12.
4. TIMOTHY FERRIS, *The Whole Shebang: A State-of-the-Universe(s) Report* (London: Phoenix, 1997), 170–171.
5. FERRIS, 111.
6. PAUL DAVIES, "The Synthetic Path," in *The Third Culture: Beyond the Scientific Revolution*, ed. John Brockman (New York: Simon & Schuster, 1995), 306–307.
7. DAVID LAYZER, *Cosmogenesis* (Oxford: Oxford University Press, 1990).
8. ERIC CHAISSON, *The Life Era: Cosmic Selection and Conscious Evolution* (New York: W. W. Norton, 1987), 3–4.
9. LEE SMOLIN, "A Theory of the Whole Universe," in Brockman, 292.
10. MARTIN GARDNER, quoted in Tony Rothman, "A 'What You See Is What You Beget' Theory," *Discovery*, May 1987, 96.
11. J. ROBERT OPPENHEIMER, *Science and the Common Understanding* (New York: Oxford University Press, 1954), 8–9.
12. NIELS BOHR, *Atomic Physics and Human Knowledge* (New York: John Wiley & Sons, 1958), 20.

13. CAPRA, 70–71.

14. RICHARD DAWKINS, *Unweaving the Rainbow: Science, Delusion and the Appetite for Wonder* (Boston: Houghton Mifflin, 1998), 245.

15. HENRY STAPP, quoted in Robert Nadeau and Menos Kafatos, *The Non-Local Universe: The New Physics and Matters of the Mind* (New York: Oxford University Press, 1999), 80.

16. NADEAU and KAFATOS, 81.

CHAPTER 7. THE MYSTERIOUS MATERIAL MIND.

1. DANIEL DENNETT, *Consciousness Explained* (Boston: Little, Brown, 1991), 33.

2. TOR NORRETRANDERS, *The User Illusion: Cutting Consciousness Down to Size* (New York: Viking, 1998), 167.

3. BRUNO SNELL, *The Discovery of the Mind* (Cambridge, Mass.: Harvard University Press, 1953), chap. 1.

4. FRANCIS CRICK, *The Astonishing Hypothesis: The Scientific Search for the Soul* (New York: Touchstone, 1995), 3.

5. DENNETT, 106.

6. J. B. WATSON and WILLIAM McDOUGALL, *The Battle of Behaviorism* (London: Kegan Paul, Trench, Trubner, 1928), 17–19.

7. B. F. SKINNER, *Walden Two* (New York: Macmillan, 1948), 262.

8. KARL MANNHEIM, *Ideology and Utopia: An Introduction to the Sociology of Knowledge* (New York: Harcourt Brace Jovanovich, 1949), 46.

9. DENNETT, 106.

10. MICHAEL GAZZANIGA, *The Social Brain: Discovering the Networks of the Mind* (New York: Basic Books, 1985), x.

11. STEVEN PINKER, *How the Mind Works* (New York: W. W. Norton, 1997), 21.

12. EDWARD O. WILSON, *Consilience: The Unity of Knowledge* (New York: Knopf, 1998), 132.

13. DENNETT, 113.

14. KENNETH J. GERGEN, *The Saturated Self: Dilemmas of Identity in Contemporary Life* (New York: Basic Books, 1990).

15. ALEXANDRA DAVID-NEEL, *Buddhism* (New York: St. Martin's Press, 1939), 123.

16. NORRETRANDERS, 143–44.

17. NORRETRANDERS, 187.

CHAPTER 8. BEING CONSTRUCTIVE.

1. RICHARD RORTY, *Contingency, Irony, and Solidarity* (Cambridge: Cambridge University Press, 1989), 3.

2. HUMBERTO R. MATURANA and FRANCISCO J. VARELA, *The Tree of Knowledge: The Biological Roots of Human Understanding* (Boston and London: Shambhala, 1987), 25–26.

3. ROBERT KEGAN, *In Over Our Heads: The Mental Demands of Modern Life* (Cambridge, Mass.: Harvard University Press, 1994), 34.

4. GIAMBATTISTA VICO, quoted in Ernst von Glazersfeld, "An Introduction to Radical Constructivism," in *The Invented Reality*, ed. Paul Watzlawick (New York: W. W. Norton, 1984), 27.

5. MATURANA and VARELA, 26.

6. MORTON HUNT, *The Universe Within: A New Science Explores the Human Mind* (New York: Touchstone, 1982), 80.

7. ZEN MASTER GENSHA, quoted in Alan Watts, *This Is It* (New York: Collier Books, 1958), 25.

8. ERNEST BECKER, *The Birth and Death of Meaning* (New York: The Free Press, 1962), 139.

9. JOHN L. PHILLIPS, JR., *The Origins of Intellect: Piaget's Theory* (San Francisco: W. H. Freeman, 1969), 7.

10. JEAN PIAGET, *The Moral Judgment of the Child*, trans. Marjorie Worden (New York: Harcourt, Brace & World, 1932).

11. LAWRENCE KOHLBERG, "Stage and Sequence: The Cognitive-Developmental Approach to Socialization," in *Handbook of Socialization Theory and Research*, ed. David A. Gosling (Chicago: Rand McNally, 1969), 347 passim.

12. CAROL GILLIGAN, *In a Different Voice: Psychological Theory and Women's Development* (Cambridge: Harvard University Press, 1982).

13. MARY FIELD BELENKY, Blythe McVicker Clinchy, Nancy Rule Goldberger, and Jill Mattuck Tarule, *Women's Ways of Knowing: The Development of Self, Voice, and Mind* (New York: Basic Books, 1986), 15.

14. MATURANA and VARELA, 245.

CHAPTER 9. ALL THE THINGS YOU ARE.

1. RICHARD DAWKINS, *River out of Eden: A Darwinian View of Life* (New York: Basic Books, 1995), 46.

2. WALT WHITMAN, *Leaves of Grass,* "Song of Myself."

3. DAWKINS, 45–46.

4. JENNIFER ACKERMAN, *Chance in the House of Fate: A Natural History of Heredity* (New York: Houghton Mifflin, 2001), 161–162.

5. M. MITCHELL WALDROP, *Complexity: The Emerging Science at the Edge of Order and Chaos* (New York: Touchstone, 1992), 145–147. The scheme of properties of complex adaptive systems is based on the work of John Holland. See Holland, *Hidden Order: How Adaptation Builds Complexity* (Reading, Mass.: Addison-Wesley, 1995).

6. DAWKINS, 1–2.

7. GERALD M. EDELMAN and GIULIO TONONI, *A Universe of Consciousness: How Matter Becomes Imagination* (New York: Basic Books, 2000), xii.

8. KENNETH J. GERGEN. *The Saturated Self: Dilemmas of Identity in Contemporary Life* (New York: Basic Books, 1991), 71–72.

PART THREE:
DARING TO KNOW IN THE TWENTY-FIRST CENTURY.

CHAPTER 10. THE SOCIAL RAMBLE OF EGO AND IDENTITY.

1. MASLOW, *Toward a Psychology of Being,* 11.

2. GERGEN, *The Saturated Self,* 7.

3. F. SCOTT FITZGERALD, *The Great Gatsby,* chapter 6.

4. *Great Gatsby,* chapter 7.

5. LEO BRAUDY, *The Frenzy of Renown: Fame and its History* (New York: Vintage, 1986).

6. Quoted in David Giles, *Illusions of Immortality: A Psychology of Fame and Celebrity* (New York: St. Martin's Press, 2000), 29.

7. Quoted in Giles, 22.

CHAPTER 11. UP AND DOWN WITH
RELIGION AND SPIRITUALITY.

1. ALAN WATTS, *The Book: On the Taboo Against Knowing Who You Are* (New York: Vintage, 1989), 10.

2. JOEL KRAMER and DIANA ALSTAD, *The Guru Papers: Masks of Authoritarian Power* (Berkeley: Frog, Ltd., 1993), 43.

3. Quoted in MARY LUYTENS, *Krishnamurti: The Years of Awakening* (New York: Farrar, Straus and Giroux, 1975), 272.

4. Huston Smith, *The Religions of Man* (New York: Harper & Row, 1958), 7.
5. Amy Waldman, "Word for Word: Taboo Heaven," *The New York Times,* Dec. 2, 2001, wk 7.
6. Steven Pressman, *Outrageous Betrayal: The Dark Journey of Werner Erhard from est to Exile* (New York: St. Martin's Press, 1993).
7. B. A. Robinson, "Osho, Formerly Known as Bhagwan Shree Rajneesh." http://www.religioustolerance.org/rajneesh.htm (accessed February 27, 2003).
8. Quoted in Alexandra David-Neel, *Buddhism* (New York: St. Martin's Press, 1939), 123.

CHAPTER 12. REAL PEOPLE, TRANSCENDENT MOMENTS.

1. Maslow, *Toward a Psychology of Being* (New York: Van Nostrand, 1962), 74.
2. Nitin Trasi, *The Science of Enlightenment* (New Delhi, D. K. Printworld, 1999), x–xi.
3. William James, *The Varieties of Religious Experience: A Study in Human Nature* (New York: New American Library, 1958), 395.
4. Maslow, *Toward a Psychology of Being*, 164–165.
5. Mihaly Csikszentmihalyi, *Flow: The Psychology of Optimal Experience* (New York: Harper and Row, 1980), 6.
6. Csikszentmihalyi, 64–65.
7. Douglas Harding, *On Having No Head: Zen and the Rediscovery of the Obvious* (London: Arkana, 1961), 11–12.
8. TASTE—The Archive of Scientists' Transcendent Experiences. http://www.issc-taste.org (accessed February 27, 2003).
9. Huston Smith, *Cleansing the Doors of Perception: The Religious Significance of Entheogenic Plants and Chemicals* (New York: Tarcher/Putnam, 2000), 142.
10. James H. Austin, *Zen and the Brain: Toward an Understanding of Meditative Consciousness* (Cambridge: MIT Press, 1998), 19–21.

CHAPTER 13. PERSONAL EVOLUTION:
BECOMING WHO YOU ARE.

1. AUSTIN, *Zen and the Brain,* 74.
2. THADDEUS GOLAS, *The Lazy Man's Guide to Enlightenment* (Palo Alto: The Seed Center, 1971), 72.
3. SUZANNE SEGAL, *Collision with the Infinite: A Life Beyond the Personal Self* (San Diego: Blue Dove Press, 1996), 15.
4. TRASI, *The Science of Enlightenment,* 186.
5. ARNOLD BEISSER, "The Paradoxical Theory of Change," in *Gestalt Therapy Now: Theory, Techniques, Applications,* eds. Joen Fagan and Irma Lee Shepherd (New York: Harper Colophon, 1970), 77.
6. For extensive references to such research see Austin, *Zen and the Brain;* and Charles Tart, *Altered States of Consciousness: A Book of Readings* (New York: John Wiley & Sons, 1969).
7. SRI NISARGADATTA MAHARAJ, *I Am That,* translated by Maurice Frydman, revised and edited by Sudhakar S. Dikshit (Durham, NC: Acorn Press, 1973), 18.
8. FREDERICK PERLS, RALPH H. HEFFERLINE, and PAUL GOODMAN, *Gestalt Therapy: Excitement and Growth in the Human Personality* (New York: Delta, 1965), 108.
9. WILLIAM JAMES, *The Varieties of Religious Experience: A Study in Human Nature* (New York: New American Library, 1958), 298.
10. ALAN WATTS, *The Joyous Cosmology: Adventures in the Chemistry of Consciousness* (New York: Vintage, 1962), 17.
11. MARY BARNARD, "The God in the Flowerpot," *The American Scholar* 32, no. 4 (Autumn 1963): 584, quoted in Smith, 19.

CHAPTER 14. THE EMERGING ENLIGHTENMENT PROJECT.

1. CARL SAGAN, *The Cosmic Connection: An Extraterrestrial Perspective* (New York: Anchor Press, 1973), 5.
2. CHRISTOPHER WILLS, *Children of Prometheus: The Accelerating Pace of Human Evolution* (Reading, Mass: Perseus Books, 1998), 261.
3. O. B. HARDISON Jr., *Disappearing Through the Skylight: Culture and Technology in the Twentieth Century* (New York: Viking, 1989), 5.
4. DENNIS OVERBYE, "A New View of Our Universe: Only One of Many," *The New York Times,* October 29, 2002, D1.

5. LESTER THUROW, "Voices of the Revolution," *Forbes ASAP* (Feb. 21, 2000): 82.

6. National Science Foundation, *Converging Technologies for Improving Human Performance* (2002).

7. RAY KURZWEIL, "No Sharp Distinction Between Human and Machine Intelligence," quoted from Tech TV interview, Jan. 11, 2001. http://www.kurzweilai.net/news/news_single.html?id=748 (accessed February 27, 2003).

8. RAY KURZWEIL, *The Age of Spiritual Machines: When Computers Exceed Human Intelligence* (New York: Penguin, 1999), 126.

9. KURZWEIL, *Age of Spiritual Machines,* 220.

10. FRANCIS HEYLIGHEN and JOHAN BOLLEN, "The World-Wide Web as a Super-Brain: From Metaphor to Model." http://www.pespmc1.vub.ac.be/SUPBRAIN.html (accessed February 9, 2003).

11. M. BROOKS, "Global Brain," *New Scientist,* (24 June 2000): 22.

12. Anonymous, "The Social Superorganism and its Global Brain," http://www.pespmcl.vub.ac.be/SUPORGLI.html (accessed February 9, 2003).

13. AC/UNU Millennium Project. Available from: http://www.acunu.org/millennium/m3000-scenarios.html (accessed February 9, 2003).

14. WALTER TRUETT ANDERSON, "Augmentation, Symbiosis, Transcendence: Technology and the Future(s) of Human Identity," in *Futures* 35, no. 5 (June 2003): 535–546.

15. MARSHALL MCLUHAN, *Understanding Media: The Extensions of Man* (New York: McGraw-Hill), 1965.

16. RICHARD DAWKINS, *The Extended Phenotype* (New York: Oxford University Press, 1982).

17. MERLIN DONALD, *Origins of the Modern Mind: Three Stages in the Origin of Culture and Cognition* (Cambridge, Mass: Harvard University Press, 1991), 356.

18. BRUCE MAZLISH, *The Fourth Discontinuity: The Co-evolution of Humans and Machines* (New York: Yale University Press, 1993).

19. ALEXANDER CHISLENKO, "Legacy Systems and Functional Cyborgization of Humans," http://www.lucifer.com/;~sasha/articles/Cyborgs.html (accessed February 27, 2003).

20. THEODORE ROSZAK, *Person/Planet: The Creative Disintegration of Industrial Society* (Garden City, N.Y.: Doubleday, 1978).

21. GREGORY STOCK, *Metaman: The Merging of Humans and Machines into a Global Superorganism* (New York: Simon & Schuster, 1993).

22. J. E. LOVELOCK, *Gaia: A New Look at Life on Earth* (Oxford: Oxford University Press, 1979), 148.

23. JAMES N. ROSENAU, "The Future of Politics," *Futures* (Nov.–Dec. 1999): 1005–1016.

24. ROBERT KEGAN, *In Over Our Heads: The Mental Demands of Modern Life* (Cambridge, Mass.: Harvard University Press, 1994), 352.

INDEX